In the Highest Degree

IN THE HIGHEST DEGREE

Essays on C. S. Lewis's Philosophical Theology—
Method, Content, & Reason
Volume II

P. H. Brazier

Foreword by Gregory Hagg

SERIES: C. S. LEWIS: REVELATION AND THE CHRIST
www.cslewisandthechrist.net

◆PICKWICK *Publications* · Eugene, Oregon

IN THE HIGHEST DEGREE. VOLUME II
Essays on C. S. Lewis's Philosophical Theology—Method, Content, & Reason

Copyright © 2018 Paul H. Brazier. All rights reserved. Except for brief quotations in critical publications or reviews, no part of this book may be reproduced in any manner without prior written permission from the publisher. Write: Permissions, Wipf and Stock Publishers, 199 W. 8th Ave., Suite 3, Eugene, OR 97401.

Pickwick Publications
An Imprint of Wipf and Stock Publishers
199 W. 8th Ave., Suite 3
Eugene, OR 97401

www.wipfandstock.com

PAPERBACK ISBN: 978-1-5326-5888-4
HARDCOVER ISBN: 978-1-5326-5889-1
EBOOK ISBN: 978-1-5326-5890-7

Cataloging-in-Publication data:

Names: Brazier, P. H., author. | Gregory Hagg, foreword writer.

Title: In the highest degree. Volume II : essays on C. S. Lewis's philosophical theology—method, content, & reason / P. H. Brazier, with a foreword by Gregory Hagg.
Description: Eugene, OR : Pickwick Publications, 2018 | Includes bibliographical references and index.
Identifiers: ISBN 978-1-5326-5888-4 (paperback) | ISBN 978-1-5326-5889-1 (hardcover) | ISBN 978-1-5326-5890-7 (ebook)
Subjects: LCSH: Lewis, C. S. (Clive Staples), 1898–1963—Religion. | C. S. (Clive Staples), 1898–1963—Theology. | Philosophical theology. | Apologetics.

Classification: LCC BX5199.L53 B639 2018 (print) | LCC BX5199.L53 (ebook)

Manufactured in the U.S.A.

For Hilary

Contents

Acknowledgements / ix

Foreword / xv

Introduction / 1

1 *Praeparatio Evangelica*: C. S. Lewis as a Catholic Evangelical,
Defined by Method, Technique, and Form / 9

2 Christological Prefigurement: the Incarnation-Resurrection Narrative—
History and Reality, Imagination and Mythopoeic Intimation / 31

3 Revelation and Second Meanings:
A Philosophical and Pneumatological Justification / 73

4 A Doctrine of Transposition:
Towards a Philosophy of the Incarnation / 95

5 The Actuality of the Incarnation:
Triune Simultaneity and the Will of God—Lewis . . . and Shakespeare / 127

6 Election and Predestination:
Decision, Faith, and Responsibility—Whither Humanity / 145

Bibliography / 179

Indices / 189

Sectional Contents / 207

Acknowledgements

First an apology. Lewis's doctrine of transposition and his philosophy of the incarnation inevitably occur in a number of these essay: they are central to his thinking. These papers were originally self-contained and published in original/earlier form in various journals. Lewis's doctrine of transposition and his philosophy of the incarnation are dealt with proper here in Vol. II, essay/chapter 4; any mention in the other essays has been reduced to an absolute minimum so as to avoid repetition. This editing also applies where components of Lewis's philosophical theology occur in more than one essay

With one exception (Vol. II, essay 6, doctrine of election, recently completed) all of these papers were conceived and researched, initially, up to twenty years ago. Written and published in academic journals between 2007 and 2015, the material was then re-assessed. The editions in these two volumes are related to the original published editions, but much of the material has been revised and extended in the light of research and conclusions in recent years; in addition the titles and structure of the papers, in most cases, have changed.

I here acknowledge and thank most gratefully the editors and publishers of the original papers for permission to reuse and develop the original papers.

First, my thanks and acknowledgement are to Dr. Pat Madigan, S.J., editor of *The Heythrop Journal* for having published the following papers, which appear here in developed form:

> P. H. Brazier, "C. S. Lewis and Christological Prefigurement," *The Heythrop Journal* 48.5 (2007) 742–75.
> (Here, essay/chapter Vol. II.2)

Acknowledgements

> P. H. Brazier, "C. S. Lewis: A Doctrine of Transposition," *The Heythrop Journal* 50.4 (2009) 669–88.
> (Here, essay/chapter Vol. II.4.)

> P. H. Brazier, "'God . . . or a Bad, or Mad, Man': C. S. Lewis's Argument for Christ—A Systematic Theological, Historical and Philosophical Analysis of *aut Deus aut malus homo*," *The Heythrop Journal* 55.1 (2014) 1–30.
> (Here, essay/chapter Vol. I.2.)

> P. H. Brazier, "C. S. Lewis: The Question of Multiple Incarnations," *The Heythrop Journal* 55.3 (2014) 391–408.
> (Here, essay/chapter Vol. I.6.)

> P. H. Brazier, "C. S. Lewis on Atonement: A Unified Model and Event, the Drama of Redemption—Understanding and Rationalizing the Tradition," *The Heythrop Journal* 56.2 (2015) 285–305.
> (Here, essay/chapter Vol. I.3.)

My thanks also goes to Laura Birrell of Sage Publishing for permission and acknowledgement to reuse the article on the actuality of the incarnation (here, essay/chapter Vol. II.5) originally published in *The Downside Review*, by the monks of Downside Abbey in Somerset:

> P. H. Brazier, "C. S. Lewis on the Actuality of the Incarnation: Triune Simultaneity and the Will of God," *The Downside Review* 131.463 (2013) 87–102.

My thanks also goes to Professor Judith Wolfe editor of *The Chronicle of the University of Oxford C. S. Lewis Society* for permission and acknowledgement to reuse the articles on Lewis's debate with Pittenger (here, essay/chapter Vol. I.5), and on second meanings (here, essay/chapter Vol. II.3):

> P. H. Brazier, "The Pittenger-Lewis Debate: Fundamentals of an Ontological Christology," *The Chronicle of the Oxford University C.S. Lewis Society* 6.1 (2009) 7–23.

Acknowledgements

> P. H. Brazier, "C. S. Lewis on Revelation and Second Meanings: A Philosophical and Pneumatological Justification," *The Chronicle of the Oxford University C. S. Lewis Society* 7.1 (2010) 18–35.

My thanks also goes to Professor Judith Wolfe editor of *The Journal of Inklings Studies* (the successor to *The Chronicle of the University of Oxford C. S. Lewis Society*) for permission and acknowledgement to reuse the article on Lewis and Anscombe (here, essay/chapter Vol. I.1):

> P. H. Brazier, "C. S. Lewis and the Anscombe Debate: from analogia entis to analogia fidei," *The Journal of Inklings Studies* 1.2 (2011) 69–123.

My thanks also goes to Dr. Calvin L. Smith of King's Evangelical Divinity School, editor of *The Evangelical Review of Theology and Politics*, for permission and acknowledgement to reuse the article on Lewis methodology (here, essay/chapter Vol. II.1):

> P. H. Brazier, "C. S. Lewis. praeparatio evangelica: a Catholic Evangelical Defined by Method, Technique, and Form," *The Evangelical Review of Theology and Politics* 1 (2013) A1–17. Online Journal: www.evangelicalreview.com.

My thanks also goes to Bruce Johnson editor of *Sehnsucht The C. S. Lewis Journal* for permission and acknowledgement to reuse the article on Lewis's doctrine of scripture (here, essay/chapter Vol. I.4):

> P. H. Brazier, "C. S. Lewis on Scripture and the Christ, the Word of God: Convergence and Divergence with Karl Barth," *Sehnsucht* 4 (2010) 89–109.

Acknowledgment and thanks is given to the C. S. Lewis Co. Pte., for permission to quote from the following works used in Vol. II.

C. S. Lewis. *Collected Letters, Vol. I—Family Letters 1905–1931*. Edited by Walter Hooper. San Francisco: Harper San Francisco, 2004. Extracts by C. S. Lewis, copyright © C. S. Lewis Co. Pte. Extracts reprinted by permission.

Acknowledgements

C. S. Lewis. *Collected Letters, Vol. II: Books, Broadcasts and War 1931 1949*. Edited by Walter Hooper. San Francisco: Harper San Francisco, 2004. Extracts by C. S. Lewis, copyright © C. S. Lewis Co. Pte. Extracts reprinted by permission.

C. S. Lewis. *Collected Letters, Vol. III: Narnia, Cambridge and Joy 1950–1963*. Edited by Walter Hooper. San Francisco: Harper San Francisco, 2007. Extracts by C. S. Lewis, copyright © C. S. Lewis Co. Pte. Extracts reprinted by permission.

C. S. Lewis. *Letters of C. S. Lewis*, 2nd edition. Revised and enlarged. Edited by Walter Hooper. London: Fount, 1988. Extracts by C. S. Lewis, copyright © C. S. Lewis Co. Pte. Extracts reprinted by permission.

C. S. Lewis. *Surprised by Joy*. London: Bles, 1955. Extracts by C. S. Lewis, copyright © C. S. Lewis Co. Pte. Extracts reprinted by permission.

C. S. Lewis. *The Pilgrim's Regress*. London: J. M. Dent and Sons, 1933. Extracts by C. S. Lewis, copyright © C. S. Lewis Co. Pte. Extracts reprinted by permission.

C. S. Lewis. *Miracles* (1st ed., 1947). London: Bless, 1947. Extracts by C. S. Lewis, copyright © C. S. Lewis Co. Pte. Extracts reprinted by permission.

C. S. Lewis. *An Experiment on Criticism*. Cambridge: Cambridge University Press, 1961. Extracts by C. S. Lewis, copyright © C. S. Lewis Co. Pte. Extracts reprinted by permission.

C. S. Lewis. *Mere Christianity*. London: Bles, 1952. Extracts by C. S. Lewis, copyright © C. S. Lewis Co. Pte. Extracts reprinted by permission.

C. S. Lewis. *The Chronicles of Narnia—The Lion, the Witch and the Wardrobe*. London: Bles, 1950 Extracts by C. S. Lewis, copyright © C. S. Lewis Co. Pte. Extracts reprinted by permission.

C. S. Lewis. *The Chronicles of Narnia—The Voyage of the Dawn Treader*. London: Geoffrey Bles, 1952. Extracts by C. S. Lewis, copyright © C. S. Lewis Co. Pte. Extracts reprinted by permission.

Acknowledgements

C. S. Lewis. *The Chronicles of Narnia—The Silver Chair*. London: Bles, 1953. Extracts by C. S. Lewis, copyright © C. S. Lewis Co. Pte. Extracts reprinted by permission.

C. S. Lewis. *The Chronicles of Narnia—The Horse & his Boy*. London: Bles, 1954. Extracts by C. S. Lewis, copyright © C. S. Lewis Co. Pte. Extracts reprinted by permission.

C. S. Lewis. *The Chronicles of Narnia—The Magician's Nephew*. London: Bles, 1955. Extracts by C. S. Lewis, copyright © C. S. Lewis Co. Pte. Extracts reprinted by permission.

C. S. Lewis. *The Chronicles of Narnia—The Last Battle*. London: Bles, 1956. Extracts by C. S. Lewis, copyright © C. S. Lewis Co. Pte. Extracts reprinted by permission.

C. S. Lewis. *Reflections on the Psalms*. London: Bles, 1958. Extracts by C. S. Lewis, copyright © C. S. Lewis Co. Pte. Extracts reprinted by permission.

C. S. Lewis. *Transposition and Other Addresses*. London: Bless, 1949. Extracts by C. S. Lewis, copyright © C. S. Lewis Co. Pte. Extracts reprinted by permission.

C. S. Lewis. *They Asked for a Paper: Papers and Addresses*. London: Bles, 1962. Extracts by C. S. Lewis, copyright © C. S. Lewis Co. Pte. Extracts reprinted by permission.

C. S. Lewis. *Christian Reflections*. Edited by Walter Hooper. London: Fount, 1967. Extracts by C. S. Lewis, copyright © C. S. Lewis Co. Pte. Extracts reprinted by permission.

C. S. Lewis. *The World's Last Night and Other Essays*. New York: Harcourt, Brace and World, 1960. Extracts by C. S. Lewis, copyright © C. S. Lewis Co. Pte. Extracts reprinted by permission.

C. S. Lewis. *The Screwtape Letters*. London: Geoffrey Bles, The Centenary Press, 1942. Extracts by C. S. Lewis, copyright © C. S. Lewis Co. Pte. Extracts reprinted by permission.

Acknowledgements

C. S. Lewis. *Undeceptions: Essays on Theology and Ethics*. London: Bles, 1971. **Extracts by C. S. Lewis, copyright** © **C. S. Lewis Co. Pte. Extracts reprinted by permission.**

C. S. Lewis. *The Problem of Pain*. London: Centenary Press, 1940. **Extracts by C. S. Lewis, copyright** © **C. S. Lewis Co. Pte. Extracts reprinted by permission.**

C. S. Lewis. *The Great Divorce: A Dream*. London: Macmillan, 1945. **Extracts by C. S. Lewis, copyright** © **C. S. Lewis Co. Pte. Extracts reprinted by permission.**

C. S. Lewis. *Of Other Worlds. Essays and Stories*. edited by Walter Hooper. London: Bles, 1966. **Extracts by C. S. Lewis, copyright** © **C. S. Lewis Co. Pte. Extracts reprinted by permission.**

Foreword

In preparation to provide a foreword to this two-volume work, *In the Highest Degree*, it seemed appropriate to review the previous five-volume series from P. H. Brazier, *C. S. Lewis: Revelation and the Christ*. This series of five books on C. S. Lewis is like the picture on the box of a jigsaw puzzle. Without the picture we might piece together part of the puzzle like a quadrant that forms a spectacular cloud formation. Separately, another section might focus on a pastoral scene of absolute serenity, or to the left might be a well-lit chapel spilling over with people of all races and creeds. However, when we see the whole picture on that box, there is the satisfaction of understanding the artist's cohesive plan for the puzzle, or how things fit together. The parts are now related to the whole.
Others have written on the theology of Lewis, but Brazier's contribution is unique in its format and exhaustive in its content. Nearly everyone who teaches Bible and theology in the classroom or the pulpit has some form of the "quotable Lewis" at his disposal—pieces of the jigsaw puzzle that may be organized according to topic. He gives us the picture on the box. By systematizing the theology of C. S. Lewis, Brazier helps the reader see the entire picture. He puts the testimony of one of history's greatest thinkers in a format that benefits all.

It is not as though Lewis himself did not have a system. He probably did, although the outline was not prominent in his teaching. His literary acumen led him to tell the story first, use an allegory first, grab the attention of the reader first, or solidly capture the imagination first. The didactic comes later. This may reflect the account of his own conversion, and to a greater degree the experience of his wife, Joy Davidman. They both experienced the "baptism of the imagination" as he calls it, an experiential encounter with Jesus Christ prior to learning salvific doctrine. Even after coming to a conscious decision to accept the claims of Christ based upon

Foreword

argumentation and reason, the apologist continued to express his faith in one of his most celebrated works of fiction, *The Chronicles of Narnia*, reaching the imagination of the readers, young and old alike—first. Lewis describes his own experiences as *praeparatio evangelica* or the preparation for the gospel witness. This was so dramatic for his Jewish-born wife, that we may see a hint of fulfillment of the apostle Paul's generalization, "The Jews require a sign, but the Greeks seek after wisdom" (1 Cor 1:22). God has often gotten the attention of Jewish people through a unique spiritual experience prior to coming to faith in Messiah *Yeshua*.

These conversion accounts of Lewis and Davidman form one of the outstanding features of the first of the five volumes, *C. S. Lewis: Revelation, Conversion, and Apologetics*. They are compared with the likes of Augustine, Karl Barth, Simone Weil (a converted French Jewish philosopher), and Edith Stein (a Jewish convert to Catholicism, holocaust martyr, and later sainted Teresa Benedicta of the Cross). They have in common an encounter with Christ. This seems to underscore Lewis's emphasis on the *analogia fidei* as compared to the *analogia entis*. The latter asserts that man comes to understand God through analogy to God's creation, but not all see God there. Some see only a mechanism of nature. This can lead to the kind of atheism that characterized Lewis in his early years. The *analogia fidei*, however, requires a touch of the Divine, a revelation through Christ and his Word, which also reveals the triunity of God, the sinful predicament of mankind, and the sacrifice of the Lamb of God for sins. Lewis seems much more Augustinian in this emphasis on faith. On the other hand, his love of reasoned debate and apologetics paint him more as a Thomist who is committed to fideism but who is also an evidentialist!

The comparison and contrast between Barth and Lewis, from their conversion accounts to their theological convictions, is worth the price of the book. Swiss Reform *versus* Anglican, professor of dogmatics *versus* popular apologist, yet both experiencing the Christ-encounter, and both unabashedly denouncing the creeping liberalism of their day. They united in their insistence upon a Christocentric Christianity. They both were ecumenical enough to focus on the unifying, non-negotiable aspects of mere Christianity. Brazier gives an astute rendition of the contributions of these two giants upon whose shoulders many stand.

Throughout all five volumes that precede *In the Highest Degree* he highlights the beautiful works of fiction by Lewis. He will often deftly

Foreword

explain the profound allegories that Lewis used. From *The Pilgrim's Regress* to *The Great Divorce* to *The Screwtape Letters*, etc., the strategy of Lewis was to stimulate the enlightened imagination of the reader in order to teach truth. He whets the appetite for further exploration of Christianity in much the same way as his friend J. R. R. Tolkien did in his works. Then he provides the rational, biblical evidence for the faith. Many have traversed the trail from the winters of Narnia and the rebellion of Edmund to the essentials of the faith and forgiveness in Aslan/Christ.

Lewis certainly went beyond allegory to more precise apologetics. Brazier correctly repeats the theme of "philosophical theology" when speaking of the contributions of Lewis. It is the study of God via the love of wisdom. Reason must be applied to understand Revelation. Lewis championed the idea of viewing reason as part of revelation in order to come to the point of conversion. But he was a different kind of apologist than most of his day, one who could leave the rarified air of the academic ivory tower to "write the vision, and make it plain upon tablets, that he may run that reads it" (Hab 2:2).

As is often the case, the student becomes like his teacher. One gets the feeling that due to his exhaustive knowledge of Lewis, Brazier would be able to finish Lewis's sentences if they were together at a social gathering. Both Lewis and Brazier are capable of disentangling very complex theological matters in order to reach the common man. Although it is a testimony to his theological philosophy, Lewis's *Mere Christianity* is comprehensible to the non-theologian. How many non-scholars have joined the family of God through reading this work of art? The book was not intended to be a treatise on theology, even though many evangelicals, Catholics, and others have labeled it so. Lewis was not attempting to write to the professors of religion in his day, he was warning a radio audience that the time to believe in Jesus Christ was now, before the Nazis took their possessions and their very lives! He wanted to strip away all but the essentials of the faith and communicate them persuasively to a modernist/liberal England.

Likewise, in his first five volumes, Brazier has been writing for the non-professional, non-academic reader of Lewis who loves his apologetics and literary artistry. He provides the hooks upon which to hang Lewis's lofty ideas, and throughout his explanation of Lewis's philosophical theology, he makes plain the simplicity of Christian truth. Both the layman and the trained theologian greatly benefit from these

Foreword

five volumes. One wonders how many non-scholars will join the family of God through reading Brazier's works.

Of particular interest to this writer is the emphasis on the Jewish backgrounds of Christianity as found in the first five volumes. Even the book covers indicate that Brazier appreciates the Jewishness of Jesus as they are clear depictions of Christ Pantocrator as a Jew, and he emphasizes this fact in comments on his own ink drawings. (See the outstanding little volume devoted to the Lewis bibliography, *C. S. Lewis—An Annotated Bibliography and Resource*, 13.) A cursory reading of the index of any of the volumes reveals a considerable number of references to Israel, Jews, and Judaism. Lewis had much to say about the Jewish people (notwithstanding N. T. Wright's criticism of Lewis for failing to emphasize the Jewishness of Jesus sufficiently, a topic too extensive to cover in this foreword).

For example, Lewis felt a kinship with the serious members of all denominations and religions, whether Jews, Muslims, or Roman Catholics. Genuine belief in areas of commonality was to be preferred over liberal lack of faith. This, of course, earned Lewis criticism from evangelical separatists as being too ecumenical. Furthermore, when asked about those Jews who are still waiting for the Messiah, having rejected the claims of Jesus to that title, Lewis said that God accepts serious prayer even if the prayer is to a false god or to the true God, who is incompletely understood. He also implied that Christ saves those who do not think they know Him, (from *Collected Letters* cited by Brazier in volume four, *C. S. Lewis—On the Christ of a Religious Economy*, 3.2, 191). Just how wide is the wideness in God's mercy? It seems as though he is promoting a kind of unconscious mediation in which the atonement avails for the salvation of those who have not and will not accept the Messiah.

However, Brazier points out in the same context of his discussion of Lewis's leniency that he was not shy about challenging all people to believe. Jewish people knew the radical nature of the claims of *Yeshua* (Jesus). He entered the world claiming (among other things) to be one who existed always, who could forgive the sins of man, and who would return to judge the world—truly a liar, lunatic, or Lord. Yet, while Lewis believed that no one could be saved apart from the atoning work of Christ, he also said that we do not know exactly how this applies to those without the knowledge that we possess. In other words, God alone is the ultimate judge.

Foreword

The true identity of Jesus will be known when he returns. Lewis said that this will strike "either irresistible love or irresistible horror into every creature. It will be too late then to choose your side. . . . Now, today, this moment, is our chance to choose the right side. God is holding back to give us a chance. It won't last forever. We must take it or leave it" (from *Mere Christianity*, cited by Brazier in *C. S. Lewis—On the Christ of a Religious Economy*, 3.2, 196). Lewis spoke and wrote with evangelistic zeal. Brazier aptly reminds us that Aslan will be loved, thanked, and saved by some; loathed, hated, and condemned by others when all stand before him.

Now we move on to consider *In the Highest Degree*. The thoroughness of the five-volume series, *C. S. Lewis: Revelation and the Christ*, causes one to wonder how more could be said, but Brazier follows up with this two-volume work. *In the Highest Degree: Essays on C. S. Lewis's Philosophical Theology—Method, Content, and Reason, Volumes 1 and 2* is targeted at a different audience. The five-volume series was intended for academics as well as any who loved the works of Lewis but needed appropriate categories in systematic theology to sort out his ideas. The layman, the trained cleric, and the seminary professor have all genuinely prospered through studying that series. Most of what has been said in this foreword draws upon Brazier's treatment of Lewis in those books. Likewise, many of the topics found here in *In the Highest Degree* draw upon material developed in the five-volume series. Volume 1 covers the same ground such as the Anscombe Debate, the *aut Deus aut malus homo* argument ("God . . . or a Bad, or Mad, Man"), the atonement, Barth and Lewis, the Pittenger Debate, and multiple incarnations. In Volume 2 the topics include *praeparatio evangelica*, where Lewis's catholic/evangelical identification is discussed, Christological prefigurement, transposition, the actuality of the incarnation, and Lewis's views on election and predestination.

The differences, however, are significant. New arguments, more academic in nature, are employed to provide the essence of Lewis's philosophical theology. They come from the original journal articles that Brazier published over the years, which were directed toward the academy rather than the church.

The present work, *In the Highest Degree*, seeks to go deeper into the underpinnings of Lewis's thought. Here we are provided more

Foreword

background about the theories of atonement and the unique nuance of "triune simultaneity," where Lewis explains how God can be both eternal and actual. We are taken further into the views of Lewis concerning election, namely his idea of "infernal voluntarism" in which some choose to exclude themselves from heaven because they prefer hell. Brazier seeks to marshal new evidence to support the veracity of these views. We are provided with an in-depth treatment of Lewis's concept of transposition, a Platonic understanding of the incarnation, which informs his views of revelation, Scripture, and reason.

Of particular interest is the article about how the Holy Spirit may have been involved in the "prefigurements" that Lewis found in other religions. Do myths contain intimations of the salvation that ultimately comes through the work of Christ? Given the fallenness of the human intellect, could the Spirit use that flawed mind to adumbrate the work of the Son? Is reason part of the common grace given to all men that enables the understanding of revelation? Although there is a the divinely inspired revelation found in the Scriptures, one wonders if we have limited our understanding of pneumatology by reducing the work of the Spirit to the pages of Holy Writ. Brazier explores this concept by asking if there is internal evidence for a mythopoeic interpretation within the incarnation-resurrection narrative.

These are heady issues intended to arrive at the essential, highest degree, of the philosophical theology of C. S. Lewis. While Brazier wants to reach perhaps a more intellectually sophisticated audience this time around, the lucidity in his writing will attract the same readers of his earlier works who want even more Lewis as seen through the clarifying lens provided by Brazier. We are indebted to him. The volumes are enhanced by splendid synopses, introductions, outlines (sectional contents at the end of each book), indices, tables, artwork, figures, a glossary, biographies, and bibliographies, all of which make this contribution a "go to" resource for Lewis studies. Time invested in these wonderful books on C. S. Lewis will reap huge dividends. One will sense that he has taken a master's level course on Lewis.

Gregory Hagg, Ph.D.
Professor, Biola University, Talbot School of Theology
Director, The Feinberg Center for Messianic Jewish Studies,
Brooklyn, New York

"In the Highest Degree:"
Essays on C. S. Lewis's Philosophical Theology—
Method, Content, & Reason Vol I.

"In the Highest Degree:"
Essays on C. S. Lewis's Philosophical Theology—
Method, Content, & Reason Vol II

Essential: from the Middle English (c. 1066 to 1500),
in the sense of "in the highest degree;" from late Latin, *essentia*—
the essence of an existing entity.
Analogical formation based on *esse* ("to be"), present active infinitive
of *sum* ("I am"); *essentia, ae,* f. *sum*, is the being or essence of a
thing; originally from the Greek, οὐσία (substance, property)

So, essence, substance, being, actuality,
essential thing, existing entity, whole:

... how do we analyze and present the essentials
of C. S. Lewis's theological and philosophical thinking?

"Reason is given before Nature
and on Reason our concept of Nature depends."

C. S. Lewis, *Miracles* (2nd ed. 1960).

"Neither *will* nor *reason* is the product of nature."

C. S. Lewis. "Bulverism" (1941 and 1944).

P. H. Brazier, "C. S. Lewis,"
Oil on Linen, 13.38 x 9.84 cm, June 2018

www.cslewisandthechrist.net

"In the Highest Degree" Vol. II Introduction

It has often been stated and acknowledged that C. S. Lewis, while being subject to a profound encounter with the Holy Spirit as a young man, which led to his conversion, actually *thought* his way to faith, to being a Christian, and accepting that God is God, a God who as Lord, laid claim to his life. Lewis submitted to *El Shaddai*, Almighty God, the Lordship of Yhwh, but he had undergone a long, difficult period in having to sort out in his mind the why, the wherefore, the reasoned logic of faith. From his teenage years Lewis had been a stubborn, logical atheist (and like most reasoned atheists, there lay hidden subjective psychological issues, a legion of confused and disordered factors in his life and mind, that had led to and bolstered his atheism). Lewis from his time at the University of Oxford specialized in English literature and philosophy, including "Greats." His entire worldview was reasoned-out, logically—or so he thought. This had to be dismantled brick-by-brick before he could allow God in, though as he later acknowledged, God was already "in" and had been most unscrupulous: as he commented, "Really, a young atheist cannot guard his faith too carefully."[1]

So Lewis was no stranger to reasoning-out beliefs, to logical reasoning, so it is no wonder that when he came to write theology and to argue in the common rooms of Oxford, his position was one of a philosophical theologian. As such, philosophical theology can be seen as a branch of theology, but also—arguably, though disputed by some philosophers—of philosophy. Philosophical theology is therefore a form of theology in which philosophical methods are used in developing

---

[1] Lewis, *Surprised by Joy* (1955), 219.

and analyzing theological concepts: it is an attempt to explicate, to find rational proofs for faith. Many modern, Western philosophers appear to regard atheism as a pre-requisite for philosophical thinking, for faith is often regarded as a denial of academic neutrality. But this position is, as we shall see, contestable..

C. S. Lewis was a trained philosopher; indeed he taught philosophy at Oxford in the 1920s, early in his career. In philosophical terms, Lewis was unashamedly a Platonist (drawing inspiration from the writings of the ancient Greek philosopher Plato [c.424–348BC]). The term also applies to later systems of philosophy developed from Plato's work and ideas, for example, Neoplatonism or Platonic realism. Central to Platonism is the theory of forms. The forms are transcendent archetypes; the objects we take for reality—the things we see, hear, touch, taste, and smell—are in some way a pale imitation of the forms: reality relates to the forms as an imperfect copy does to an original. The forms tell us that what we take for reality is perceivable but not intelligible, but that there is another higher reality that is intelligible but not perceivable. Platonism is a type of philosophy that Lewis not only subscribed to but which characterized his work throughout his life. And in this he was holding fast to the classical Christian heritage. Most patristic theologians were Platonists, to varying degrees; Neoplatonism was in many ways part of patristic theology. However, many Protestant, Reformed, or Evangelical supporters of Lewis's work today object strongly to his Platonism not realizing that it is fundamental to Lewis's interpretation of the gospel and is at the heart of his understanding of revelation. The precise nature of Lewis's Platonism will become clear in the subsequent chapters of this work.

Platonism, as distinct from modern philosophy (if by modern we are citing the numerous ideas and theories of philosophy that pervaded post-Reformation thought in the West[2]), defines the form and method of Lewis's thinking and therefore the particular character of his apologetics. Lewis was not, however, immune from modern philosophy. He was schooled in, and to a degree a follower of, logical positivism

---

2   Many philosophers in the seventeenth through nineteenth centuries held some respect and place for Platonism, but the era was dominated more and more by rationalism, empiricism, political philosophy and pragmatism, existentialism and phenomenology, and analytic philosophy (against what is left of idealism), also the closed-world of Kant's mature philosophy.

in the immediate years after World War I.[3] However, his philosophical education had begun in earnest when he was invalided out of the First World War. Wounded near Arras on April 15, 1918, Lewis developed a serious interest in philosophy while recovering in Étaples hospital. He read and studied John Locke's *Essay Concerning Human Understanding*.[4] Lewis absorbed Locke's proposition that reality cannot be comprehended totally by the mind; this was in many ways a preparation for the influence of the Platonist Bishop Berkeley. Therefore, we need to focus particularly on Lewis the philosopher: his understanding of truth and reason, his Platonic idealism, and especially the proximity of his thought to that of the seventeenth-century Cambridge Platonist Henry More and the eighteenth-century philosopher Bishop George Berkeley, both of whom Lewis valued greatly.

His relationship with modern philosophy will be seen from his very public encounter in the Socratic Club with Gertrude Elizabeth Anscombe (a young philosophy don, trained in analytic philosophy, and a follower of Ludwig Wittgenstein, but also a believing and traditional Roman Catholic).

Post-conversion, Lewis was firmly grounded in theological and philosophical orthodoxy by his reading of many patristic theologians and philosophers, essentially, Augustine of Hippo (a rhetorician in the classical tradition, adult convert, as well as a theologian and philosopher). In the early years after his conversion he read, studied, and translated Augustine's *City of God*, a massive and seminal work, which also defined much of his argumentative method, and his respect for reason.[5] Furthermore, he used as a reference and source, Aquinas' *Summa* on an almost daily basis in the 1940s when writing much of his corpus.[6] The

---

3   Central European in origin, logical positivism had taken a generation to travel from the salons of Vienna to take root in the fertile post-WWI nihilism of what was left of the intelligentsia at the University of Oxford.

4   Locke, *Essay Concerning Human Understanding*.

5   Lewis studied Augustine's *Confessions* in 1936, and *The City of God* (*de civitate Dei*) in 1937, both in the original Latin, returning to them regularly over the next decade, as well as translating *The City of God* for his own use. See, Lewis writing to Dom Bede Griffiths, April 24, 1936, and, Lewis writing to Dom Bede Griffiths, May 23 1936, in, C. S. Lewis, *Collected Letters*, Vol. II (2004), 187–90 and 191–95.

6   In the 1940s, when he was working at his most apologetic, he read Thomas Aquinas's *Summa theologiae* on a daily basis, in the original Latin (a work regarded by many as a foundational work of philosophical theology).

early patristic theologian Tertullian may have argued that the temple (Jerusalem) has nothing to do with the academy (Greek philosophy),[7] but Lewis saw, accepted, and promoted *reasoning* as essential to the preaching and promotion of the gospel.

So why Lewis and philosophical theology? Because he never missed an opportunity to spell out his beliefs, to analyze his beliefs in a reasoned and logical manner, to justify before the atheistic common rooms of Oxford, the reasoned evidence for the gospel—even in his children's stories, *The Chronicles of Narnia*!

So, *In the Highest Degree: Essays on C. S. Lewis's Philosophical Theology—Method, Content, Reason Vol. I and Vol. II*: the term "essential," in middle English, evoked, "in the highest degree"; from late Latin, *essentia*, what we find here in these essays is the essence of C. S. Lewis's philosophical theology by analyzing his method, content, and form. The sum total (*summa*; feminine of *summus*, "highest"), gives us the being or essence of a thing, so, the essence, substance, being, actuality, essential thing, existing entity, whole: the highest degree, the highest essentials of C. S. Lewis's theological and philosophical thinking.

In this second volume, we open with C. S. Lewis's method, technique, and form, defined by the Christ-event, derived from the patristic theologian Vincentius of Lérins (the Scripture-imbued authority of the church, "what has been held always, everywhere, by everybody") and the Puritan Richard Baxter (from whom he acknowledges the term "mere Christian"—a sheer core to the faith, *merus*). This paper demonstrates a thread of systematic ground and continuity to Lewis's writings: a content-led bipartite method and bipartite technique, unified by a universal Platonic principle, realized through the form of the *analogia entis–analogia fidei*—derived from the Catholic and Puritan traditions, but Evangelical in mission. Therefore, Lewis defines his work as *praeparatio evangelica*: preparation for the Holy Spirit. In this he is neither an Enlightenment-led modernist, nor a disparate and relativistic liberal postmodernist, but an

---

[7] Tertullian, *De praescriptione haereticorum*, ch. 7: "Our instruction comes from 'the porch of Solomon,' who had himself taught that 'the Lord should be sought in simplicity of heart.' Away with all attempts to produce a mottled Christianity of Stoic, Platonic, and dialectic composition! We want no curious disputation after possessing Christ Jesus, no inquisition after enjoying the gospel! With our faith, we desire no further belief." Betty, Tertullian's *Prescription against Heretics* . . . (1722).

orthodox theologian-philosopher in the patristic tradition, grounding his writings in Scripture.

The second essay is an examination of the Christology and pneumatology that C. S. Lewis read from the apparent prefiguring of elements of the incarnation-resurrection narrative in religious myths; this leads us to consider Lewis's assertion that the incarnation-resurrection narrative operates on us both as fact and myth. Lewis's writings on the myth that became reality (the Christ-event) are discussed along with examples of prefigurement. Through his understanding of natural theology and his cautious respect for human imagination and in contrast to his earlier deference (during his atheistic period) for the conclusions of the Victorian religionist and social anthropologist James George Frazer, Lewis came to regard these prefigurements as the work of the Holy Spirit, intimations of God's salvific action in Christ, though Lewis's orthodoxy saw human imagination as flawed through original sin. This raises three questions. How do these prefigured ideas come to be in these myths and how do these intimations, splintered fragments of the true light, relate to Lewis's understanding of Christ as the light of the world? How does the incarnation-resurrection narrative act/operate on us as a myth, whether spoken or read (a baptized imagination is crucial here for Lewis in both the creation and receiving/hearing of such narratives)? Is there internal evidence for a mythopoeic interpretation within the incarnation-resurrection narrative?

In the third essay, following on from Lewis's proposition of Christological prefigurement, we may ask, does such a doctrine appear to do an injustice to the original aims and intentions of the author of the myth in asserting a second, a subsequent, Christological level of meaning? Lewis thought not, and could defend such an interpretation. Is it possible for anyone today to view such myths without considering what has happened in the intervening time? Regardless of concerns over purity, there is an indelible connection that must be explained. For example, the apparent connection between ancient writings—Plato, Socrates, etc.— and what happened to the Christ in his passion. Lewis therefore posits an alternative option to prophecy or chance coincidence: to previse may be the result of wisdom.

In the fourth essay, we can consider Lewis's doctrine of transposition, referred to by him as a contribution to the philosophy of the incarnation. This is rooted in Lewis's Platonism, in his reading of the works of Henry

More and Bishop Berkeley, and how it discloses his understanding of Scripture, revelation, and reason. In taking the analysis beyond the limited number of theologians who have attempted to unravel what Lewis's proto-doctrine was in this field, we describe Lewis's view of revelation as *supra-theological*. Is the doctrine of transposition a key to all of Lewis's work (literary, apologetic, and philosophical); or, more pertinently, a "flawed" doctrine of transposition, itself transposed platonically? Lewis's doctrine is designed to explain how revelation works, how it is communicated—and, paradoxically, why revelation can never be fully imparted. We can trace this back to the *communicatio idiomatum*, Trinitarian ontology, and human epistemic limitations.

C. S. Lewis eschewed the multifarious and apparently contradictory atonement theories, yet he implicitly promulgated specifically "debt" and "ransom" models. In the fifth essay, we can examine how, within his understanding of the cross as the central mechanism of atonement, Lewis tackled the paradox of incarnation through a proposition, almost a motif, of analogical narrative in which he sought to explain the actuality of the incarnation: that is, how God could be made in human flesh (John 1:14a), grounded in triune simultaneity—and how God could be both eternal and actual. After examining the "why" and "how" of revelation, we can analyze Lewis's statement: "if Shakespeare and Hamlet could ever meet, it must be Shakespeare's doing." Lewis's proposition raises questions about temporality, and modernist objections to theistic belief.

In the final essay in this volume we examine C. S. Lewis's doctrine of election: the paradox of free-will and predestination? For Lewis, the self-determination/determinism that issues from the fall (original sin) relates closely to judgment and responsibility. Comparably Arminian, Lewis asserts, across his works, in summary (though not his words): grace is resistible, judgement is final, there is no election outside of faith—and yet, for Lewis, we are "decided upon." Heaven is open to us all, but hell is forced segregation through what the individual has become, defined by *infernal voluntarism*.[8] Through faith we elect for Christ: God's elect. However, some choose to exclude themselves—they prefer hell to heaven (and if the desire for heaven is sufficient in the human, what heaven is it that is desired? Sometimes this idea of "heaven," from a human perspective, is actually a region of hell?).

8   Not Lewis's own terminology, but that of twenty-first-century scholars of Lewis' work.

Introduction

If Jesus Christ is the *Logos*, the Word of God, then was Lewis right to focus on the reasoned, intellectual, logical veracity of theological statements about God and God's dealings with humanity? The theological and philosophical works of C. S. Lewis were grounded in the argument from reason. To him, reason is a form of revelation that predates nature and relates to the divine: the Word of God, the *Logos* of Christ. These essays seeks to provide some understanding of the essentials to Lewis's philosophical theology. Ultimately Lewis is a teacher/preacher: at the center of his work is Jesus Christ, God Almighty incarnate, *El Shaddai*, Yhwh—Lord—crucified, ascended, and resurrected for our salvation.

1

Praeparatio Evangelica:
C. S. Lewis as a Catholic Evangelical, Defined by Method, Technique, and Form

SYNOPSIS

As an Anglican C. S. Lewis was at one and the same time *intensely* evangelical and *intensely* catholic. The method, technique, and form of his work was likewise catholic-evangelical: his method was defined by the Christ-event, derived from the patristic theologian Vincentius of Lérins (the Scripture-imbued authority of the church: "what has been held always, everywhere, by everybody") and the Puritan Richard Baxter (from whom he acknowledges the term "mere Christian"—a sheer core to the faith, *merus*). This paper demonstrates a thread of systematic ground and continuity to Lewis's writings: a content-led bipartite method and bipartite technique, unified by a universal Platonic principle, realized through the form of the *analogia entis–analogia fidei*—derived from the Catholic and Puritan traditions, but Evangelical in mission. Lewis's theological and philosophical writings frame a Christian *Weltanschauung*: "the creation, the fall, the incarnation, the resurrection, the second coming, and the four last things." Therefore he defines his work as *praeparatio evangelica*: preparation for the Holy Spirit. In this, he is neither an Enlightenment-led modernist, nor a disparate and relativistic liberal postmodernist, but an orthodox theologian-philosopher in the patristic tradition, grounding his writings in Scripture. Lewis could therefore be described as a catholic-evangelical.

I. INTRODUCTION

As an apologist and theologian, C. S. Lewis is often considered something of a dilettante who dabbled in theology as a popularizer, whose work demonstrates scant evidence of a system or of any philosophical ground.

IN THE HIGHEST DEGREE

Was Lewis an occasional theologian who wrote idiosyncratic (and sometimes linguistically quirky) apologetics that certainly captivated his audience, brief theological excursions focused on a particular question but not underpinned by an overarching system that ordered his theological *corpus* as a whole? The aim of this paper is to show that Lewis did exhibit a system. His method, technique, and form was consistently employed, and was characterized by a deep obligation to primary axioms and propositions, by a coherent thread of evangelical truth, defined by a seam of clarity discernible throughout his work.

Lewis was an Anglican, a communicant member of the Church of England. Evangelicals may not like the way Lewis subscribed to what can be considered a traditional Catholic position on the sacraments and on *post mortem* purgation. Likewise, Roman Catholics would do well to see how Lewis could get beyond the external structure of religion to appreciate the immediacy of relationship any believer can have with the Lord Jesus, which in some ways by-passes the structures and authority of the church(es). Lewis was, therefore, a catholic-evangelical[1] who went to great lengths to exclude the establishment middle ground along with the modernist liberal wings of the Church of England from his works—leaving the (Anglo-) Catholic and Evangelical. Writing to *The Church Times* in 1952, Lewis commented that what unites the Evangelical and the Anglo-Catholic against the liberal or modernist is that both are thoroughgoing supernaturalists who believe in the biblical witness to salvation history.[2]

II. BIBLE, TRADITION, AND CREED: HOW SYSTEMATIC WAS LEWIS?

But what do we make of Lewis as a theologian? Was Lewis a systematic theologian? Many patristic theologians started life as trained rhetoricians and philosophers: for example, Justin Martyr. Aquinas' theology was systematic: coherent and interconnected at multiple levels, based on the application of philosophical analysis. Many theologians, even

---

[1] When stated with an initial capital/upper-case letter **Catholic** and **Evangelical** refer to the Roman Catholic Church and the Evangelical movement. Where stated in lower-case, I am referring to the general nature of Lewis's beliefs and faith, doctrine and philosophy as "**catholic**" and "**evangelical**;" Lewis belonged to neither the Roman Catholic Church nor the Evangelical movement.

[2] C. S. Lewis to The Church Times, Feb. 8, 1952, in *Collected Letters* Vol. III (2007), 164.

1. Praeparatio Evangelica: C. S. Lewis as a Catholic Evangelical

Schleiermacher, can be seen as systematic. In the twentieth century many of a Reformed, Protestant, and Evangelical persuasion look to Louis Berkhof in the 1930s[3] as providing a model for systematic thinking in theology: that is, systematic theology championed (in a Barthian context) by late twentieth-century neo-orthodox theologians such as Colin E. Gunton and Robert Jenson as a relatively unique form of doctrine and teaching. Practitioners of systematic theology both within the church and the academy endeavor to formulate an orderly, rational, and coherent account of the Christian faith, often as a *Weltanschauung*, often drawing on philosophical techniques within an evidential framework. As such, systematic theology is essentially rooted in the Bible and the creeds (and therefore should be by default evangelical). Such ancient texts form a type of foundation, along with the declared philosophical techniques.[4]

Nicholas M. Healey distinguishes three types of systematic theology: first, official, generated by the churches; second, ordinary theological reflection produced by virtually all believers; and third, what can be described as professional-academic systematic theology.[5] It is the latter that essentially claims a developed method, systematically applied to the individual's work: coherence and constancy are defining principles. Can this be said of Lewis's apologetics and seemingly disparate philosophical-theological essays? Is Lewis's corpus essentially in the first two categories—churches and ordinary believers who attempt to order their doctrine and ethics? Although attempts at defining systematic theology have been disparate and therefore inconclusive, we can, as a working definition, reiterate Colin E. Gunton's comment that, "systematic theology is what happens when theology engages with philosophy: therefore reason should be discussed theologically."[6] A trained philosopher, a *literatus*, and Professor of Medieval and Renaissance Literature, C. S. Lewis was awarded an honorary Doctor of Divinity degree by the University of St. Andrews in 1946 in recognition of his work in theology and apologetics. Although he had no formal training in theology, his intellect was

---

3   See Berkhof, *Systematic Theology* (1938). Also, Barth, *Church Dogmatics* (1936–77). Post-WW2 we find Paul Tillich, Systematic Theology (1951–63).

4   Attempts at defining systematic theology have been inconclusive. See, for example, Gunton, "A Rose by any Other Name?" (1999); Healey, "What Is Systematic Theology?" (2009); Jenson, *Systematic Theology* (1997).

5   Healey, "What Is Systematic Theology?" (2009), 24–33.

6   Gunton, *Revelation and Reason* (2009), 13.

confirmed in that he received, within four years of study, two B.A. Hons degrees from the University of Oxford (having passed all three required public examinations with first-class honors) in Greats (Greek and Roman literature and classical philosophy) and in English. Lewis's training in classical philosophy was similar to, and as an apologist places him with, Justin Martyr, and many others in the early church. Lewis was technically an amateur (not a salaried religious professional), yet he had, in effect, erected an elaborate smokescreen to separate himself from a clerical elite in the Church of England and in the academy of his day because he categorized this elite as self-proclaimed modern and/or theologically liberal. Unlike many intellectuals, he made no secret of his conversion and his faith, indeed Lewis was at one and the same time *intensely* evangelical and *intensely* catholic. In considering Lewis as a theologian we shall first establish the ground and influence on Lewis as a philosophical theologian and apologist, then extrapolate—essentially from his own words—what the method, technique, and form in his *corpus* was.

III. THEOLOGICAL AND PHILOSOPHICAL GROUND: 1. THE POST-WAR ZEITGEIST

The depth, sharpness, and piercing perception of Lewis's intellect was primarily the result of "The Great Knock," William T. Kirkpatrick, who tutored Lewis for Oxford. Kirkpatrick, though an atheist, had a passionate love of truth, and veracity was not defined by, or curtailed according to, social etiquette: if your opponent was wrong you had a duty before truth to say so. Writing to his father on hearing of Kirkpatrick's death in 1921, Lewis wrote: "It is however no sentiment, but the plainest fact to say that I at least owe to him in the intellectual sphere as much as one human being can owe another. . . . It was an atmosphere of unrelenting clearness and rigid honesty . . . and this I shall be the better for as long as I live."[7] Lewis's philosophical education had begun in earnest when he was invalided out of the First World War. Wounded in the Battle of Arras, Lewis developed a serious interest in philosophy whilst recovering in Étaples hospital: he read and studied John Locke's *Essay Concerning Human Understanding*.[8] Amongst many young students who returned from the trenches, Lewis,

---

7   C. S. Lewis to his father, March 28, 1921, in *Collected Letters*, Vol. I (2004), 534–36, quotation, 534–35.

8   Locke, *Essay Concerning Human Understanding* (1997).

1. Praeparatio Evangelica: C. S. Lewis as a Catholic Evangelical

in the early 1920s, was part of the parochial Oxford post-war spirit of the age, who modelled themselves on an earlier mid-European pre-WW1 Viennese generation defined by logical positivism. After the First World War, the philosophical establishment at Oxford was still characterized by continental idealism and the English idealist philosopher, advocate of temperance, and political radical T. H. Green, but positivism was taking hold. This affects Lewis and accounts for his realist period, characterized by his atheism. Thus far Lewis was in many ways a product of the post-war spirit of the age: a brutal positivistic logic based on what was immediately perceivable to the senses derived from the concept of closed universe, which was seen as a meaningless, brute fact, not the product of a wise and intelligent creator. But Lewis started to become religious: first a theist, then a Christian. Lewis identified the rejection of the ancient religions generally, and Christianity specifically, by an intellectual elite at Oxford in the 1920s as a chronological-intellectual position. That is, a proposition characterized by "the uncritical acceptance of the intellectual climate of our own age and the assumption that whatever has gone out of date is on that count discredited."[9] Seen as an unswerving faith in the modern and contemporary, this chronological-intellectual proposition was expressed thus: if one argues that A implies B, and if A implying B is an old argument from the times when people also believed C, then A implying B is false, because C was found to be untrue; furthermore, Lewis asserted that this argument implied that such propositions are to be mistrusted if they are religious or relate to a religious mind-set, because the modernist (mistakenly) believes that humanity progresses from crude ignorance, year by year. Identifying the arrogance of this flawed modernist argument helped Lewis extricate himself from a plethora of philosophies and belief systems at Oxford in the 1920s. It was, moreover, the inverse of this chronological-intellectual argument that characterized his Christian apologetic: anything modern should be mistrusted because it is contemporary, and must first to be measured against the former, the old. Lewis mistrusted modern philosophy and theology, and through

9   See Lewis, *Surprised by Joy* (1955), ch. 13, specifically 206–8, quotation, 207. Along with Owen Barfield and J. R. R Tolkien, Lewis would then raise the question of why did a particular thought system cease to be fashionable, and whether it was ever refuted, and if so, how. See also, Lewis, *Mere Christianity* (1952), ch. 7. See also, the first volume of *The Space Trilogy*, Lewis, *Out of the Silent Planet* (1938), where the anti-heroes, Devine and Weston, assume all ideas that have gone before are inferior and flawed, even in relation to alien species on another planet. See also, Lewis, *The Pilgrim's Regress* (1933).

his training in classical philosophy he drew upon Plato, avoiding the continental Cartesian and Kantian schools and their derivative thought systems. Parallel to his development towards becoming a Christian was his development in pre-modern idealism as a philosophical foundation, together with his understanding of and respect for reason. Idealism was for Lewis contrary to the closed universe of positivistic realism.

IV. THEOLOGICAL AND PHILOSOPHICAL GROUND: 2. IDEALISM AND PLATONISM

Much of the philosophical ground of Lewis's work was formulated in the 1920s, during his period as an apostate atheist as part of his early employment at Oxford teaching philosophy. Lewis's doctoral research at Oxford was on the seventeenth-century Cambridge Platonist Philosopher Henry More, who contrasted with the continental school of philosophy: "What Lewis found in More was an anti-Cartesian rationalist, someone who understood reason not as an abstract, analytic faculty presiding over an indeterminate field of extension, but as the consubstantial light joining the intellect to reality."[10] In contrast to the continental school, Lewis simply went back to Henry More, and to Plato; when he became a Christian this extended to patristic theologians, medieval scholasticism, and seventeenth-century Protestants: "More's thought . . . pointed beyond the merely rational and merely material, and in him Lewis found an idealist who believed in God, in reason as a living principle, in nature as alive with Logos."[11] Lewis the philosopher was therefore brought to a degree of intellectual maturity by his study of the seventeenth-century Platonists; this gave him a ground, a philosophical framework, which remained constant for the rest of his life.

Lewis's studies exposed him to many thought systems. As a naive philosophy teacher at Oxford in his mid-twenties, he owned to subscribing to what he termed philosophical idealism. In addition to the fundamental grounding he drew from Henry More, this intellectual development was influenced by Plato, the Irish philosopher George Berkeley, Bishop of Cloyne, and indirectly, and to a lesser extent, by Georg Hegel, though it

---

10 Patrick, "C. S. Lewis and Idealism" (1998), 160. See also, on the relationship between More's philosophy and the continental school, Walker, "Scripture, Revelation and Platonism in C. S. Lewis," (2002).

11 Patrick, "C. S. Lewis and Idealism" (1998), 161.

1. Praeparatio Evangelica: C. S. Lewis as a Catholic Evangelical

is questionable as to how much Lewis really did draw on the continental school, noted for absolute idealism and dialectic. In his assertion of the forms, Lewis is an orthodox Platonist (with Tolkien, he used the term "shadowlands" for this world, this reality, to contrast with the real, when the real is intuited, but beyond our immediate sense perception). From his conversion on, Lewis is a Christian Platonist in a manner similar to many patristic theologians. After Henry More, it is Bishop George Berkeley's writings on perception and epistemology that Lewis draws on, specifically Berkeley's theory of immaterialism—subjective idealism—encapsulated in the dictum, *esse est percipi* (to be is to be perceived), which had a profound effect on the young Lewis, because of the argument from Berkeley that we can only know sensations and ideas of objects.

V. THEOLOGICAL AND PHILOSOPHICAL GROUND: 3. THEOLOGICAL INFLUENCES

Though trained in philosophy (classical philosophy—as were most of the patristic theologians, in particular Justin Martyr, Athanasius, and Augustine, who had been trained in the secular academy of their day) Lewis's primary aim was to glorify God, and inform people about the salvific actions of God in the Christ-event. Therefore, he is a theologian-philosopher, not a philosophical theologian: the emphasis on the primacy of theology is important. Whereas, for example, Athanasius (following his philosophical training) was prepared by the Catechetical School in Alexandria in the early fourth century as a theologian, Lewis was essentially self-taught theologically: he read widely and deeply from patristic to medieval theologians. Lewis laid out his theological influences, and the education he received from them, in a letter in response to an enquiry from a reader, in 1958. When the correspondent questions the complexity of the debts Lewis owes to modern theologians, he comments that his debt to the moderns is hardly anything at all, that he knows not the moderns and what they stand for, that Christianity reached him initially through the literature he taught in the 1920s: Dante, Spenser, Milton, George Herbert, and so forth.[12] After his conversion he drank in Augustine of Hippo, Richard Hooker, Thomas Traherne, and the work of many medieval mystics, also the church fathers, the patristic

---

12   C. S. Lewis to Corbin Scott Carnell, Oct. 13, 1958, in, *Collected Letters*, Vol. III (2007), 978–98.

theologians. He admits his ignorance of many modern theological works, with the exception of Anders Nygren's *Agape and Eros*, and Gustaf Aulén's seminal work on Christ's sacrifice, *Christus Victor* (both works drew heavily on the patristic tradition, but also on the Reformation tradition from the sixteenth and seventeenth centuries). A key to Lewis's beliefs and therefore his theology is an orthodox doctrine of original sin. Much of Lewis's doctrine of the fall is derived specifically from Augustine's *de civitate Dei*. Lewis studied Augustine's *confessiones* in 1936, and *de civitate Dei* in 1937, both in the original Latin, returning to them regularly over the next decade, as well as translating the massive *de civitate Dei* for his own use.[13] In addition, Lewis read and studied Aquinas's great *summa theologiae* on a daily basis in the 1940s, in its original Latin, which gave his apologetics and philosophical theology a distinctively sharp logical edge.

VI. SYSTEMATIC METHOD, TECHNIQUE, AND FORM

If apologetics are broadly to be considered as arguments in justification of a theory or doctrine, and if Christian apologetics are to be qualified as reasoned arguments to explicate orthodox Christian faith, and if an apologist confronts the disagreements between differing theistic and non-theistic belief systems, then defense is at the heart of apologetics. Given the origins of the term in the Greek *apologia*, Lewis as a Christian apologist wrote and spoke in defense of the truth of the gospel, justifying it in the face of self-confessed atheists, scientists, and philosophers, but also in relation to other religions and belief systems. Because he was, so to speak, preparing the way—*praeparatio evangelica*—he also confronted the inertia and apathy of many ordinary people who considered themselves neither Christian, nor anti-Christian. Lewis commented that "Mine are *praeparatio evangelica* rather than *evangelium*, an attempt to convince people that there is a moral law, that we disobey it, and that the existence of a Lawgiver is at least very probable and also (unless you add the Christian doctrine of the atonement) that this imparts despair rather than comfort."[14] Therefore, Lewis saw himself as preparing his

---

13   C. S. Lewis to Dom Bede Griffiths, April 24, 1936, and, C. S. Lewis to Dom Bede Griffiths, May 23, 1936, in, *Collected Letters*, Vol. II (2004), 187–90 and 191–95.

14   C. S. Lewis to Sister Penelope CSMV, May 15, 1941, in *Collected Letters*, Vol. II (2004), 484–85. See also, Lewis, "Preface to the Third Edition," in *The Pilgrim's Regress*, xvii. See also, Heck, "*Praeparatio Evangelica*" (1997).

1. Praeparatio Evangelica: C. S. Lewis as a Catholic Evangelical

readers for the gospel, not necessarily converting them. Lewis saw his role, public and private, in bearing witness to Christ: he was in effect a pre-evangelist.[15] Lewis wrote and broadcast popular apologetics, but he also wrote serious philosophical theology. It would give a false picture to consider one without the other. If apologetics is considered different to academic theology, and in particular from philosophical theology then we need to consider what techniques Lewis used to assert orthodox Christian doctrine—whether philosophical theology or apologetics—whilst attempting to be true to the core of established faith.

Lewis's method was defined by content: the nature of the content was derived from the fifth-century patristic theologian Vincentius of Lérins and the seventeenth-century Puritan Richard Baxter. Lewis's content-led method in his theology is two-fold: one element is broadly *catholic* (pertinently, patristic), the other broadly *evangelical* (pertinently, Puritan). In terms of how he presented this content in his apologetics, Lewis relied on two identifiable philosophical techniques: first, *reductio ad absurdum*, and, second, the law of excluded middle.

VII. CONTENT-DEFINED METHOD:
1. WHAT HAS BEEN HELD ALWAYS, BY ALL

First, was an appeal to the basic core of the faith established in the centuries after Christ's resurrection, a basic core that was essentially complete by the mid-fifth century, but with much of the detail worked out by the mid-eighth century, this common core to the faith was endorsed by Scripture and by the developing church tradition. Writing to *The Church Times* in 1952, Lewis commented that,

> To a layman, it seems obvious that what unites the Evangelical and the Anglo-Catholic against the Liberal or Modernist is something very clear and momentous, namely, the fact that both are thoroughgoing supernaturalists, who believe in the Creation, the Fall, the Incarnation, the Resurrection, the Second Coming, and the Four Last Things. This unites them not only with one

---

15   Lewis probably discovered the phrase from Eusebius of Caesare's, *Proparaskeuē Euangelikē* (*Preparation for the Gospel*, written sometime between 313 and 324 AD), usually known by its Latin title, *Praeparatio Evangelica* was written to demonstrate the veracity of the gospel over and against pagan religion through clear and sustained argument, as such it complements Lewis's apologetic defense of Christianity. See Johnson, Ethnicity and Argument in Eusebius' *Praeparatio Evangelica* (2006).

another, but with the Christian religion as understood *ubique et ab omnibus*.[16]

The phrase *ubique et ab omnibus* is important. It is from Vincentius of Lérins, who was asserting that we should hold on to that which has been believed by all. Lewis is referring to Vincentius's key work, *The Commonitory* (written in 434 AD), which was written to establish a general or common rule to identify truth from falsity. Vincentius's rule is in essence succinct and simple: it is the authority of the Bible. All questions of doctrine and ethics must be measured against the canon of Scripture, answered from the Bible. But this, Vincentius acknowledges, is problematic because there are so many interpretations of Scripture. The rule of Scripture is then qualified by an appeal to that which has been endorsed universally since the earliest days of the church: the rule of faith guides readers to the correct interpretations of the Bible—the authoritative ones. But the Bible's authority does not depend on the rule of faith: it is not the clergy as such but the whole church that is spoken of—"all, everywhere, always," thus: "*quod ubique, quod semper, quod ab omnibus*" ("what has been held always, everywhere, by everybody").[17] In other words, there is a body of doctrine/belief, particularly about Jesus of Nazareth, the Christ, which is non-negotiable, authenticated by Scripture, held in faith by all, always, everywhere (hence, universally consented to from antiquity), which was established in the centuries after Christ, in the patristic era, that emerged from the apostles as the authority of the church.

VIII. CONTENT DEFINED METHOD: 2. A MERE CORE

The second element to Lewis's method was, like Vincentius of Lérins, to identify a common ground or core, but in this instance to name it and in so doing identify some of its characteristics: "*Mere Christianity*." This common core, this "*Mere Christianity*," is then to be used as a measure of

---

16   C. S. Lewis to *The Church Times*, Feb. 8, 1952, in, *Collected Letters* Vol. III (2007), 164.

17   Vincent of Lérins, *The Commonitory of Vincent of Lérins* (trans. Heurtley, 2002). For the statement, "*quod ubique, quod semper, quod ab omnibus*," quoted by Lewis, see, ch. 2, §. 6 "A General Rule for Distinguishing the Truth of the Catholic Faith from the Falsehood of Heretical Pravity," 214, also, 219 and, 223. An online text can be consulted at the Christian Classics Ethereal Library: www.ccel.org.

1. Praeparatio Evangelica: C. S. Lewis as a Catholic Evangelical

doctrine and ethics. Lewis continued in the letter sent to *The Church Times* from 1952, quoted above, "Perhaps the trouble is that as supernaturalists, whether 'Low' or 'High' Church, thus taken together, they lack a name. May I suggest 'Deep Church'; or, if that fails, in humility, Baxter's 'mere Christians?'"[18] Lewis is deliberately invoking the work of the seventeenth-century English Puritan Richard Baxter:

> You know not of what Party I am of; nor what to call me; I am sorrier for you in this than for myself; if you know not, I will tell you, I am a CHRISTIAN, a MEER* CHRISTIAN, of no other Religion; and the Church that I am of is the Christian Church, and hath been visible where ever the Christian Religion and Church hath been visible: But must you know of what Sect or Party I am of? I am against all Sects and dividing Parties: But if any will call *Mere Christians* by the name of a Party, because they take up with *Mere Christianity*, *Creed*, and *Scripture*, and will not be of any dividing or contentious Sect, I am of that Party which is so against Parties: If the name CHRISTIAN be not enough, call me a CATHOLIC CHRISTIAN; not as that word signifieth an hereticating majority of Bishops, but as it signifieth one that hath no Religion, but that which by Christ and the Apostles was left to the Catholic Church, or the body of Jesus Christ on Earth.
>
> I am sorry that you are not content with meer Christianity.... I would say also that (nor as Protestants) did I not take the religion called Protestant (a name which I am not fond of) to be nothing but *simple Christian*.[19]
>
> (Baxter's emphasis and capitalization.
*: early modern English spelling.)

Therefore, a "mere"[20] core of orthodoxy informed Lewis's method, that which had been held by all during the patristic era, a "mere" core that developed in the early centuries of the church, and could be identified as a true seam of orthodoxy through church history. Content was doctrinal; content defined method—and method was therefore by definition orthodox.

18 C. S. Lewis to *The Church Times*, Feb. 8, 1952, in, *Collected Letters* Vol. III (2007), 164.

19 Baxter, "What History Is Credible, and What Not," Introductory essay in, *Church History of the Government of Bishops and their Councils* (1680), xvii.

20 "Mere," from, the medieval Middle English "pure," "sheer," or "downright," "meer," from the Latin, merus, undiluted.

Lewis set out the principle underlying his bipartite method and bipartite technique in a letter to an American Episcopalian, Hart Lyman Stebbins, who had written to him asking what would be "the arguments which throw the decision to the Anglican and against the Roman Catholic Church."[21] Lewis's reply uses an image, a metaphor, almost a parable, inevitably Platonic. He writes that if he sought the fullest and truest interpretation of what Plato taught then he would be confident in accepting the interpretation which is common to all those who either claim to be Platonists or subscribe to his teaching, those who agree on what he took to be true Platonism: "Any purely modern views which claim to have discovered for the first time what Plato meant, and say that everyone from Aristotle down has misunderstood him, I reject out of hand."[22] Lewis then tackles the balance between the churches of his day, of the denominations in the twentieth century.

> I should approach them with great respect. But if I found that their teaching in many ways was curiously unlike his actual text and unlike what ancient interpreters said, and in some cases could not be traced back to within 1000 years of his time, I should reject these exclusive claims: while still ready, of course, to take any particular thing they taught on its merits.
>
> I do the same with Christianity. What is most certain is the vast mass of doctrine which I find agreed on by scripture, the Fathers, the Middle Ages, modern RCs, modern Protestants. That is true "catholic" doctrine. Mere "modernism" I reject at once.[23]

Therefore, we have Lewis's content-driven method succinctly stated in one principle: continuity and agreement of a core of belief, agreed on by scripture, the Fathers, the Middle Ages, contemporary Roman Catholics and Protestants and tracing its heritage back to the apostles: this is true "catholic" for him. This is a universal principle, where universalism lies beyond any particularly denomination.[24] Because Lewis's reply was in the

---

21 C. S. Lewis to H. Lyman Stebbins, May 8, 1945, in, *Collected Letters* Vol. II (2004), 645–47. The essential substance of Stebbins letter is presented on 645 at the beginning of the reply Lewis sent to him.

22 C. S. Lewis to H. Lyman Stebbins, May 8, 1945, 645–46.

23 C. S. Lewis to H. Lyman Stebbins, May 8, 1945, 646.

24 It is in this context that Lewis uses the hall metaphor in the preface to *Mere Christianity*: the individual denominations and churches are like rooms leading off from a hall or lobby, where the hall represents this mere core of orthodoxy (*Mere Christianity*

1. Praeparatio Evangelica: C. S. Lewis as a Catholic Evangelical

context of Stebbins enquiry of the relationship between the Anglican and the Roman Catholic churches he did continue to explain how he rejected Roman Catholicism where it differed and dissented from this universal tradition and in particularly from apostolic Christianity, citing examples relating to Mary and Mariology, the papal principle, and the doctrine of transubstantiation, in relation to—importantly—the New Testament. We need to remember that Lewis is writing in the context of pre-Vatican II Rome. "In a word, the whole set-up of modern Romanism seems to me to be as much a provincial or local variation from the central, ancient tradition as any particular Protestant sect is. I must therefore reject their claim: though this does not mean rejecting particular things they say."[25] This is not simply an anti-Roman polemic; Lewis equally applied this universal principle to Protestantism. For example, writing to his life-long friend Arthur Greeves there are detailed criticisms of the Puritan and more extreme Protestantism evident in their Ulster heritage, where such Puritanism departs from this universal principle and becomes provincial, parochial, and local, a variation from this central and mere, simple and sheer, core.[26] We may ask, importantly, what is the source of this unifying universal principle? For Lewis this is Christ: the universal Christ from all eternity to all eternity, the second person of the Trinity, co-eternal with the Father and the Holy Spirit, the Word of God, who through and in the Spirit will lead us into all truth, that governs all truth, who for Lewis is biblically endorsed as the way, the truth, and the life (John 16:13; cf. John 8:32; 14:16.)

IX. CONTENT DEFINED METHOD:
3. REGULA FIDEI

Lewis's writings were content-driven: as the Christ-event is an occurrence, an incident in history, the method is primarily defined by this event. This event leads into church history, the content issuing—in part—from Jesus' request to his followers to remember him.[27] Therefore, Lewis's method is

---

[1952], viii–ix).

25 C. S. Lewis to H. Lyman Stebbins, May 8, 1945, in, *Collected Letters* Vol. II (2004), 646–47.

26 C. S. Lewis to Arthur Greeves, Dec. 6, 1931, in *Collected Letters*, Vol. II (2004), 22–25.

27 Matt 26.26–28; Mark 14.22–25; Luke 22.14–19; See also 1 Cor 11:24.

to identify a body of knowledge and understanding that exists outside of human consciousness. This had led to the formulation of the creeds. To go beyond this, to expand and expound on the creeds, is then to codify this understanding into a body of knowledge and understanding, propositions and doctrine. Primarily this body of knowledge and understanding is attested to by Scripture, it is endorsed by Scripture, and it is about God's dealings with humanity culminating in the incarnation, crucifixion, and resurrection. Secondarily, when there are questions that cannot be directly answered by appeal to Scripture, this developing body of doctrine is secondarily endorsed by appeal to the developed patristic tradition—the early church. Therefore, there is identified a "*meer*"/"*merus*," a sheer, pure, simple, undiluted core, a basic core of "*Mere Christianity*," which is at the heart of the Christian faith and provides the foundation, the ground, for theological apologetics: Scripture, backed-up by the patristic tradition, identifies a mere core. This underpins all of Lewis's work as a theologian.

This relates closely to the *regula fidei* (rule of faith), which was established in Lewis's work from early on, though it becomes more and more important in his mature work: that which evaluates theological opinion and the life of the church by measuring against what has been firmly established and believed—that is, Lewis's content-driven method derived from the patristic theologian Vincentius of Lérins and the seventeenth-century Puritan Richard Baxter, his "mere" core of orthodoxy. This rule of faith was rooted in Scripture: in Paul's comments in Romans, where all is to be seen in proportion to faith: in the Greek New Testament, *analogian tēs pisteōs*—literally, the "*analogy of faith*" (Rom 12:6).

Lewis saw Christianity as the *Weltanschauung*. This "mere" core was the meta-narrative, above all competing meta-narratives. Richard Baxter's work, from which Lewis derived the concept of "*Mere Christianity*," was a work of church history and he, like Lewis, realized the importance of identifying what was and what was not part of this salvation history. Baxter wrote:

> But it is not all history that is needful or useful to us: there are many things done which we are not concerned to be acquainted with. But the history of the Church, of the propagation of the Christian faith, and what the doctrine was that was then received, and how it was practiced, promoted and defended, and how it was corrupted, invaded and persecuted, is of so great use to posterity,

1. Praeparatio Evangelica: C. S. Lewis as a Catholic Evangelical

that next to the scripture and the illuminations of God's Spirit, I remember nothing more needful to be known.[28]

This is remarkably similar to Vincentius of Lérins balance between Scripture and the developing patristic church tradition. Baxter saw this as important because, he argues, that mere Christians should know about the past, about church history, as they need to be "truly acquainted how things have gone in the Church from the beginning,"[29] thus the records and documents from the patristic period are of immense importance. This was also so for Lewis: history was not relative, our perception may, to a degree, be relative to our personal interests, but there was a thread—as Vincentius of Lérins had identified—of truth, of the emergence of sound beliefs about Christ, which was of importance.

X. TRANSPOSITION: A UNIFYING UNIVERSAL PRINCIPLE

Lewis is identifying the universal testimony of the church as the ground and as an indicator of doctrine where theology is a word of the church, issuing from the Word: the *Logos*. The Word is defined by what flows from the revelation of the Christ-event, through the authority of the church, bound by the Holy Spirit. There is therefore a unifying universal principle against which all modern or contemporary forms of theology are measured. This unifying universal principle is at its strongest in the early and patristic churches where Scripture is developed as a validating mechanism (Vincentius) and is at its purest and simplest, later, in a mere core (Baxter). This issues from a doctrine of revelation. Lewis's understanding of revelation, where revelation is at the heart of doctrine, is governed—pneumatologically—by transposition.[30]

If idealism is incarnational (the ideal, the eternal, descended to earth, to live amongst us and die for our sins, to raise us up again and draw us up

---

28   Baxter, "Preface," in *Church History of the Government of Bishops and Their Councils* (1680), iv.

29   Baxter, "Preface," in *Church History of the Government of Bishops and Their Councils* (1680), vi vii.

30   Lewis, "Transposition," a sermon given in Mansfield College, Oxford on Whit Sunday, May 28, 1944; published in *Transposition and Other Addresses* (1st ed., 1949). A reworked and extended edition of the sermon as an academic paper ("Transposition," 2nd ed., 1962) was published in *They Asked for a Paper*. All references are to this 2nd edition.

out of the mire heavenward[31]), it is important to remember that, for Lewis, any revelation is transposed. Described by Lewis as his contribution to the philosophy of the incarnation, a doctrine of transposition relates closely to a kenotic Christology (Phil 2:6–11), to the *communicatio idiomatum* (the communication of attributes), the knowability of God (which is both a veiling and an unveiling), and how human fallibility can lead us to misread what is communicated to us.[32] In a doctrine of transposition, the hard-and-firm division and separation posited by Platonic idealism between eternity and our reality, between the forms and the physical world, is blurred; it is seen as a gradation. Therefore, transposition explains, to a degree, what is happening in revelation: transposition makes gradual, it theologizes this hard-and-fast Platonic dualism. Lewis argues that the knowledge and understanding that is imparted in divine revelation is transposed:[33] it is changed, diminuted, diluted, *through our reception* of revelation, like a symphony for full orchestra transposed for solo piano, or a drawing (sometimes pencil, other times pen-and-ink, then charcoal or pastel—each different) as compared to the landscape depicted or the person portrayed. However, something of the essence, the essential spirit, is communicated, relayed, *revealed*. The fine drawings by Leonardo da Vinci are an example of how, despite the limitations of the medium, the drawing still conveys something of the essential *beauty* and *spirit* in a person, in the face, and not just the physical form but the *essence*. This is "how" revelation is imparted. As a key to all of Lewis's work, a doctrine of transposition is itself transposed, reduced, lessened, and changed, but essentially still true to the original. This is broadly Platonic in the manner in which the transposed is defined by the truly real in eternity. Lewis's doctrine is designed to explain how revelation works, how it is communicated, and, paradoxically, why revelation can never be fully imparted. Jesus is therefore a transposition of the eternal *Logos*, the second person of the Trinity, into the human. Moses knew that no human could look God in the face and live. Therefore, such an incarnational transposition is by necessity veiled—simply so we can begin to discern, to know, and understand something of the revelation of the Christ. If God

---

31 Lewis draws heavily on Athanasius (c.297–373) in this proposition.

32 Lewis, "Transposition," (2nd ed.; 1962), 166. For a detailed exposition of this, see Brazier, "C. S. Lewis: A Doctrine of Transposition" (2009). See also, Ch. 4 in this volume.

33 Lewis, "Transposition," (2nd ed.; 1962).

had descended, un-transposed, two thousand years ago, then it would have been the end of the world (as it will be in the *eschaton*, with the second coming).

XI. APOLOGETIC TECHNIQUE:
1. *REDUCTIO AD ABSURDUM*

In formal disputation and logic—and especially beloved by barristers in court—*reductio ad absurdum* (reduction to the absurd) is a type of argument that refutes an opponent's proposal by demonstrating that it is either rooted in, or leads inevitably to, an absurd or self-contradictory conclusion. If such a proposition is shown to be absurd and untenable then Lewis has, so to speak, won the day, or so he believed. Lewis excelled at reducing the opposition's arguments to nothing, demolishing their case and showing what they believed to be absurd: *reductio ad absurdum*. Such a technique is valued by Lewis in an apologetic discussion. Such a technique is grounded in logic. Lewis was no fideist who shied away from logic and reason. Logic is inherent to the natural sciences, but also in finding out about the truth of God: "One of the objections to studying logic most often cited is that logic does not apply to God or to any of the mysteries of the Christian faith, such as the Trinity or the Incarnation, ... [but] even those who claim, 'Logic does not apply to God,' use logic in that very statement. Logic is unavoidable. ... Theology is a rational discourse about God."[34] Geisler and Brookes continue by reiterating, derived from Aristotle, the four basic laws, self-evident and self-explanatory: the law of non-contradiction (A is not non-A, no two contradictory statements can be simultaneously true in the same sense); the law of identity (God is God); the law of excluded middle (A is either A or non-A, there is no compromise); the law of rational inference (inferences can be made from what is already known to what is not yet known).[35] Therefore, "Theological method builds on these elementary laws of logic. If logic is

---

34   Geisler and Brookes, *Come Let Us Reason. An Introduction to Logical Thinking*, Ch. 1 "The Whats and Whys of Logic," 11–20, specifically, 15–17, referring to John 1, the Logos.

35   Geisler and Ronald , *Come Let Us Reason* (1990), 16–17. The law of rational inference is at the heart of Lewis's *The Chronicles of Narnia*, what Lewis called a "supposal," a "what if," in this case, what if Christ was incarnate in a totally alien reality, another world outside of our universe, and died to save creatures there? What would happen: analogy by inference.

a necessary precondition of all thought, then it must also be necessary for all thought about God."[36] This does not deny that in many instances our human fallibility and fallenness may lead to an apparent paradox, which we cannot resolve through logic: logic is not God.

XII. APOLOGETIC TECHNIQUE:
2. LAW OF EXCLUDED MIDDLE

Reductio ad absurdum relates, in terms of philosophy and logic, to the *law of excluded middle* (C. S. Lewis is mortal, or he is immortal, there is no third option, logic excludes that Lewis is neither mortal nor immortal[37]). Again rooted in philosophical logic the law of the excluded middle is the technique used to show that an argument or proposition is either true or not true. In its purest form, because truth can appear ambiguous, this is expressed as "either-or." Ambiguity is then dismissed by logical argument. Lewis almost certainly derived this technique from his reading of Aristotle. Lewis excelled at excluding the grey, nuanced, middle ground where ambiguity thrived; he excluded this in favor of the "either-or." He did not necessarily insist on one option being acknowledged as truth, but left the defeated opponent to see that if absurdity was to be avoided they had to make a decision. This comes into its own with Christian apologetics because whatever beliefs we hold Jesus confronts us with the need to make a decision. This "either-or" is at the heart of Lewis's most popular and in some ways controversial apologetic: that Jesus was "Mad, Bad, or God" (that is, *aut Deus aut malus homo*—Jesus was God, or he cannot be considered a good man).[38] The picture given to us by Scripture, the witness and testimony of the evangelists, is of a man who audaciously forgave people their sins, when such was God's prerogative, a man who claimed pre-existence to Abraham, who *acted as if* he was God. Scripture also shows how those who encountered Jesus, or those who exercised power and control over him (the Scribes and Pharisees, the Chief Priests, the Romans), were forced to make a decision about him: either Jesus is

---

36 Geisler and Brookes, *Come Let Us Reason* (1990), 16–17.

37 If Lewis were an inanimate thing, like a rock, then he would be neither mortal nor immortal. Both categories only apply to living things

38 See Brazier, *C. S. Lewis—The Work of Christ Revealed* (2012), "Part Two The Revelation of Christ—God, or a Bad Man," chs. 4–8, 89–188, also, Brazier, "God . . . or a Bad, or Mad, Man" (2014).

1. Praeparatio Evangelica: C. S. Lewis as a Catholic Evangelical

a "liar," he is "unbalanced," he cannot be considered sane, or he has a "demon," he is "possessed," he does these things by Beelzebub, or he is the God of Israel, the Lord, walking among them, he is truly the divine "light of the world."[39]

Lewis's two-fold method and two-fold technique was not forcing the hearer to the point of conversion, it was merely setting out the options, clearly, without a nuanced, grey, middle-ground confusion. Therefore, Lewis's method and technique simply prepared the hearer to make a decision, Lewis's apologetics and theology were evangelical but, as he asserted, they were *praeparatio evangelica*.

XIII. ANALOGIA ENTIS–ANALOGIA FIDEI

Lewis's work develops from the assertive, even aggressive, apologetic of the 1940s into something characteristically and methodologically dissimilar (though not poles apart, or diametrically different), and the progress of that change can be attributed to a greater or lesser degree to the Anscombe-Lewis debate (1948), though proving such an assertion is riddled with the problems of causation that the debate was about.[40] The form of Lewis's work is defined within this bipartite method and technique *by analogy*. In the 1930s and 1940s his apologetics and philosophical theology are defined by grounding propositions in creation, and therefore in reason—the *analogia entis*; by the 1950s Lewis sees the primary link between God and humanity for our theologizing as in and through the Christ: the *analogia fidei*.

In the 1930s and 1940s (the early and middle period works) Lewis's championing of apologetics is through the *analogia entis*: for example, *The Problem of Pain* (1940), and especially in the BBC radio programs, *The Broadcast Talks* (1941–44). It is in these works that he applies *reductio ad absurdum* to its fullest, forcing the reader and listener to reject the irrationality and illogicality of the alternative position, and excluding any grey middle-ground compromise. There is some evidence of the *analogia fidei* in this early and middle period—analogical narratives, theologically charged parable and story—characterized by the form of the *analogia*

---

39 John 8:49 and 10:21, also, Matt 11:18 and Luke 7:33, and, Mark 3:20–22.

40 See Brazier, "C. S. Lewis and the Anscombe Debate" (2011).

fidei, for example, *The Space Trilogy* (1938–45), *The Screwtape Letters* (1942), and *The Great Divorce* (1945).

In the mature period works, late 1940s and the 1950s, after the Anscombe-Lewis debate (1948), which did not refute his argument from reason, but exposed a badly worked-out premise in his understanding of causation,[41] he took a more cautious and reflective approach, wisdom becomes the touchstone, complemented by the *analogia fidei*. It is faith now that leads to understanding, but faith is the ground from which reason can work, where reason predates creation, where the reason of God is infused into the human. To reject the Christ is *absurdum*, Christ is the universal *Weltanschauung*; to try to pursue a middle ground is flawed. The *analogia fidei* is demonstrated in his use of analogical narrative. For example, *The Chronicles of Narnia* (1950–56), *Till We Have Faces* (1956), *Reflections on the Psalms* (1958), and *Letters to Malcolm: Chiefly on Prayer* (1964, posthumously published). Lewis continues to value the *analogia entis* throughout his mature work, for example, the many carefully structured essays of philosophical theology, *Mere Christianity* (1952) and the second edition of *Miracles* (2nd ed. 1960); however, it is fair to say that the form of the *analogia fidei* occupies a much greater role in his work in the 1950s. This development probably owes some of its impetus to the Anscombe-Lewis debate, but the evidence is there for a more gradual change, initiated from before his encounter with the young linguistic philosopher Elizabeth Anscombe. In addition, the move from an emphasis on the *analogia entis* to the *analogia fidei* may have been, to a degree, the result of maturity as Lewis grew older; and there is also the effect his love for Joy Davidman had on him, and her subsequent death from cancer.

XIV. CONCLUSION

Lewis gets close to producing a *summa* (if a *summa* can be considered part of the aim and objective of a systematic theology) in *Mere Christianity*,[42] which was based on the wartime BBC radio broadcasts (1941–44),

---

[41] Brazier, "C. S. Lewis and the Anscombe Debate" (2011), specifically, 83–83, also, 96–104.

[42] Lewis, *Mere Christianity* (1952).

1. Praeparatio Evangelica: C. S. Lewis as a Catholic Evangelical

which dealt with the Christian *Weltanschauung*: the creation and the fall into original sin, salvation history, God's revelation and economy with humanity and the world, the incarnation, crucifixion, resurrection, and second coming of God in Christ, the church, all leading teleologically to usher in the *eschaton*: death, judgement, heaven, and hell. *Mere Christianity* was a relatively short work compared to the lengths Thomas Aquinas and Karl Barth went to, yet it is, perhaps, more complete than many systematic theologies (though it does have its detractors who will point to a personal bias in Lewis, a criticism that can be levelled at any theologian, systematic or otherwise).

Lewis was an intensely private and reticent man, who disliked his fame, but nonetheless he produced a considerable *corpus* of work that still today communicates orthodox, creedal, traditional, Christian doctrine to many millions of people. Disparate though his work may appear to some, taken as a whole there is a thread of continuity throughout that indicates a systematic basis to his theological and philosophical writings, there is even the framework of a systematic theology (however, it is incomplete, as can be said with Aquinas, Barth, Gunton, and many others). It can be argued that Lewis lacks the pretense that many official theologians use to give their work credibility before an often overtly atheistic and seemingly disinterested academy. Then there are those who are quite justifiably skeptical of the concept of systematic theology, that it is just an academic pretense grafted onto basic Christian doctrine, especially when it is difficult to get systematic theologians to agree on a single unifying definition of systematic theology. This notwithstanding, Lewis did exhibit something of a system, consistently applied, with a steady and predictable logical ordered and reasoned thread of method, technique, and form, across his work. Lewis did exhibit, often veiled, this content-led bipartite method and bipartite technique that worked together in the form of the *analogia entis–analogia fidei*, unified by a universal Platonic principle, that may be considered to represent the pneumatological action of the economic Trinity: Lewis's Platonic commerce can, in effect, be seen as a somewhat mechanistic description of the action of the Holy Spirit within salvation history. Lewis was intensely serious and reserved, whose work was deeply considered and thought-out. What is important is not whether Lewis can be classified as a systematic theologian but that he had a carefully thought-out method and technique, consistently applied to his popular apologetics, his philosophical theology, and his confessional writings. We must not be beguiled by the popular conception of Lewis, the seeming dilettante who dabbled in theology as a popularizer; underlying Lewis's *corpus* is a depth and consistency, a coherence, that is often normally associated with high-ranking professional academic theologians.

2

Christological Prefigurement: the Incarnation-Resurrection Narrative— History and Reality, Imagination and Mythopoeic Intimation

SYNOPSIS

This paper is an examination of the Christology and pneumatology that C. S. Lewis read from the apparent prefiguring of elements of the incarnation-resurrection narrative in religious myths, and also his assertion that the incarnation-resurrection narrative operates on us both as fact and myth. After an initial examination of the term myth and mythopoeia, Lewis's writings on the myth that became reality (the Christ-event) are discussed along with examples of prefigurement. Through his understanding of natural theology (rooted in that of Augustine, though fed by Lewis's daily reading of the *Summa theologiae*) and his cautious respect for human imagination (from the poet, theologian, and philosopher Samuel Taylor Coleridge) and in contrast to his earlier deference for the conclusions of the Victorian religionist and social anthropologist James George Frazer, Lewis came to regard these prefigurements as the work of the Holy Spirit—intimations of God's salvific action in Christ—though Lewis's orthodoxy saw human imagination as flawed through original sin. This leads us to ask three questions: First, how do these prefigured ideas come to be in these myths and how do these intimations, splintered fragments of the true light, relate to Lewis's understanding of Christ as the light of the world? Second, how does the incarnation-resurrection narrative act/operate on us as a myth, whether spoken or read (a baptized imagination is crucial here for Lewis in both the creation and receiving/hearing of such narratives)? Third, is there internal evidence for a mythopoeic interpretation within the incarnation-resurrection narrative? Our conclusions can be illustrated by a brief examination of Lewis's own Christian myth— Aslan from *The Chronicles of Narnia*—originally written for a Christian audience but now read by mainly non-Christian/post-Christian children and adults.

PART I.
A CRITICAL EVALUATION OF LEWIS'S PROPOSITION THAT THE INCARNATION-RESURRECTION NARRATIVE IS BOTH MYTH AND HISTORY

I. INTRODUCTION

On the evening of his conversion from theism to Christianity C. S. Lewis is recorded as having described myths as beautiful and moving, though they were "lies and therefore worthless, even though breathed through silver . . . ."[1] His understanding of myth was to change during his life as a result of his adoption and championing through apologetics of an orthodox Christian faith, centered as it is on the death and resurrection of God-incarnate. Myth was, and continued to be, very important to him—primarily the Northern European myths, closely followed by Hinduism and Greek mythology. Professionally, his work was in mediæval and Renaissance literature, he therefore had a very good understanding of myth, story, and the effect such narratives have on us.[2] The aim of this paper is broadly twofold: a critical evaluation of Lewis's identification of a mythopoeic (as he termed it) element in the incarnation-resurrection narrative, and a systematic examination of the relationship between myth and event in Lewis's Christology and pneumatology. Lewis's theories were derived from his reading of religious myths from outside of the Judaeo-Christian tradition: what he termed pagan myths, though it is important to remember that the term pagan is used here with no derogatory intent, nor as a term of abuse. Lewis used the term simply to refer to those peoples and cultures outside of the Judaeo-Christian tradition and revelation (Oriental, Middle Eastern, Indian, and European tribes and

---

1 Quoted by Tolkien in his poem "Mythopoeia" (1978), reflecting Lewis's position up to the point of his conversion. Note "Mythopoeia" (1978), footnote 4. See also, C. S. Lewis to Arthur Greeves from the Kilns, Oct. 18, 1931, in *Letters of C. S. Lewis* (ed. W. H. Lewis, revised by Walter Hooper; 1993). See also: Lewis, *They Stand Together: The Letters of C. S. Lewis to Arthur Greeves 1914–1963* (1979).

2 In particular, see Lewis, *Studies in Mediaeval and Renaissance Literature* (1966); also, Lewis, *The Discarded Image* (1964). For a good introduction to Lewis's use of story see Huttar and Schakel, *Word and Story in C. S. Lewis* (1991).

2. Christological Prefigurement: The Incarnation-Resurrection Narrative

nations, particularly in the ancient world). Initially, I shall look at some definitions of myth, and then proceed to examine what Lewis actually wrote. Defining what is meant by the incarnation-resurrection narrative will lead us to appraise examples of prefigurement. Lewis's position will then be examined in the light of his views on natural theology (particularly noting the influence of Plato and Augustine) and his theories about imagination and inspiration, illumination and revelation (essentially from the influence of the poet, philosopher, and theologian Samuel Taylor Coleridge). At the heart of Lewis's understanding of story—whether real or fictitious—is a concept he adopted from the Roman Catholic scholar John Ronald Reuel Tolkien: mythopoeia. The noun mythopoeia—the creating of myths—was developed from the late nineteenth century by many English-speaking writers; however, it is in the work of Tolkien (both as Professor of Anglo-Saxon at Oxford and in his mythological work in scripting the Middle Earth sagas, including *The Lord of the Rings*) that it is imbued with theological meaning and significance, relating to divinely gifted, prevenient inspiration.[3]

II. MYTH

C. Stephen Evans in his work on Christology[4] argues for the historicity of the Gospel accounts, as against much modern scholarship, which calls into question the reliability of the church's version of the story of Jesus. Evans argues for the historical basis of Christianity, that the religious significance of this story cannot be adequately captured by the category of non-historical myth. Like many others who assert an orthodox Trinitarian account, he identifies that the category of myth has been employed as a means of dealing with the particular genre of the Gospels by a number of theologians. To this end, he briefly examines C. S. Lewis's proposition that the incarnation-resurrection narrative is both myth and history: a myth

---

3   Mythopoeia, mythopoesis, is derived from the Greek *mythos* (myth) + *poien* (to make); in Platonic Greek, *mythopoios, -on*, (*poieō*), the term is essentially restricted in use to British academics and writers circa 1870–1960. The adjective mythopoetical, from the Greek *mythopoiia*, is from the 1950s. Myth is derived from the Greek *mythos*: in New Testament Greek, *a myth, fanciful story*; in Homeric Greek, *a tale, story, narrative, a legend or fable*.

4   Evans, *The Historical Christ and the Jesus of Faith* (1996). See also Evans, "The Incarnational Narrative as Myth and History" (1994); Evans, "Mis-using Religious Language" (1979).

that has been historically enacted without ceasing to be a myth. Before turning to C. S. Lewis in chapter 3 of his work, Evans briefly sets out four definitions of myth, which are pertinent to this investigation:[5] first, myths as pre-scientific explanations, bad explanations of phenomena in the natural world (fanciful stories to explain rainfall, the movement of the sun, etc.); second, the sociological function (to reinforce the identity of a group of people and explain cohesive ritual practices); third, myths as embodying psychological truth, which may be crucial to the value of the myth (pre-scientific explanations are seen as wrong and irrelevant, but psychological truths touch a deeper level of humanity and may give insights that cannot be obtained through other means, for example, the story of Oedipus); four, such stories express in a dramatic fashion some abstract metaphysical truth, though historically false. Evans explains that these four definitions are not mutually exclusive. Someone who holds that a particular myth may express metaphysical or psychological truth may also assert that it may be a pre-scientific explanation of some phenomenon. He quotes the work of Joseph Campbell as an example that reflects a Jungian view, that myths can embody both a psychological function as well as metaphysical one.[6] The term myth is therefore a rich depository of meanings and nuances—quite different from the way some contemporary theologians have used the term. In the twentieth century, myth was often, simplistically, taken to mean that something is fiction, a story with no basis in real events: a misconception, a misrepresentation of the truth. For example, John Hick in the preface to *The Myth of God Incarnate* asserts that the conception of Jesus "as God incarnate, the Second Person of the Holy Trinity living a human life, is a mythological or poetic way of expressing his significance for us."[7] This represents a uniquely modern, Enlightenment approach to Christology based upon a particularly narrow definition of myth. Such definitions do not always take into account the full richness of myth—especially from a metaphysical perspective. The term myth was essentially introduced into theology in

---

5   Evans, *The Historical Christ and the Jesus of Faith* (1996), ch. 3, "Why the Events Matter: 1. History, Meaning Myth."

6   See Campbell, *The Hero with a Thousand Faces* (1968); also, Campbell, "Mythological Themes in Creative Literature and Art" (1970).

7   Hick, "Preface," in The Myth of God Incarnate (1977), ix. See also: Hick, *The Metaphor of God Incarnate* (1993).

2. Christological Prefigurement: The Incarnation-Resurrection Narrative

the nineteenth century.⁸ By contrast, Lewis is often critical of progressive Protestant theologians for failing to understand the genre of myth from a literary perspective. It must be remembered that Lewis knew story and knew myth—after a lifetime lecturing on the subject of literature at Oxford he was appointed Professor of Mediæval and Renaissance Literature at Cambridge. In *Modern Theology and Biblical Criticism*⁹ he criticizes Bultmann, Lock, and Vidler for not understanding literary genre when they attempt to approach the Gospels as non-historical records and classify them according to literary genre. He is particularly scathing of Lock's assertion that John's Gospel is a spiritual romance.¹⁰

III. LEWIS ON MYTH

Lewis proposes a definition of myth in an essay on literary criticism published in 1961.¹¹ He notes that there is a particular kind of story that has a value in itself—a value independent of its embodiment in any literary work. Lewis quotes the story of Orpheus in a summary of an hundred words, showing how it still has an extraordinary power: "it strikes and strikes deep."¹² Lewis then lays out six characteristics of myth: i) they are extra literary; ii) the story does not depend upon the usual literary attractions such as suspense or surprise—there is a sense of inevitability about mythical stories; iii) human sympathy is at a minimum, the characters are like shapes moving in another world—they have a profound relevance to our lives, but we do not necessarily identify with them, "The story of Orpheus makes us sad; but we are sorry for all men rather than sympathetic with him"; iv) myth is always fantastic—it deals with "impossibilities and preternaturals"; v) the experience of listening to or reading a myth is always grave; vi) importantly we find this experience to be awe-inspiring: "we feel it to be numinous; it is as if something of

---

8 Wiles, "Myth in Theology" (1977), 149.

9 Lewis, "Modern Theology and Biblical Criticism," a paper read at Westcott House, Cambridge, 11th May 1959, published in *Christian Reflections* (1967). (Note that in later editions the title of this paper is changed to "Fern-Seed Elephants"). See also Christensen, *C. S. Lewis on Scripture* (1980); Harries, *C. S. Lewis: The Man and his God* (1987).

10 See Lock, *The Gospel according to St John* (1928); also Vidler, *Windsor Sermons* (1958).

11 Lewis, *An Experiment in Criticism* (1961): see ch. 5 "On Myth," 40f.

12 Lewis "On Myth" (1961), 41

great moment has been communicated to us." Therefore to Lewis, a myth is more than just a fanciful story that did not happen; however, a myth which is also an account of an historical event is something other.[13]

IV. MYTH BECAME REALITY

As an eighteen-year-old apostate and atheistic student Lewis wrote to Arthur Greeves that "All religions, that is, all mythologies to give them their proper name, are merely man's own invention—Christ as much as Loki."[14] He proceeded to explain the origin of such "mythologies," particularly Christianity—basically expounding a view culled from the work of the religionist Victorian anthropologist Sir James George Frazer. Frazer's massive twelve-volume work, *The Golden Bough*,[15] was the product of an academic life spent travelling the world recording the religious-folk mythology of primitive tribes: he spent decades observing various customs, rituals, beliefs, and myths from the standpoint of the emerging discipline of social anthropology. Frazer's position is Feuerbachian and to a degree Freudian: religion is a human projection, a response to a hostile world; Frazer is also a high-Victorian projecting cultural and racial superiority as he travelled the British Empire. Lewis's intellectual starting point is therefore that all religion is a human product, constructed from observing and relating to this aggressive and unsympathetic world. At this time Lewis would have subscribed to a view of natural theology similar to that of Feuerbach that God exists only as a psychological projection and hence all theology is a human product. Lewis was therefore dismissive of natural theology because there was

---

13   Jonathon Miller—scientist, doctor, media celebrity, and self-confessed atheist—has commented of his own piety towards the Christian story: "If there is a God then he could have thought of no more powerful, creative and imaginative way of expressing his presence than through his incarnation in Christ, an 'ordinary' man." Quoted in Appleyard, "The True Face of Art" (2000).

14   C. S. Lewis to Arthur Greeves from Great Bookham, Oct. 12, 1916, in, *Letters of C. S. Lewis* (1993).

15   Frazer, *The Golden Bough* (1911–15). Initially published in two volumes in 1890, the work then grew to the final twelve-volume 3rd edition published 1911–15: volume 1–2, part I, *The Magic Art*; volume 3, part II, *Taboo and the Perils of the Soul*; volume 4, part III, *The Dying God*; volume 5–6, part IV, *Adonis, Attis, Osiris Studies in the History of Oriental Religion*; volume 7–8, part V, *Spirits of the Corn and of the Wild*; volume 9, part VI, *The Scapegoat*; volume 10–11, part VII, *Balder the Beautiful the Fire-Festivals of Europe and the Doctrine of the External Soul*; volume 12, *Bibliography and General Index*. See also Frazer, *The Golden Bough* (abridged edition; 1922).

2. Christological Prefigurement: The Incarnation-Resurrection Narrative

no God; further that all our supposed knowledge of God is merely an enlargement of ideas about human experience. As a young scholar Lewis would have concurred with Feuerbach when the latter wrote, "the secret of theology is nothing else than anthropology—the knowledge of God is nothing else than the knowledge of man."[16] Feuerbach was a profound influence on Frazer; Frazer likewise on Lewis's intellectual development. Lewis came to adopt a diametrically opposite view of natural theology in his thirties after his conversion initially to theism and then to Christianity. Shortly after his conversion he again wrote to Arthur Greeves in 1931 commenting about how profound and suggestive of meanings beyond his grasp the myths of dying and reviving gods were, and how the story of Christ was simply a true myth—"a myth working on us in the same way as the others, but with this tremendous difference that it really happened[;] ... it is God's myth where the others are men's myths."[17] Therefore, he was adopting something approaching a Barthian position in respect to natural theology—God's self-revelation in Christ was the only true story, the actuality. The other stories/myths were to be dismissed as the mere product of humanity striving to perceive a transcendent God—these were only "men's myths." Much of the formulation of these ideas is in reaction to Frazer, hence the idea of the one true (that is, historical) myth. However, this Barthian-type position was to soften with maturity, as we shall see later. Lewis's Christological ideas and his understanding of natural theology were to undergo change and development over a thirty-year period; his understanding of Christological prefigurement and myth developed from 1931 to 1961: the evidence is in his writings.[18] A paper

16   Feuerbach, *Das Wesen des Christentums*, (1973), 121, 207.
17   C. S. Lewis to Arthur Greeves from the Kilns, Oct. 18, 1931, in *Letters of C. S. Lewis* (1993).
18   1931: C. S. Lewis to Arthur Greeves from The Kilns, Oct. 18, 1931, in *Letters of C. S. Lewis* (1993).
1933: *The Pilgrim's Regress* (1933).
1940: "The Kappa Element in Romance," a paper written in 1940, later published as "On Stories" in Lewis, *Essays Presented to Charles Williams* (1947).
1942: "Miracles'—preached in St Jude on the Hill Church, London, and appeared in St Jude's Gazette, number 73, Oct., 1942, 4–7; a shorter version published in *The Guardian*, Oct. 2, 1942, was later published in Lewis, *Undeceptions* (1971).
1944: "Myth Became Fact" first appeared in *World Dominion* XXII, September-October 1944, 267–70; later published in *Undeceptions* (1971).
1944: "Is Theology Poetry?" read as a paper to the Socratic Club in Oxford and first appeared in print in *The Socratic Digest* 1944; published in Lewis, *Screwtape Proposes a Toast* (1965).

read to an undergraduate literary society in 1940 contains a kernel of his developing ideas, particularly his understanding of the relationship between natural theology and myth.[19] However, it is in his understanding of miracles that we find the best exposition of his ideas about the mythical-historical nature of the incarnation. Lewis spoke and wrote on several occasions during the 1940s on the subject of the incarnation (the grand miracle as he called it) as well as miracles generally culminating in the essay, *Myth Became Fact*.[20] This is the central text to what I shall call his proposition of Christological prefigurement, though Lewis never gave the proposition a definite title. Lewis opens the essay with a criticism of modern intellectuals, personified by one of his academic colleagues, who though having abandoned the Christian faith persisted in clinging on to something of the form—such modern intellectuals were moved, asserted Lewis, by the mythical qualities of the story. It is the myth, Lewis asserts, that gives life. He then examines the distinction between abstract and concrete experience (which we will come to later) and how this allows myths to express something experiential to us, which we could not grasp otherwise:

> The old myth of the dying God, without ceasing to be myth, comes down from the heaven of legend and imagination to the earth of history. It happens—at a particular date, in a particular place, followed by definable historical consequences. We pass . . . to a

---

1945: "The Grand Miracle" was preached in St Jude on the Hill Church, London, and appeared in *The Guardian*, April 27, 1945; published in *Undeceptions* (1971).

1946: "Religion without Dogma?" a paper read to the Socratic Club on May 20, 1946 in answer to a paper of Professor H. H. Price, "The Grounds of Modern Agnosticism," delivered on Oct. 20, 1944. Both were later published in the *Phoenix Quarterly* (1.1, 1946). "Religion without Dogma" was then published in Lewis, *Undeceptions* (1971); amendments and responses from the floor are in the minute's book of The Socratic Club, published, along with the paper in, Lewis, *Compelling Reason* (1996).

1947: "The Grand Miracle," an expansion on the kernel of material initially presented in 1942 at St Jude on the Hill Church, published in, Lewis, *Miracles* (1st ed. 1947), ch. 14.

1955: Lewis, *Surprised by Joy* (1955), Lewis's spiritual autobiography written during the early 1950s.

1959: "*Modern Theology and Biblical Criticism*," a paper read at Westcott House, Cambridge, May 11, 1959; published in Lewis, *Christian Reflections* (1967).

1961: "On Myth," published in Lewis, *An Experiment on Criticism*, (1961).

19   Lewis, "The Kappa Element in Romance" (1940).

20   Lewis, "Myth Became Fact" (1944).

2. Christological Prefigurement: The Incarnation-Resurrection Narrative

> historical person crucified under Pontius Pilate. By becoming fact it does not cease to be a miracle.[21]

Lewis continues by showing how many derive sustenance from a story's mythical qualities even if they do not assent to its factuality and historicity. But these mythical qualities in the story of Christ are not equal to the reality:

> Those who do not know that this great myth became fact when the Virgin conceived are, indeed, to be pitied, ... that it carries with it into the world of facts all the properties of myth. God is more than a god, not less; Christ is more than Balder, not less. We must not be ashamed of the mythical radiance resting on our theology. We must not be nervous about "parallels" and "pagan Christs": they ought to be there—it would be a stumbling block if they weren't.[22]

These ideas around prefigured Christology were in part referred to and further developed in a paper read to The Socratic Club in Oxford—"Religion without Dogma?"—in 1946; however, Lewis devoted the fullest exposition of the proposition a year later in chapter 14 of the book *Miracles* (1st ed. 1947).[23] There are also key remarks in his autobiography, *Surprised by Joy*, published in 1955—chiefly explaining how he came to see the incarnation-resurrection narrative as the one true myth (in this case refuting Frazer).

V. MYTH AND EVENT—A KEY TO LEWIS'S CHRISTOLOGY

Lewis is a classic orthodox theologian in his Christology; however, two propositions distinguish him from the mainstream in orthodoxy: he is prepared to tackle the question of narrative prefigurement, which most other theologians either dismiss or shy away from; also, he is prepared to write about the mythological/mythopoeic effect the incarnation-resurrection narrative has on us. There is something of a dialectic here (not a method usually associated with Lewis) in his use of myth and event: the former represents the historic event prefigured in religious

---

21 Lewis, "Myth Became Fact" (1944).
22 Lewis, "Myth Became Fact" (1944).
23 Lewis, *Miracles* (1st ed. 1947).

stories/myths; the latter encompasses the myth derived from the event. Lewis writes of the idea, the content of the story of Jesus (the incarnation-resurrection narrative) being prefigured in pre-Christian myths; he also writes about the effect that the story of Jesus (again the incarnation-resurrection narrative) has on us even if we do not believe in the historical reality. There are therefore two different propositions here, not mutually exclusive, but nonetheless dealing with different concepts. To proceed with an analysis of these propositions it is necessary to address two questions: What is meant by the phrase I have been using thus far, the incarnation-resurrection narrative? and What exactly are these examples of prefigurement that Lewis alludes to, and what do we mean by prefigurement?

VI. THE INCARNATION-RESURRECTION NARRATIVE

Many see the phrase incarnational narrative as encompassing the whole of Christ's life on earth; Lewis refers generally to the Christian story and specifically to either the incarnation or the resurrection. But he is actually quite vague as to what constitutes the subject and object of prefigurement. This will be encountered later when we examine the examples of prefigurement that he cites. At its most concise, the incarnation narrative, or story, is encapsulated in John 1:14a. The question then arises, what exactly is encompassed by the incarnational narrative when Lewis writes of prefigurement. At times he talks of the incarnation and the virginal conception; at other times the idea of a dying and reviving god. For the purposes of this study we will refer to the incarnation-resurrection narrative as the two points in Christ's earthly life that Lewis regarded as critically fundamental to the faith and to God's salvific action with the world and humanity: first, the Virginal conception-incarnation and, second, the cross-resurrection. There are numerous allusions pointing towards the incarnation and resurrection in Jewish history and in the Old Testament. Frazer in effect ignores these; Lewis accepts them in faith. What preoccupied Lewis was the evidence of prefigurement in the ancient pagan oral traditions. Therefore, it is pertinent to examine some of the myths that Lewis alludes to.

2. Christological Prefigurement: The Incarnation-Resurrection Narrative

VII. IDEAS OF PREFIGUREMENT: 1. INCARNATION

Lewis cites specific pagan myths/gods: for example, Balder, Adonis, and Osiris. In this, Lewis draws on three volumes of Frazer's work.[24] Frazer's work was central to Lewis in his pre-theistic/Christian period. He supported the concepts and historicism inherent in Frazer's agenda. After conversion he sought to accommodate Frazer's material—he knew he could not simply dismiss it—so he revised it from a Christocentric position. Frazer recorded innumerable examples of stories/myths of what can be considered gods in human form, deified humans, and dying and reviving gods. Of great importance to both Frazer and Lewis was the Northern myth of Balder

There are cases cited by Frazer of what he terms incarnate gods, though these are in many respects examples of individuals possessed either temporarily or permanently by a presumed divine source. Often these gods are no more than invisible magicians who work behind the veil of nature using a man or woman as means of temporality. When possessed, the host personality is nearly always in abeyance. There is then another class of incarnate gods where the host is inspired—again temporarily or permanently—acquiring both divine knowledge and divine power, though this stops short of omniscience and omnipotence. Often these incarnate gods or possessed individuals assume magical powers over nature and the community and exercise awesome political powers within tribal societies: omnipotence (sociologically, anthropologically), but never omnipresence. In the case of a more organized and mature religion, Hinduism, there are prolific examples of human gods. For example, the belief in Chinchvad, near Poona in Western India, is that since the seventeenth-century AD there has been an incarnation of the elephant-god Gunputty. The piety, abstinence, mortification, and prayer of a Brahman of Poona was such that the god promised a portion of his holy spirit to abide with him and each of seven generations thereafter—so that the light of the god should be transmitted to a dark world.[25] There are, it can be argued, countless examples of deification of an individual, or possession either wholly or partly, temporarily or permanently, by spirits or divine powers or gods;

---

24 Frazer, *The Golden Bough* (1911–15), vol. 4, part III: The Dying God; Frazer, *The Golden Bough* (1911–15), vol. 9, part VI: The Scapegoat; Frazer, *The Golden Bough* (1911–15), vols. 10–11, part VII, Balder the Beautiful the Fire-Festivals of Europe and the Doctrine of the External Soul.

25 Frazer, *The Golden Bough* (abridged; 1922), 121.

but is this the same as the Christian incarnation? Is there anything resembling the incarnation in form or typology?[26] Avatars in Hinduism represent the descent of a god to earth in incarnate form. This is often an incarnation or embodiment, or a manifestation. For example, Krishna was the eighth avatar of Vishnu, incarnated to help the five brothers regain their kingdom. Sometimes these gods appear in human form. An Avatar (descent in Hinduism) was usually to counteract some evil in this world. However, "descending," "appearing," or "abiding" is not ontologically synonymous with the nature of incarnate being in Jesus of Nazareth. There are similarities, but the two are not synonymous: being made flesh with all that is implied in being human—the apparent self-emptying of God—is a different concept of ontology altogether. According to a kenotic Christology, God empties himself and is incarnated, humbled, and vulnerable in the form of a human baby. Possession or deification imparts divine properties; the Christian incarnation divests! That is, although Jesus of Nazareth was both fully human and fully divine, we can assert that *kenosis* divests, likewise the adoption of specifically human limitations constitutes disempowerment rather than empowerment. Macquarrie writes that "any revelation of God must be a veiled revelation, for God cannot be revealed directly in a finite earthly medium."[27] Therefore, there is a measure of ambiguity even in the revelation of Christ. Barth writes: "God is always God even in his humiliation. The divine being does not suffer any change, any diminution[;] . . . God cannot cease to be God."[28] Humility and weakness are as much a part of God as are power and transcendence. Incarnation in the Hindu traditions, as well as Oceanic traditions, empowers and gives virtual messianic, dictatorial powers over tribal communities; by comparison, the Christian incarnation involves self-restraint: power and authority are marked by humility and forgiveness. The idea of an avatar appearing in human form is to a degree Docetic. Once God is incarnate—not just *appearing* human or abiding, but born as a human—then there is risk. This idea would seem to have absolutely no precedent in mythology and religion. Examples of incarnational prefigurement regard the indwelling of the divine as empowering;

---

26 This issue has been dealt with by Scott, David, and Selvanayagam, (eds.), *Re-visioning India's Religious Traditions* (1996); see also, Ward, God, Faith *The New Millennium* (1998).

27 Macquarrie, *Jesus Christ in Modern Thought* (1990).

28 Barth, *Church Dogmatics* IV/1 §59 The Obedience of the Son of God, 179f.

2. Christological Prefigurement: The Incarnation-Resurrection Narrative

despite the divestment that God undergoes, the Gospel writers witness to a glory that is absent in prefigurement (John 1:14b). Is it fair to Lewis's Christology to speak of *kenosis* and divestment? Yes. In many of his writings he comments on God's restraint and divestment, likewise God's humiliation in taking on the human frame.[29] For example, Lewis cites the literary motif of the ruler who disguises himself to go amongst his people, as one of them. Kierkegaard took this further when he extends the analogy to the folk tale of the king who divests himself of his royal regalia to don the clothes of an ordinary citizen to woo the woman he loves, and then having won her heart reveals himself as her Lord and king.[30] This is reminiscent of the courtship of the Hebrew people in the Old Testament, but God does not hide, he is revealed as YHWH throughout, the one true God, the lord who made heaven and earth. (Though it is important to remember the Barthian principle that this unveiling also involves a veiling: God is revealed on God's terms only and in freedom—revelation as a vulnerable human baby.) The idea of the self-emptying of God in the Christian incarnation is beyond human imagination and comprehension—it is sheer madness from a human perspective. Though if we accept that humility and weakness are as much a part of God as are power and transcendence then we can see how the Christian incarnation transcends the stories/myths quoted by Frazer. Lewis does write in his book *Miracles* (1st ed. 1947) about how the incarnation is prefigured in nature—in general revelation—in the sense that there is a descending in the cycle of life: a seed falls to the ground and so forth.[31] This is, however, more of an analogy than a prefigurement and there is still no ontological parallel with the self-emptying and self-restraint seen in the Christian incarnation.

As can be seen from the example quoted in the above paragraph, Kierkegaard has written on the question of Christological prefigurement. Whatever the differences are between Lewis and Kierkegaard I propose that there is no actual parallel of the Christian incarnation in Frazer's evidence specifically, in the work of ethnographers or social anthropologists generally, or even in Lewis's writings. This is another way

---

29   Lewis, "The Grand Miracle," in *Miracles* (1st ed. 1947), ch. 14.
30   Kierkegaard, *Philosophical Fragments* (trans. Hong and Hong; 1985), ch. 2.
31   Lewis, *Miracles* (1st ed. 1947), ch. 14, 117–18.

of reconciling Lewis and Kierkegaard when the latter asserts in the guise of his pseudonym, Johannes Climacus, that:

> Christianity is the only historical phenomenon that despite the historical—indeed, precisely by means of the historical—has wanted to be the single individual's point of departure for his eternal consciousness. . . . No philosophy (for it is only for thought), no mythology (for it is only for the imagination), no historical knowledge (which is for memory) has ever had this idea—of which in this connection one can say with all multiple meanings that it did not arise in any human heart.[32]

It is further proposed that there is also no evidence in any of Lewis's writings, correspondence, or papers that I have examined that he had thought through the implications of incarnational prefigurement to this degree. There may be analogies, pointers, but there is no parallel—ontologically, epistemologically, or, more important, soteriologically—with the Christian incarnation: none of the examples in Frazer of incarnate gods generally[33] or a Hindu avatar specifically can atone and reconcile for original sin, for the fall. What Lewis does is point to analogies, figurative similarities. Why these are there will be considered later when we examine Lewis's concept of imagination. Let us move on to the idea of a dying and reviving god.

VIII. IDEAS OF PREFIGUREMENT: 2. RESURRECTION

Generally speaking there is greater evidence of prefigurement in the examples of dying and *reviving* (not necessarily *resurrected*) gods. Lewis was a classicist and knew his Greek myths. For example, the story of Adonis, a beautiful youth beloved by the goddesses Aphrodite and Persephone, slain by a wild boar while hunting. Following Aphrodite's pleas, the god Zeus restored him so he should spend the winter months with Persephone in Hades and the summer months with Aphrodite. The story was considered symbolic of the natural cycle of death and rebirth. Another example: the myth of Balder, upon which Lewis and Frazer place a great emphasis.[34] The god of light and joy in Norse mythology (son of

---

32 Kierkegaard, *Philosophical Fragments* (1985), 35–36, examined in Evans, *Historical Christ and the Jesus of Faith* (1996), 53–56

33 Frazer, *The Golden Bough* (abridged; 1922), ch. VII, 109–27.

34 Frazer, *The Golden Bough* (1913), part VII: Balder The Beautiful Vol I Vol II;

2. Christological Prefigurement: The Incarnation-Resurrection Narrative

Odin and Frigga, king and queen of the gods) Balder—or Baldhr—was regarded as beautiful, compassionate, and graceful in comparison to the other gods. Frigga, having dreamed that Balder's life was threatened, extracted an oath from the forces and objects in nature that they would not harm him, but overlooked the mistletoe. The gods, thinking Balder safe, rained blows and objects at him. Loki maliciously placed a twig of mistletoe in the hands of the blind Hoder, "god" of darkness, and directed his aim against Balder. Balder fell, mortally wounded, pierced to the heart. After his death, Odin sent another son the messenger Hermod to the underworld to plead for his return. Balder's release was conditional on everything in the world weeping for him. Everything wept except one old woman in a cave, and so Balder could not return to life. Balder's characteristics are in many ways similar to those of Christ—love, joy, light, beauty, compassion; there are also similarities with the *Logos*, the Word. Furthermore, similarities can be seen with the suffering Christ, though more with the Hebrew concept of the scapegoat. Balder, however, does not take on death voluntarily—he is tricked by Loki, unaware that he is not immune to mistletoe. Jesus wrestled with his fate in the Garden of Gethsemane but accepted what was to befall him. What is more, there is the potential for Balder being revived or restored, but this falls short of resurrection: it does not happen. There is a similar potentiality with the Egyptian god Osiris: he is tricked into death, like Balder, by an evil brother. Because of the love and lamentations for Osiris, the sun-god Ra initiates the restoration of the broken and fragmented body of the murdered god—Isis fanned the cold clay with her wings, Osiris is revived and thenceforth reigned as king over the dead in the other world. Again similarities, but does this constitute a parallel? Furthermore, neither in the story of Balder or Osiris (nor the many other stories of dying and *reviving* gods) is there an explicit reference to the *resurrection* of an *incarnate* god. Such a story is beyond human comprehension or invention (part of Kierkegaard's paradox). Lewis and Kierkegaard are looking at different elements of the incarnation-resurrection narrative—Kierkegaard focuses on the detail, Lewis looking at generalizations. Kierkegaard holds to the uniqueness of the incarnational narrative (the Word became flesh) and in a specific sense he is right—a critical evaluation of the supposed parallels in pagan and Hindu mythology confirm Kierkegaard's reservations. Lewis

also Frazer, *The Golden Bough* (abridged; 1922).

was talking in terms of generalizations. He uses the term *"prefigurement"* to indicate foreshadowing. To be more specific, prefigurement indicates a similarity, figuratively, or by type; that is, to be like metaphysically, psychologically, and for that matter sociologically. In one sense, dreams prefigure reality; in another sense, the whole of the Old Testament prefigures Christ. This raises the question, to what extent do these pagan myths prefigure Christ? Is this an example of natural theology, or general revelation, or echoes of a specific revelation? There is the analogy with death and resurrection in the natural world. Is this an example of general revelation? That is, the idea of seeds dying to bring forth new crops. There are myths the world over of corn gods, but it is difficult to justify the idea of mythological parallels of the incarnation of God or the death and resurrection of Christ. These parallels do not hold when systematically analyzed, epistemologically, ontologically, soteriologically; but there are prefigurements, echoes—indicative, characteristically, of type and form, relating to the one story that was rooted historically in an actuality.

IX. LEWIS AND NATURAL THEOLOGY, REVELATION, AND IMAGINATION

Lewis places great emphasis on prefigurement in the sense that I have just outlined: that these pagan Christs are a foreshadowing of the incarnation-resurrection, relating figuratively to it. Lewis's mature beliefs about natural theology generally, and on revelation, inspiration, and imagination specifically, will be examined so as to ascertain what value he placed on prefigurement.

After his conversion, and in contradiction to the Feuerbachian-Freudian atheism already noted, Lewis assigned a value to natural theology in keeping with his churchmanship, central Anglican with leanings towards the (Anglo-)Catholic. Lewis read and was influenced by the Greek philosophers, but also Aquinas' *Summa theologiae*. Although Aquinas had formulated the distinction between natural and revealed theology (a distinction hardened by theologians in response to the Enlightenment), Lewis subscribed to the older Augustinian view that there is no unaided knowledge of God. Lewis was therefore profoundly influenced by Augustine in the value he gave to natural theology, also the deep respect he held for Platonic idealism. Hence, we find the post-conversion Barthian-type rejection softening as he absorbs this other,

2. Christological Prefigurement: The Incarnation-Resurrection Narrative

older approach to natural theology. For example, Augustine, writing to Deogratius comments:

> Therefore, from the beginning of the human race, whosoever believed in Him, and in any way knew Him, and lived in a pious and just manner according to His precepts, was undoubtedly saved by Him, in whatever time and place he may have lived.[35]

Hence, there is Lewis's respect for natural theology and natural law. Augustine continued:

> For as we believe in Him both as dwelling with the Father and as having come in the flesh, so the men of the former ages believed in Him both as dwelling with the Father and as destined to come in the flesh.... Wherefore the true religion, although formerly set forth and practiced under other names and with other symbolical rites than it now has, and formerly more obscurely revealed and known to fewer persons than now in the time of clearer light and wider diffusion, is one and the same in both periods.[36]

Therefore, the true religion was perceived in part, or "more obscurely revealed" prior to the specific revelation of Christ. This is the position Lewis came to hold. The question then arises, what form did these intimations take? Or, more pertinently, what is the means whereby such ideas can feature in the thought of men and women? To answer this, it is necessary to examine the place of imagination generally in theology, and in particular, to focus on Lewis's understanding of imagination and how it relates to revelation, inspiration, and illumination.

Imagination is rooted in creativity—where do ideas come from? Imagination has had a troubled standing in Western philosophy and theology. In the Reformed tradition imagination was considered suspect. Calvin wrote, "God rejects without exception all shapes and pictures, and other symbols by which the superstitious believe they can bring him near to them. These images defile and insult the majesty of God."[37] In the Reformed tradition this suspicion of images influenced not only architecture and decoration but also created a highly conceptualized form of articulation that sought to reduce image-type thinking amongst theologians. When he embraced Christianity it was as an Anglican—

---

35 Augustine, "Letter no 102 to Deogratius...," 409 CE (1979), 819–20.
36 Augustine, "Letter no 102 to Deogratius...," 409 CE (1979), 820
37 Calvin, *Institutes of the Christian Religion* (1995), 1:xi.1.

pertinently it is his professional work in literature rather than this Anglican tradition that influences his ideas about imagination. In sharp contrast to the negative view of imagination in the Reformed tradition there exists a very positive tradition. For example, the romantic idealists such as Samuel Taylor Coleridge and Friedrich Schelling, who regarded a form of imagination derived from Kant's aesthetic idealism as important. As poet, philosopher, and theologian, Coleridge distinguished "primary imagination," from "secondary imagination" and/or "fancy." Coleridge wrote:

> The primary imagination I hold to be the living power and prime Agent of all human perception, and as a repetition in the finite mind of the eternal act of creation in the infinite I AM. The secondary imagination I consider as an echo of the former, coexisting with the conscious will, yet still as identical with the primary in the kind of its agency, and differing only in degree, and in the mode of its operation. It dissolves, diffuses, dissipates, in order to re-create; or where this process is rendered impossible, yet still at all events it struggles to idealize and to unify. It is essentially vital, even as all objects (as objects) are essentially fixed and dead. Fancy, on the contrary, has no other counters to play with but fixities and definites. The fancy is indeed no other than a mode of memory emancipated from the order of time and space; and blended with, and modified by that empirical phenomenon of the will which we express by the word choice. But equally with the ordinary memory it must receive all its materials ready-made from the law of association.[38]

The ideas in Coleridge's account of primary imagination (relating to the *imago Dei* in so far as through imagination men and women are made in the image of God, reproducing the mind of God in miniature) were a profound influence on Lewis.[39] He cites them obliquely as instrumental in his intellectual and religious development on a number of occasions in his spiritual autobiography.[40] George MacDonald, whom Lewis regarded

---

38   Coleridge, *Biographia Literaria* (1956), 175, see also 77. See also Barfield, *What Coleridge Thought* (1972).

39   For Lewis on imagination see, Schakel, *Reason and Imagination in C. S. Lewis* (1984); also Lewis, "Psycho-analysis and Literary Criticism" (1969). See also: Swinburne, *The Concept of Miracle* (1970); Swinburne, *Revelation: from Metaphor to Analogy* (1992).

40   Lewis, *Surprised by Joy* (1998 [1955]), 10–11, 25–26, 63, 130, 132, 140, 153, 158, 164.

2. Christological Prefigurement: The Incarnation-Resurrection Narrative

as a profound influence on his understanding of myth, saga, and story, wrote a full exposition on Coleridge's ideas in an essay published in 1895.[41] This is almost certainly the point of contact Lewis had initially with these ideas. For MacDonald, the imagination is the medium by which we enquire into God's creation. Imagination therefore occupies a central place in enquiry, in hypothesizing, in creating mental-images (for example, mental model-making and conceptualization as practiced by scientists and historians, but also by theologians).[42] Methodologically, from the perspective of the philosophy of theology, David Kelsey writes, "At the root of any theological position, there is an imaginative act in which a theologian tries to catch up in a single metaphorical judgment or model the full complexity of God's presence."[43] In this respect, it may be valid to consider that those who composed (or imagined) the stories of incarnation or dying and reviving gods, myths of prefigurement, are methodologically operating in a similar way to contemporary theologians. It has been argued that a theologian of whatever persuasion (for example, Catholic or Calvinistic) undertakes an act of imagination. A theologian will usually select from the culture and tradition within which he/she operates those structures which are to form the system behind a theological position. By comparison, Calvin Seerveld, writing from the viewpoint of a Reformed tradition, distinguishes on the one hand between imagining that is perceptual error and on the other hand imagining that is an oracle of truth.[44] Lewis wrote, "I think that all things reflect heavenly truth, the imagination not least."[45] Further, "that imagination is distinct from thought; thought may be sound while accompanying images are false."[46] Lewis acknowledges that the mind is illuminated by the divine

41   MacDonald, "The Imagination" (1895) (written in 1867). See also Barfield, *Poetic Diction* (1973).

42   For the role of imagination in historical thinking, see, for example, ideas indicative of the time when C. S. Lewis was at the peak of his creative writing, Collinwood, *The Idea of History* (1946); or, Kroner, *The Religious Function of Imagination* (1941). In the field of philosophy of science, see: Black, *Models and Metaphors* (1962); also, indicative of the understanding around the time of Lewis's intellectual formation, see: Lewes, *Comte's Philosophy of the Sciences* (1904).

43   Kelsey, *The Use of Scripture in Recent Theology* (1975), 163.

44   See Seerveld, "Imaginativity" (1987).

45   Lewis, *Surprised by Joy* (1955), 167.

46   Lewis, "God in the Dock," in, *Lumen Vitae* 3, September 1948, reprinted in *Undeceptions* (1971); sentiments also expressed in *Miracles* (1st ed. 1947) and

and that this leads to a degree of understanding—theological activity is not solely the result of human striving and searching. The imagination can, under certain circumstances, be an oracle of truth where general cognitive activities fail.

Therefore, for Lewis there is still the possibility of prevenient grace allowing inspiration and intimation, though as we shall see, such revelatory reception is still subject to the fall: Lewis talks of the pagan imagination being baptized to a degree, though such minds continued to be corrupt after the event, misinterpreting and misusing what was given—they became "corrupt in their imaginations . . . one road leads home and a thousand lead into the wilderness."[47] Generally speaking, from a Reformed position, the imagination is indelibly corrupted by original sin. Calvin, as we saw, dismissed images or mental pictures/models, the product of human imagination, where humanity believed it could bring God near.[48] Lewis would not necessarily have disagreed with this. What he did assert was that God used this fallen human imagination, images, and mental pictures/models to communicate some sort of intimation of God's salvific actions: the prefiguring images/myths were for Lewis pneumatologically given, not humanly invented.

PART II:
CHRIST AS THE LIGHT OF THE WORLD IN REALITY AND IN MYTHOPOEIC INTIMATIONS

X. RE-INTRODUCTION: INTERIM CONCLUSION

So, to summarize, many theologians of whatever persuasion may use "secondary imagination" (or Coleridge's "fancy") to create conceptual models relating to Christological theories. Likewise, the imagination can, under certain circumstances, be an oracle of truth that may give some

---

"The Weight of Glory" (an address first delivered at St Mary the Virgin, Oxford, 13th September 1941, published in Lewis, *Screwtape Proposes a Toast* (1965). "God in the Dock," was later published in Lewis, *God in the Dock* (1979).

47 Lewis, *The Pilgrim's Regress* (1933), Book VIII, ch. 8, 193.
48 Calvin, *Institutes of Christian Religion* (1995), 1:xi.1.

2. Christological Prefigurement: The Incarnation-Resurrection Narrative

understanding or intimation of a revelatory nature. Such revelation, however implicit and ambiguous, must surely be seen as relating to God's salvific redemptive action in Jesus Christ. Often these revealings are amongst prophets and mystics (a word that would need serious qualification). Such revealings may also be subject to the taint and limits imposed on the mind by the fall. Furthermore, all is subject to the specific self-revelation of God in Jesus Christ; all valid natural theology is reliant upon grace. If this is all so, then we can cautiously postulate that there is validity in Lewis's general proposition of prevision—his doctrine of christological prefigurement. That is, that throughout many cultures, societies, and religions there have been intimations relating to the specific self-revelation of God in Christ, transpositions of the divine theme of redemption, fragments of the truth that point to Christ whether the arose pre- or post-incarnation-resurrection (the myth of Osiris is pre-incarnation-resurrection and hence a prefigurement; many Hindu avatars are both pre- and post-incarnation-resurrection, and are hence both prefigurements and echoes). In narrative form these intimations can have a power similar to the actual Gospel narratives; however, the fullness of the historic actuality of the incarnation-resurrection is unique and has not, could not, as Kierkegaard asserted, be prefigured or replicated.

So if it is accepted that there is a degree of prefigurement relating to the story of Christ's incarnation, death, and resurrection, though there are no direct or indirect parallels ontologically, epistemologically, and soteriologically. If it is also accepted that Lewis had a broad respect for natural theology, in keeping with Augustine, and that his appreciation saw natural theology not merely as intellectual/philosophical speculative gropings for an understanding of God but rather as bound up with the revelation in Christ (because a distinction should not be made between general and specific revelation, but rather the degree to which God reveals himself in a multitude of instances), then it can be accepted that the imagination should not be seen as completely lost because it is intrinsically flawed and evil, but can under certain circumstances be an oracle through which God gives some understanding of a revelatory nature.

We can now proceed to three questions: first, how do these prefigured ideas come to be in the pagan myths and how do these intimations relate to Lewis's understanding of Christ as the light of the world; second, how does the incarnation-resurrection narrative act/operate on us as a myth, whether spoken or read? And finally, is there internal evidence for a mythopoeic interpretation within the incarnation-resurrection narrative? Along the way we need to examine the perlocutionary effect these stories have and the sanctifying work of the Holy Spirit; also Lewis's Neo-Platonic assertion that where there is light, there is Christ—that as the light of the world, Jesus Christ illumines the minds of those outside cognitive knowledge of the historic actuality of the incarnation-resurrection. Furthermore, we can examine C. S. Lewis's own mythopoeic creation, his "supposal": Aslan from *The Chronicles of Narnia*. How much is Aslan an accurate intimation, echo of the divine truth of Jesus Christ crucified and resurrected for our redemption?

XI. SPLINTERED FRAGMENTS OF THE TRUE LIGHT: HOW DO THESE PREFIGURED IDEAS COME TO BE IN PAGAN MYTHS?

Although as an eighteen-year-old atheistic apostate Lewis viewed all mythology and Scripture as a human creation, Lewis's position changed as his faith and his theology developed. By the time of his mature writings he believed that such myths, stories, and ideas (prefigurement and echoes of the incarnation-resurrection narrative) were inspired by God: God was the source and ground of the meaning and intention behind the story of Balder or Osiris, or the intimations of incarnation in Hindu avatars. In this sense, he draws on Tolkien's concept of mythopoeia and on Coleridge's definition of imagination. Lewis did not, as we have seen, subscribe to a wholly Reformed position with regard to natural theology and revelation. However, Lewis agreed with Augustine that there is no unaided knowledge of God. This is close to a Reformed position, but Lewis gave credit to natural theology, and to the imagination that many in the Reformed tradition would not; furthermore he believed that there is value, even intimations of a revelatory nature, in other religious experience, though any value in such general revelation is in relation to and qualified by the specific self-revelation of God in Christ Jesus (again a point of confluence with Augustine). Lewis explicitly ascribes mythopoeia to God: God is the creator and author of these myths. Lewis was deeply influenced here by Tolkien's theory of sub-creation,[49] that it is from God that people draw their ultimate ideals—especially some of

---

49   See Tolkien, "On Fairy Stories" (1947).

2. Christological Prefigurement: The Incarnation-Resurrection Narrative

their imaginative inventions which if they originate with God must reflect something of divine truth, or as Tolkien put it, "splintered fragment of the true light."[50] To Tolkien, all "storytellers" are "sub-creators" under God the "prime-creator" and hence "pagan myths are never just lies—there is always something of the truth in them. . . . God [was] expressing himself through the minds of poets, and using the images of their 'mythopoeia' to express fragments of His eternal truth."[51] Lewis argues in "Myth Became Fact" that our only response to God acting mythopoeically is for us to be mythopathic, sympathetic, and empathetic to these intimations: "If God chooses to be mythopoeic—and is not the sky itself a myth?—shall we refuse to be mythopathic? For this is the marriage of heaven and earth: perfect myth and perfect fact."[52] As we have seen, Lewis often refers to Coleridge's concept of imagination. Human perception of God acting mythopoeically would appear to be an example of Coleridge's "secondary imagination"—like the "primary imagination" but less like it only in degree and operating as an echo of the "primary imagination" in the conscious mind. Such intimations of the incarnation-resurrection, inspired by the Holy Spirit, are one step removed from the actuality of the reality witnessed to by the Gospels and hence are merely echoes or prefigurements resulting from the illumination of the *Logos*—the true light that enlightens all, which was to come into the world (John 1:9). In a paper read to The Oxford Socratic Club in 1944 Lewis wrote,

> The Divine light, we are told, "lighteneth every man." We should, therefore, expect to find in the imagination of great pagan teachers and myth-makers some glimpse of that theme which we believe to be the very plot of the whole cosmic story—the theme of incarnation, death and rebirth. And the differences between the pagan Christs (Balder, Osiris, etc.) and the Christ Himself is much what we should expect to find.[53]

---

50   Tolkien, "On Fairy Stories" (1947); see also, Tolkien's poem "Mythopoeia" (1978). For a summary of these ideas on Lewis see, Carpenter, *The Inklings* (1978), 42–45.

51   Tolkien, "On Fairy Stories" (1947), 43f.

52   Lewis, "Myth Became Fact," first appeared in *World Dominion* XXII, September-October 1944, 267–70; later published in Lewis, *Undeceptions* (1971).

53   Lewis, "Is Theology Poetry?" read as a paper to the Socratic Club in Oxford and first appeared in print in *The Socratic Digest* 1944; published in Lewis, *Screwtape Proposes a Toast* (1965).

Therefore, in none of the examples of prefigurement/echoes do we find an actual self-emptying *incarnation* of God or the dying and actual *resurrection* of God incarnate. The incarnation narrative (as expressed in John 1:14a) is rooted in an historical actuality. This can only happen once; any prefigurement/echo is a pointer, a glimpse and will stop short of the true reality; this actuality is not a human invention but such prefigurements cannot exactly parallel the Christian incarnation: the paradox as Kierkegaard would put it. The light that illuminated the pagans may be considered in this context to be the same light that is referred to in the prologue to John's Gospel. Lewis goes as far as to suggest that ideas of God's saving purposes were not only foretold in the Hebrew religion but that images or mythical pictures were given within the North European pagan myths, in the ancient Egyptian religion, and in Hinduism, to name but three of the instances that Lewis alludes to. In *The Pilgrim's Regress* he wrote using allegory suggesting that God gave "the shepherds" (the Hebrew people) ideas and rules and set their feet on the road but that he gave images to the pagans. He also asserts that the mythology of the pagans contained a divine call; however, they mistook the images for what they were not and became "corrupt in their imaginations," hence "one road leads home and a thousand lead into the wilderness."[54] The degree to which the imagination can, on the one hand, be the object of divine inspiration and illumination and, on the other hand, an oracle of truth is debatable: Calvin, as we saw, was dismissive of the imagination. Broadly speaking the Reformed tradition regards both the imagination and natural theology as suspect at best and of little consequence—emphasis is placed on sin and fallenness. However, Lewis does address the question of sin and fallenness. Lewis writes both in his autobiography and in his theological writings on the concept of a baptized imagination.[55] At its most explicit, this is where the imagination (essentially a form of mental activity held to be distinct from cognitive or rational processes, a free and creative ordering of the contents of the mind) is governed by the Holy Spirit: because of original sin an unbaptized imagination fails to perceive the intrinsic value and meaning in stories and myths from a God-ward, and hence true, perspective. The hearers (and these stories were nearly

54 Lewis, *The Pilgrim's Regress* (1933), Book VIII, ch. 8, 193.
55 For instance: Lewis, *Surprised by Joy* (1955); also "Preface," in, Lewis (ed.), George MacDonald (1946); "Is Theology Poetry?" (1944); also, Lewis, *The Pilgrim's Regress* (1933), Book X, esp. ch. 2.

2. Christological Prefigurement: The Incarnation-Resurrection Narrative

always part of an oral tradition) may not "know" the details of the story of when the virgin conceived, when her Son who died on the cross for their/our sins rose from the dead, but something of the profound effect of this true story would have worked on them (and us)—and not just on a psychological level: it may be that their/our very being is reordered to a degree and reoriented towards the one true living God, despite the maze and confusion of religious ideas and gods. However, Lewis would have concurred with a Reformed position proposing that the imagination was inextricably fallen and tainted by original sin, but he would have argued that it was not irredeemable in this life. Lewis does not necessarily tie the baptism of the imagination to an explicit liturgical practice: the Spirit blows where it wills (Gen 1:2b and John 3:8). Lewis sees a baptized imagination as an essential key in comprehending ultimate reality; this knowledge of reality is apprehended by acquaintance with and participation in the divine *Logos*. A person comprehending ultimate reality, a reality illuminated by the *Logos* (in the sense of an immediate, intuitive, and imaginative capacity) has perception of God to the extent that such acquaintance and perception is considered by Lewis to be revelatory; however, the rational interpretation of such an experience may be subject to distortion while communication of the experience may be flawed. Revelation of this kind is mediated through human faculties: it is human to err; to err is to be human. Hence, Lewis explains in *The Pilgrim's Regress* that those in receipt of the Northern European myths misinterpreted and misused the images they were given. Lewis assumes that the pagan imagination (individually or collectively) was to a degree baptized when it received/perceived the images; however, we must presume that the imagination of such an individual, and those subsequently hearing the human record of these intimations were, relatively speaking, equally flawed. Lewis does not address whether epistemological baptism is permanent this side of eternity. Human epistemic limitations would seem to dismiss such a proposition; likewise the fact that we are still subject to the vagaries of sin—*simul iustus et peccator*.

Therefore, is Lewis conceiving of the universal resurrected Christ, the *Logos*, as working on people's minds regardless of whether they knew what had happened or was to happen for their redemption in Palestine two thousand years ago? Such illumination, the work of the Spirit, moves and operates where and how it will and we cannot utterly dismiss the salvific effect on—in the case of Lewis's prefigurement theories—the North

European pagan tribes who were subject to these myths (the salvation outside of knowledge in Matthew 25?). But none of these prefigurements actually replicate what happened on the cross. There is therefore something of a universal Platonic form to Lewis's understanding of the resurrected Christ. Tolkien, as we saw, referred to such intimations as splintered fragments of the true light; for Lewis, where there is enlightenment there is Christ: as the light of the world Jesus Christ illumines the minds of those outside of the cognitive knowledge of the historic actuality of the incarnation-resurrection. Karl Barth worked on the same principle but in a much more systematic way than Lewis. In the fourth volume of his *Church Dogmatics*,[56] he does not assert Jesus Christ as light and truth from the one light and truth that is God, he asserts that Jesus Christ simply is this light and truth (the one light and truth that God is). He is the light of the world; Jesus is the divine light flooding the world with his light. These other lights must be part of or related to this one true light, they are not independent. As with Lewis, this does move Barth in a universalistic direction: if Jesus Christ is the light of the world then there is a degree to which this light can be recognized anywhere—in the secular world, not necessarily only in the religious. Barth writes:

> Are these truths outside the one? Yes, for the creature has its being and existence outside God. But as lights of the creature these truths are refractions (in this connection there is a real place for the term) of the one light and appearances (this term is also justified at this point) of the one truth. If they have force, value, validity, these are not independent. Primarily and finally, they are not their own. They are merely those which are lent them by the shining of the one light of the one truth. These are lights and truths of the *theatrum of the gloria Dei*.
> ... But as this light rises and shines, it is reflected in the being and existence of the cosmos which is not created accidentally, but with a view to this action and therefore to this revelation.[57]

These *refractions* (Barth uses *Brechungen*) of the one light and truth are appearances (Barth uses *Erscheinungen*) of God's self-declaration, the self-revelation of God. Lewis and Barth are referring to truths that come

---

56   Barth, *Church Dogmatics*, IV/3i: The Doctrine of Reconciliation Part 3i (1961), §69 The Glory of the Mediator, sub-section 2. The Light of Life, 151f.

57   Barth, *Church Dogmatics*, IV/3i, §69.2, 152, 153 (Deutsch: §69. Die Herrlichkeit des Mittlers, 2. Das Licht des Lebens, 173 und 174).

2. Christological Prefigurement: The Incarnation-Resurrection Narrative

from Christ—refractions for Barth, intimations for Lewis, splintered fragments of the true light for Tolkien. They are saying that where Christ is not known or recognized, or cognitive knowledge of the event is impossible, the Christ's truth and light has to break in. The incarnation-resurrection is the one real event in this; it is part of the history of this world. Hence, for Barth these truths are refractions, because the one light is an expression of the one truth. Apart from Christ there is no light and no truth; but divine light-truth is often distinct from human light-truth, and we may filter this true light though our fallenness (also we must heed to Paul's warning about dark forces parading themselves as the light—2 Cor 11:14). As we have seen, Lewis asserted that those receiving or hearing these intimations mistook the images for what they were not and became corrupt in their imaginations—one road led home and a thousand lead into the wilderness.[58] Did this postlapsarian confusion lead to a multiplicity of gods and religious theories?—eventually to a degree of apophatic denial? This leads into the question of how the incarnation-resurrection narrative operates on us when we hear it mythopathically.

XII. HOW DOES THE INCARNATION-RESURRECTION NARRATIVE ACT/OPERATE ON US AS A MYTH, WHETHER SPOKEN OR READ?

In his essay "Myth Became Fact" Lewis deals with the question of how and why the incarnation-resurrection narrative acts upon us both mythopoeically and as the record of an actuality: an historical event. Lewis writes how the human intellect is incurably abstract yet the only realities we experience are concrete: "this pain, this pleasure, this dog, this man. While we are loving the man, bearing the pain, enjoying the pleasure, we are not intellectually apprehending pleasure, pain or personality." Lewis explains that if and when we begin to intellectualize abstractly the concrete realities are reduced to the level of mere instances or examples:

> We are no longer dealing with them but that which they exemplify. This is our dilemma—either to taste and not to know or to know and not to taste or, more strictly, to lack one kind of knowledge because we are in an experience or to lack another kind because we are outside of it. . . . But when else can you really know these

---

58   Lewis, *The Pilgrim's Regress*, (1933), Book VIII, ch. 8.

things? "If only my toothache would stop, I could write another chapter about Pain." But once it stops what do I know about pain?[59]

Lewis cites myth as a partial solution to this dilemma. In listening to and being carried by a myth he asserts that we come nearest to experiencing as concrete what can otherwise be understood only as an abstraction. While we receive a myth as story we experience the principle concretely, though as soon as we translate we get abstraction. To Lewis, it is not truth that flows into us from the myth but reality, he notes how "truth is always *about* something, but reality is that *about which* [Lewis's emphases] truth is[;] . . . every myth is the father of innumerable truths on the abstract level."[60] Therefore, the story in the Gospels generally, and the incarnation-resurrection narrative specifically, operate on us mythopoeically precisely because they convey to us the reality that they represent: whether one believes or not in the reality (the historical actuality of the incarnation and resurrection), the story acts upon us like a myth. Notice how many people today will comment about how nice it would be if the story of Jesus were true. The reality is touching them, not just the abstract truth which they choose to deny. Lewis writes further,

> Now as myth transcends thought, Incarnation transcends myth. The heart of Christianity is a myth which is also a fact. . . . I suspect that men have sometimes derived more spiritual sustenance from myths they did not believe than from the religion they professed. To be truly Christian we must both assent to the historical fact and also receive the myth (fact though it has become) with the same imaginative embrace which we accord to all myths. A man who disbelieved the Christian story as fact but continually fed on it as myth would, perhaps, be more spiritually alive than one who assented and did not think much about it.[61]

There is of course a heavy dose of Platonic idealism in this, and we must not forget the influence of classicism and the theology of the patristic era on Lewis: he wrote about how the story of the incarnation "comes down from the heaven of legend and the imagination"[62] to us to become reality. Is Lewis talking about a Platonic form? So, whether assent is given or not,

---

59 Lewis, "Myth Became Fact" (1944), 34.
60 Lewis, "Myth Became Fact" (1944), 35.
61 Lewis, "Myth Became Fact" (1944), 36.
62 Lewis, "Myth Became Fact" (1944), 36.

2. Christological Prefigurement: The Incarnation-Resurrection Narrative

the story/myth works on us concretely—the reality touches us, though we must acknowledge that for some it may not. The incarnation-resurrection narrative acting upon us mythopoeically would seem, therefore, to have a perlocutionary effect. Following Lewis's proposition through, we do not just think abstractly about this narrative and draw conclusions, it acts upon us in a perlocutionary way: in perceiving the reality the words are *doing* something, like effecting a marriage when someone suitably authorized declares a couple man and wife. For most people, this effect cannot be avoided. What is conveyed is monumental. This is related to a doctrine of illumination—how the Spirit illumines our minds, and hence the text, with understanding, how the Spirit enables us to accept the text for what it claims. This was so for the tribal warriors who listened after a feast in some great Northern hall to the story of Balder (though we saw how the story fell short of actual god-like resurrection); the story would have had a perlocutionary effect on them (intimations on a deeper level than the conscious mind of God's salvific intentions and actions in relation to human kind) similar to the way the incarnation-resurrection narrative was spoken and received as an oral tradition by the apostles and disciples in Jerusalem, Damascus, and Antioch in the immediate months and years after the resurrection: listen to what God has done for you! This leads us into questions about the nature of the incarnation-resurrection narrative.

XIII. IS THERE INTERNAL EVIDENCE FOR A MYTHOPOEIC INTERPRETATION WITHIN THE INCARNATION-RESURRECTION NARRATIVE?

If a mythopathic view of the incarnation-resurrection narrative is to be seen as valid, then the question arises as to whether the narrative itself supports such a view. There is not the scope or space within this paper to analyses both Old and New Testaments to ascertain an answer, especially considering the relationship between many of the stories in the Old Testament and myths from Middle Eastern societies and cultures; however, a brief examination of Lewis's ideas on this subject is possible. In a chapter on the incarnation-resurrection in his work *Miracles* (1st ed. 1947),[63] Lewis addresses the problem as he sees it. He writes that

---

63 "The Grand Miracle," an expansion on the kernel of material initially presented in 1942 at St Jude on the Hill Church, published in, Lewis, *Miracles* (1st ed. 1947), ch. 14.

although the story of Jesus has remarkable parallels with the principle of descending and reascending within nature myths there is no suggestion in the Gospels of a self-awareness of this parallel in Jesus or his disciples. In the Christian story God descends to reascend. This is a familiar pattern in nature—all life must descend (i.e., a seed) to reascend. Cultures all over the world have death and resurrection myths woven into their perception and understanding of the natural world, many such myths are elevated to the status of corn kings, the king must die in the ground as a seed to reascend, to grow again, to rule again. Lewis writes,

> The doctrine of the Incarnation, if accepted, puts this principle even more emphatically at the center. The pattern is there in Nature because it was first there in God. All the instances of it which I have mentioned turn out to be but transpositions of the Divine theme into a minor key.[64]

Lewis asserts that many could see Christ as simply another corn-king. Yet although Jesus was addressing an agrarian society, and although the metaphor of a seed falling and dying to rise again is used in his sayings as well as in other parts of the New Testament,[65] there is no conscious parallel drawn between this observable fact of creation and the reality of God descending to reascend taking fallen creation with him. Lewis writes, "The records, in fact, show us a Person who *enacts* [Lewis's emphasis] the part of the Dying God, but whose thoughts and words remain quite outside the circle of religious ideas to which the Dying God belongs. . . . It is as if you met the sea-serpent and found that it disbelieved in sea-serpents."[66] Lewis addresses this problem by asserting that the Christians are not simply claiming that God was incarnate in Jesus but that the one true God whom the Hebrews worshipped as yhwh had descended. On the one hand, this is the God of creation—of nature. On the other hand, this is not a nature-god. This is the God for whom the earth is his footstool, not his vesture—"Yahweh is neither the soul of nature nor her enemy . . . ."[67] We can therefore understand why Christ is at once so like the corn-king and so silent about him. He is like the corn-king because *the corn-king is a*

---

64   Lewis, *Miracles* (1st ed. 1947), ch. 14, 118.

65   For example, Matt 13; 25; Mark 4; Luke 8; 13; 17; 1 Cor 15; 2 Cor 9:10; 1 Pet 1; 1 John 3.

66   Lewis, *Miracles* (1st ed. 1947), ch. 14, 119.

67   Lewis, *Miracles* (1st ed. 1947), ch. 14, 121.

2. Christological Prefigurement: The Incarnation-Resurrection Narrative

portrait of him. Elements of nature-religion are strikingly absent from the teachings of Jesus and from Hebrew history, in particular the covenant, because of the unique calling of the Hebrew people to testify to the one true God, author and lord of creation, not merely a part of creation:

> In them you have from the very outset got in behind nature-religion and behind nature herself. Where the real God is present the shadows of that God do not appear, that which the shadows resembled does. The Hebrews throughout their history were being constantly headed off from the worship of nature-gods; not because the nature-gods were in all respects unlike the God of Nature but because, at best, they were merely like, and it was the destiny of that nation to be turned away from likenesses to the thing itself.[68]

Hence, there is no internal evidence within the Gospels of these echoes/prefigurements; likewise there is no direct parallel between the incarnation-resurrection narrative and these echoes/prefigurements, which are merely shadows, because to Lewis the Christ-event is the reality beyond the shadows breaking in to redeem: hence, Lewis at his most Platonic. Further, we find that the value he gives to prefigurement, and for that matter natural theology, natural or general revelation, is entirely subordinate to the reality of the Christ-event, which in many ways transcends religion.

XIV. A TEMPORAL PARADOX?

There is an issue/question that we alluded to: some of these prefigurements occur in ancient Egyptian myths, or in North European pagan societies and religion prior to the event of the incarnation-resurrection in Palestine two thousand years ago; others after—for example, in India, perhaps only a few hundred years ago, though they may have been received-composed in ignorance of the Christ-event. There is something of a temporal paradox here, which raises the question of time: we must see the incarnation-resurrection as being at the center of time, therefore any pneumatologically inspired intimations, echoes, and/or refractions about or related to the Christ-event are to be seen as derivative from and reliant for meaning upon this central event; indeed, they must all be seen pertinently as echoes from this single cataclysmic event. Conventionally

---

68   Lewis, *Miracles* (1st ed. 1947), ch. 14, 121.

we see time in our reality, our universe, starting with the big bang, with creation *ex nihilo*, and leading teleologically to the *eschaton*. However, Christologically we must see time starting and ending in our reality with the incarnation-resurrection, therefore all mythopoeic creations that point to or are narrative echoes of the truth of the incarnation-resurrection relate to this central event, whether they occur before or after the reality of the incarnation-resurrection according to the chronologically linear perception we appear to have of time. Christologically time must be seen as circular—everything in our reality, everything that has lived, is alive, or will live is a creation *ex nihilo* related to and radiating out like the ripples on a pool from this central point in our reality. Temporally the effect of the incarnation-resurrection can be identified like the point of disturbance from a stone touching the surface of a pool, but the shock waves radiate out in all directions—rippling the surface of the water, but also radiating into the depths and fanning out as shock waves through the air: this is how the incarnation-resurrection effects our spacio-temporal reality, because the Word was made flesh and dwelt amongst us and we crucified him, and he rose again from the dead. Generally speaking, all of these pneumatological mythopoeic intimations, echoes, and/or refractions that point to or are related to God's incarnation-resurrection are essentially formed in cognitive unawareness, inspired and composed in a lack of knowledge of the historic actuality of the incarnation-resurrection, but profoundly affected by the event nonetheless.

XV. LEWIS'S "SUPPOSAL"

Lewis went beyond an academic study characterized by Christological theorizing about the evidence or otherwise of intimations, echoes, or refractions of the Gospels' narrative in the world's religions and mythologies: he wrote his own Christian myth—*The Chronicles of Narnia*.[69] Lewis's aim was to present the love, light, and truth of God's

---

69   Lewis, *The Chronicles of Narnia* (1950–56):
The Lion the Witch The Wardrobe (1950).
Prince Caspian: The Return to Narnia (1951).
The Voyage of the Dawn Treader (1952).
The Silver Chair (1953).
The Horse His Boy (1954).
The Magician's Nephew (1955).
The Last Battle (1956).

2. Christological Prefigurement: The Incarnation-Resurrection Narrative

turn towards creation, as represented in the gospel. He did this because he believed it had been buried, even extinguished to a degree, by Victorian and Edwardian pietism, by obligation and moralizing, and by adult superiority towards children. Lewis wrote:

> I thought I saw how stories of this kind could steal past a certain inhibition which had paralyzed much of my own religion in childhood. Why did one find it so hard to feel as one was told one ought to feel about God or about the sufferings of Christ? I thought the chief reason was that one was told one ought to. An obligation to feel can freeze feelings. And reverence itself did harm. The whole subject was associated with lowered voices; almost as if it were something medical. But supposing that by casting all these things into an imaginary world, stripping them of their stained-glass and Sunday School associations, one could make them for the first time appear in their real potency? Could one not thus steal past those watchful dragons? I thought one could.[70]

Lewis's initial inspiration was with images:

> All my seven Narnia books, and my three science-fiction books, began with seeing pictures in my head. At first they were not a story, just pictures. The Lion began with a picture of a faun carrying an umbrella and parcels in a snowy wood . . . then suddenly Aslan came bounding into it.[71]

We have noted already Lewis's assertion that God gave images to the pagans, as compared to the law and revelation given to the Hebrews.[72] Lewis's more formal aim was to explore what he termed a "supposal": what if Christ became incarnate in the flesh, the physical reality of another world, as part of another sentient life. Not another world within our universe but an entirely different universe, another reality? Lewis decried the label allegory, concentrating on this term "supposal"—a "what if" supposition.[73] In writing to a parent in 1958 Lewis asserted:

> If Aslan represented the immaterial Deity he would be an allegorical figure. In reality however he is an invention giving an

---

70   Lewis, "Sometimes Fairy Stories May Say Best What's to be Said" (1966).

71   Lewis, "It All Began with a Picture . . ." (1966).

72   Lewis, *The Pilgrim's Regress* (1944), 193.

73   Walter Hooper has collated the material gleaned from various letters, essays where Lewis explains his aims, and what he meant by "supposal": Hooper, *C. S. Lewis A Companion Guide* (1996), 423–26.

imaginary answer to the question, "What might Christ become like if there really were a world like Narnia and He chose to be incarnate and die and rise again in that world as He actually has done in ours?" This is not allegory at all.[74]

Unlike the prefigurement myths which were in effect created and heard outside of cognitive knowledge *about*, or the *awareness of* the incarnation-resurrection, Aslan is a conscious attempt at Christian education within and for a society and tradition that knew about Christ Jesus' atoning sacrifice, but for Lewis had lost the plot due to pietism and moralizing. However, with over 100 million copies sold (which gives a readership of upwards of half a billion) since their original publication in the early 1950s, having been translated into most of the world's main languages, and because of the nature of a post-Christian society in Britain, it is now a fair assumption to say that most of the readers of *The Chronicles of Narnia* in the early twenty-first-century may not have heard of the gospel reality—the same sort of target audience that received and heard the prefigurement myths we have been considering.[75]

Lewis's "supposal" is therefore something of a fanciful conjecture, a "what if . . ."; he is not necessary asserting and exploring the possibility of multiple incarnations, though he did not eliminate the possibility.[76] Lewis will argue that this leaves open the possibility of theophanic incarnations to other life forms in other worlds or universes. In addition, his understanding of multiple incarnations is derived from Aquinas, and then presented in allegorical form in his science-fiction writings.[77]

74   C. S. Lewis, to Mrs Hook, Dec. 29, 1958," in *Letters of C. S. Lewis* (1993).

75   The potency and veracity of Lewis's creation of Aslan is attested to by the level of criticism emanating from secular self-confessed atheistic sources such as *The Guardian* columnist Polly Toynbee (for example, her review of the film, *The Lion, the Witch the Wardrobe*; see: "Narnia represents everything that is most hateful about religion," in, *The Guardian*, Dec. 5, 2005) and the novelist Phillip Pullman.

76   Brian Hebblethwaite has approached the idea of multiple incarnations citing C. S. Lewis as an example of the Thomist believe that although multiple incarnations are theoretically possible, there has never been more than one incarnation of the Word of God to rational humanity. See: Hebblethwaite, "Impossibility of multiple incarnations" (2001); also, Kevern, "Limping Principles: A Reply to Brian Hebblewaite" (2002). In a related field, see: Fisher and Fergusson, "Karl Rahner and the Extra-Terrestrial Intelligence Question" (2006); also Bonting, "Theological Implications of Possible Extraterrestrial Life" (2003).

77   Lewis began to explore this in one of his science-fiction books: *Perelandra* (1943).

2. Christological Prefigurement: The Incarnation-Resurrection Narrative

However, Aslan is not meant to be a separate incarnation from Jesus Christ. The two would not vie for precedence in the *eschaton*—they are one and the same. They differ only in form, the form taken—the form of a man or the form of a lion, in either case a form appropriate to each created reality. These are broadly speaking, matters beyond our present concern. The Narnian stories are like the pagan myths for Lewis, they do not exist in their own right to point to their own internal reality and logic: they exist to point to the single historic event in our reality. So how does Aslan re-present Jesus Christ as the second person of the Trinity, as God incarnate? The important issue is not about multiple incarnations, but whether we come to a much deeper, more profound understanding of the incarnation-resurrection through Lewis's Christological portrait:

> Well, I think in his religious books you tend to get a rather hard view of God, now the conception of Aslan, which you have in the children's stories, seems to me quite different and seems to me to come from a far deeper level in Lewis's character. Aslan is the deity; it is an extraordinarily original achievement. He has, Aslan has, divine qualities of awe, power and authority, yet he exudes love and is himself somehow intensely lovable, so lovable that it is possible for children to want to embrace him, to put their arms about his neck and kiss him. I think that this is perhaps Lewis's, yes, highest religious achievement.[78]

XVI. ASLAN —LEWIS'S MYTHOPOEIC SUB-CREATION

Lewis's Aslan is written in the knowledge of the Gospel narratives and is constructed to elucidate, to parallel didactically though not ontologically, the economy of God's salvation. Written into this are existential meetings between Aslan and individuals or even communities. These meetings are reminiscent of Nicodemus' encounter with Jesus in John's Gospel: these people-creatures can turn one way or the other; they can turn to Aslan, or away. There are naturally many encounters with Narnians who believe in Aslan. However, there are other encounters between people-creatures who have not heard of Aslan, or hold diametrically opposite religious beliefs, or are explicitly hostile to Aslan, having been given a false picture of him. These encounters illustrate to a degree Lewis's belief

---

[78] Comments from *Beyond Personality*—A memoir of C. S. Lewis, a documentary broadcast on BBC Radio 4, Dec. 18, 1988, compiled by Ann Bonsor.

IN THE HIGHEST DEGREE

about the intimations given to the pagans that we have been considering, and how God's salvific actions through Christ relate to, in this instance, the North European pagan tribes. We can consider two examples—Shasta and Emeth.

Shasta (from *The Horse and His Boy*) is a boy who runs away from his adoptive father (a fisherman in Calormen) so as to escape slavery.[79] He flees to Narnia with the aid of a Narnian talking horse in the company of Aravis, a Calormen high-born princess. Shasta's religious education in Calormen has been in the cult of Tash—reminiscent of North European pagan religions, but also akin to the Middle Eastern religions characteristic of the mighty nations that surrounded and preyed on the ancient Hebrews. In the temple in Tashban, the golden statue of Tash is in the form of a giant bird of prey with multiple arms/limbs. Shasta has been taught that Narnia is a land of evil magic ruled by a sorcerer in the malevolent form of a lion (Aslan). After many heroic adventures, alone and crossing the fog-bound mountains into Narnia he becomes aware of a presence by his side. At first he wonders if it is a ghost, a ghoul, or some monstrous creature. As time passes it does not attack him, and he is more and more concerned; he can hear it moving alongside him; he can sense it sigh and can feel its warm breath on his arm. He eventually plucks up the courage to speak to it, to enquire: "One who has waited long for you to speak, said the Thing." Shasta shares his woes and troubles from a cruel and bitter childhood—the thing comforts him and explains that it was he all along who has guided Shasta and Aravis in their escape, and protected him on many occasions. When he presses the thing to explain why he treated Aravis cruelly (at their first encounter Aslan draws his claws across her back in reparation for the severe flogging the slave received as a result of being drugged by Aravis during the escape), the voice answers,

> "I am telling you your story, not hers. I tell no one any story but his own."
>
> "Who are you?" asked Shasta.
>
> "Myself," said the Voice, very deep and low so that the earth shook ... and again "Myself," whispered so softly you could hardly hear it, and yet it seemed to come from all round you as if the leaves rustled with it.
>
> Shasta was no longer afraid.... But a new and different sort of trembling came over him. Yet he felt glad too.

79   Lewis, *The Chronicles of Narnia—The Horse His Boy* (1954).

2. Christological Prefigurement: The Incarnation-Resurrection Narrative

> The mist was turning from black to grey and from grey to white; . . . the whiteness around him became a shining whiteness; his eyes began to blink. He could see the mane and ears and head of his horse quite easily now. A golden light fell on them from the left. He thought it was the sun.
>
> He turned and saw, pacing beside him, taller than the horse, a Lion. It was from the Lion that the light came. No one ever saw anything more terrible or beautiful.
>
> . . . [A]fter one glance at the Lion's face he slipped out of the saddle and fell at its feet. He couldn't say anything but then he didn't want to say anything, and he knew he needn't say anything.
>
> The High King above all kings stooped towards him. Its mane, and some strange and solemn perfume that hung about the mane, was all round him. It touched his forehead with its tongue. He lifted his face and their eyes met. Then instantly the pale brightness of the mist and the fiery brightness of the Lion rolled themselves together into a swirling glory and gathered themselves up and disappeared. He was alone with the horse on a grassy hillside under a blue sky. And there were birds singing.[80]

Lewis described *The Horse and His Boy* as being about "the calling and conversion of a heathen."[81] Shasta's religious education has corrupted him from a true understanding of Aslan, yet when he eventually meets Aslan religious concepts and words become irrelevant: he senses and perceives the beauty and love of God incarnate, the fiery brightness and swirling glory, and knows that all he must do is respond in love and gratitude, obedience and commitment. Is Lewis asserting that many pagans will not only have led lives under the grace, protection, and influence of Christ but also, preveniently speaking, have become people who were ready and able to respond to Christ should he choose to reveal himself to them?

We can elucidate by examining a second example: Emeth from *The Last Battle*.[82] Set in Lewis's apocalyptic, eschatologically charged end-of-time, Emeth (Hebrew for *faithful, true*) is a Calormen warrior who along with an army has invaded Narnia. After death—his death and the destruction of the entire world that was Narnia and the surrounding

---

80   Lewis, *Chronicles of Narnia—The Horse His Boy*, ch. 11, 127f.
81   C. S. Lewis, to Anne Jenkins, March 5, 1961, quoted in Hooper, *C. S. Lewis: A Companion and Guide* (1996), 425–26.
82   Lewis, *The Chronicles of Narnia—The Last Battle* (1956), ch. 15.

lands/countries (including Calormen)—Emeth comes face-to-face with Aslan. What strikes Emeth is the size, power, and awesomeness of Aslan, but equally his beauty, glory, and truth:

> But the Glorious One bent down his golden head and touched my forehead with his tongue and said, "Son, thou art welcome." But I said, "Alas, Lord, I am no son of thine but the servant of Tash." He answered, "Child, all the service thou hast done to Tash, I account as service done to me."
>
> ... "Lord, is it then true, as the Ape said, that thou and Tash are one?" The Lion growled so that the earth shook (but his wrath was not against me) and said, "It is false. Not because he and I are one, but because we are opposites, I take to me the services which thou hast done to him. For I and he are of such different kinds that no service which is vile can be done to me, and none which is not vile can be done to him. Therefore if any man swear by Tash and keep his oath for the oath's sake, it is by me that he has truly sworn, though he know it not, and it is I who reward him. And if any man do a cruelty in my name, then, though he says the name Aslan, it is Tash whom he serves and by Tash his deed is accepted."
>
> ... But I said also (for the truth constrained me), "Yet I have been seeking Tash all my days." "Beloved," said the Glorious One, "Unless thy desire had been for me thou wouldst not have sought so long and so truly. For all find what they truly seek."
>
> Then he breathed upon me and took away the trembling from my limbs and caused me to stand upon my feet ... then he turned him about in a storm and flurry of gold and was gone suddenly.
>
> And since then ... I have been wandering to find him and my happiness is so great that it even weakens me like a wound. And this is the marvel of marvels, that he called me Beloved.[83]

At the general resurrection and judgement all come face-to-face with Aslan and as they look at his face, they either love him, or loath him, they either turn one way or the other: those who love Aslan and turn to him are not uniquely the Narnians—his followers—there are many creatures who geographically and culturally have never heard of Aslan, or more pertinently had never known him pneumatologically. These creatures turn one way or the other: to Aslan and into the new heaven and new earth, or into the darkness—the decision is Aslan's and Aslan's alone. After this Narnian *eschaton* there are a group of rebellious

---

83   Lewis, *The Chronicles of Narnia—The Last Battle* (1956), ch. 11, 152f.

2. Christological Prefigurement: The Incarnation-Resurrection Narrative

renegade dwarves who have lived in Narnia and know about Aslan but are cynical and skeptical and despite being amongst the saved, the redeemed, when they are approached by Aslan in the new heaven and earth they fear him, perceive him as a monster, as a threat.[84] They are oblivious to the goodness around them, perceiving kindness as a cruelty, and the glories of this new creation as dark, dank, and rotten. "There is no black hole, save in your own fancy" cries Tirian the last king of Narnia to them.[85] Aslan comments to Lucy, "You see they will not let us help them. They have chosen cunning instead of belief. Their prison is only in their own minds, yet they are in that prison; and so afraid of being taken in that they cannot be taken out."[86] Crucially these dwarves lack faith—primarily, faith in Aslan, but their lives, their values, their behavior betrays this lack of faith. By contrast Emeth's life, his desires, his actions, all that he was when alive, was evidence of faith in Aslan even though he was culturally and geographically isolated from the Narnia "religion" centered on Aslan (in the same way that those who composed and heard the pagan myths that for Lewis and Tolkien to some degree prefigured Christ's atoning sacrifice, were isolated from the reality that took place in Palestine two thousand years ago). Lewis's use of *account*, that is, when Aslan declares to Emeth "I account as service done to me," is comparable to Paul's use of "reckoned" in the context of Abraham's righteousness before God.[87] Pertinently, whereas Aslan declares to Tash—the demonic satanic god at the center of Calormen religion—"Begone, monster, and take your lawful prey to your own place [i.e. hell],"[88] it is the goodness (something of a Platonic norm or form, in intent?) inherent in Emeth's faith and desire that link him to Aslan, not to Tash. Otherwise, Tash would claim him for his own: "no service which is vile can be done to me, and none which is not vile can

---

84 Lewis, *The Chronicles of Narnia—The Last Battle* (1956), ch. 13, 135f.

85 Lewis, *The Chronicles of Narnia—The Last Battle* (1956), 138.

86 Lewis, *The Chronicles of Narnia—The Last Battle* (1956), 140.

87 "Abraham believed God, and it was reckoned [*elogisthē*, from *ellogeō*, to charge to one's account, to keep a record of] to him as righteousness. Now to one who works, wages are not reckoned [*logizetai*, from *logizomai*, count, reckon, calculate, take into account, credit] as a gift but as something due. But to one who without works trusts him who justifies the ungodly, such faith is reckoned [*logizetai*] as righteousness. So also David speaks of the blessedness of those to whom God reckons [*logizetai*] righteousness apart from works." (Rom 4:3–6).

88 Lewis, *The Chronicles of Narnia—The Last Battle* (1956), 125.

be done to him."⁸⁹ Therefore, it is our lives and our intentions that betray or confirm our allegiance, not necessarily our religious declarations: the sovereignty and *aseity* of God in Christ will decide. These passages are Lewis explicitly trying to spell out to his readers the implications of Matthew 25 for non-Christians. In this context Lewis wrote: "The truth is God has not told us what his arrangements about the other people are. We do know that no man can be saved except through Christ; we do not know that only those who know Him can be saved through Him."⁹⁰

This does not detract from the uniqueness of Christ, if anything it further denies a syncretistic approach to the world's religions. Lewis is therefore presenting his understanding of the eternally electing God who seeks the redemption of all creation, who seeks to be reconciled to his creatures. Aslan's sacrifice (in *The Lion, the Witch and the Wardrobe*) represents the overwhelming love of the absolute supreme transcendent God, who comes in infinite humility, meekness, and modesty in Christ Jesus, gives himself to humanity in unconditional freedom and grace, despite the venomous hatred that humanity/creation heaped on him on the cross/stone table. There are numerous illustrations given by Lewis of encounters between creatures-humans in Narnia and Aslan where the one thing the creature must do is repent of his/her sins, acknowledging in love the lordship of God incarnate: regarding her brother Edmund (for whom Aslan allows himself to be sacrificed on the stone table because of Edmund's treachery), Lucy comments to her sister, "Does he know what Aslan did for him, does he know what the arrangement with the witch really was?"⁹¹ As Lewis asserted, it is not necessarily only those who know him (in the manner of cognitive knowledge) who can be saved by him.⁹² Do we truly know him? Do we fully understand what Christ did for us? We think we do, but is our knowledge any more definite, any more certain or complete than Emeth's or Shasta's? It is only in the *eschaton* that we will know as we our known (1 Cor 13:12).

---

89   Lewis, *The Chronicles of Narnia—The Last Battle* (1956), 154.
90   Lewis, *Mere Christianity* (1952), 53.
91   Lewis, *The Chronicles of Narnia—The Lion the Witch The Wardrobe* (1950), 163.
92   Lewis, *Mere Christianity* (1952), 53.

2. Christological Prefigurement: The Incarnation-Resurrection Narrative

XVII. CONCLUSION

Lewis's initial justification for these prefiguring myths was in effect in reaction to Frazer's work: because of the value he had given Frazer's agenda and conclusions as a young atheist and apostate. However, as we have seen, Lewis's Christology soon developed a pneumatological justification and role for these myths beyond the context of Frazer's work. So, in conclusion, what does this tell us about God's salvific actions towards humanity: the intention and action to bring about redemption and salvation potentially for all? Lewis is setting out the soteriological principle that whether we are Christian or not our salvation lies not in our actions-beliefs, but in what the Lord has done for us. The most we can do is acknowledge, repent, and allow the Lord's Spirit to change us, reconcile and redeem us. In the case of those who have consciously heard of the Gospel narratives, the very story of the incarnation, passion, and resurrection should operate on us in a perlocutionary manner: awareness of the narrative is important because of the event it represents. It is because of the very importance of the incarnation-resurrection narrative that the prefiguring myths must be seen as having a relative value and significance. What of these prefiguring myths? In the case of Emeth and Shasta (who for Lewis are comparable with the pagans and heathens outside of the Judaeo-Christian revelation), this was operating on a subliminal level. Such myths will point towards something of the reality of the incarnation-resurrection and may likewise operate in a perlocutionary manner but on a subliminal level. However important these pneumatological mythopoeic echoes/intimations/refractions appear to be, their function is simply to point towards the real event: Jesus Christ, the second person of the Trinity crucified and resurrected for our salvation. If you have access to knowledge of the real story, the real event, then why bother with myths? If because of cultural, geographic, or temporal isolation these intimations come to people who can never know of the true story then the myths may have a perlocutionary effect on individuals/societies (subject to the degree of reception or rejection, which is governed by our fallen state—*simul iustus et peccator*) in accordance with the will of the Father and may or may not work towards God's loving purposes which are the potential salvation and transformation of all humankind and creation.

3

Revelation and Second Meanings: A Philosophical and Pneumatological Justification

SYNOPSIS

Some may consider there to be a problem with a doctrine of Christological prefigurement because it appears to do an injustice to the original aims and intentions of the author of the myth in asserting a second, a subsequent, Christological level of meaning? Lewis thought not, and could defend such an interpretation. Is it possible for anyone today to view such myths without considering what has happened in the intervening time? Regardless of concerns over purity, there is an indelible connection that must be explained. For example, the apparent connection between ancient writings—Plato, Socrates, etc.—and what happened to the Christ in his passion. Lewis therefore posits an alternative option to prophecy or chance coincidence: to previse may be the result of wisdom. Questions are raised as to what extent these prefigurements may be considered idolatrous? Again, Lewis could refute accusations of idolatry. Through his understanding of natural theology, revelation, and human imagination (proximately to that of Augustine, but also to the English romantics, especially the poet, theologian, and philosopher Samuel Taylor Coleridge) Lewis's esteem, prior to his conversion, for pagan myths relating to the appearing (incarnation?) and reviving from death (resurrection?) of pagan gods, avatars, and spirits, led him after his conversion to analyze why and how these religious myths/stories related to the actual Christ-event. Lewis's understanding in this is contiguous with Coleridge and George MacDonald, but also J. R. R. Tolkien (from whom he learns and uses many concepts—for example, sub-creation, mythopoeic/mythopoeia, refractions and splinters of the true light). His cautious respect for these intimations of prefigurement were as a mode of revelation rooted in Augustine's doctrine of illumination and the proposition that there is no un-aided true knowledge of God, knowledge and understanding given through prevenient grace and imbued through the faculty of the imagination.

I. INTRODUCTION: CHRISTOLOGICAL PREFIGUREMENT

A consistent element of C. S. Lewis's understanding of God's self-revelation is that intimations of the Christ-event—the incarnation-cross-resurrection—were given, often in the form of myth, to people geographically and cognitively distant from the revelation given to the Jews as God's chosen people. These intimations, in narrative form, story, myth, were also imparted, *a posteriori*, to people isolated for various reasons from the efforts of the church to attest to God's salvific actions through the Christ. These intimations we may call Christological prefigurement, part of a doctrine of Christology and pneumatology. As a working hypothesis, we may say that such intimations are eschatological, in that they draw people closer to Christ's judgement. Lewis saw many of the pagan myths amongst, for instance, North European peoples as manifestations of the universal Christ—hints and intimations of the Christ-event in stories of an incarnate "god" come to save his people, dying and raised up again. Therefore, pagans, for Lewis, were (at least potentially) people moving towards Christ without explicit knowledge. Many questions and issues are raised by Lewis's proposition. I addressed these questions in an in-depth analysis of Lewis's Christological prefigurement elsewhere, in a paper published in 2007.[1] However, one issue that was not dealt with, which was raised by that paper, was the question of second meanings. Is there a potential problem with a doctrine of Christological prefigurement because it appears to do an injustice to the original aims and intentions of the author of the myth in asserting a second, subsequent, level of meaning? Lewis thought not, and could defend such an interpretation, drawing

---

[1] For example, what does a critical evaluation of Lewis's proposition that the incarnation-resurrection narrative is both myth and history disclose? What did Lewis mean by myth, and how does myth became reality in the Christ-event? What exactly did Lewis classify as ideas of prefigurement in relation to the incarnation-resurrection narrative, and how do these intimations relate to natural theology, revelation, and imagination? What doctrine of Christ as the light of the world in reality and in mythopoeic intimations was Lewis working with—and did Tolkien's proposition of splintered fragments of the true light give Lewis a particular understanding of how these prefigured ideas came to be in pagan myths? We may also ask, how does the incarnation-resurrection narrative act/operate on us as a myth, whether spoken or read? And what internal evidence for a mythopoeic interpretation is there within the incarnation-resurrection narrative? Finally, how do our conclusions measure up to Lewis's "supposal": Aslan, Lewis's own mythopoeic sub-creation? See Brazier, "C. S. Lewis Christological Prefigurement" (2007).

3. Revelation and Second Meanings

essentially on a philosophical interpretation of the pneumatological element of the economic Trinity. This paper is an examination of this question, and outlines Lewis's defense.

II. INTENTION AND VALIDITY

There is a potential problem with Lewis's doctrine of Christological prefigurement. This problem is centered on a number of questions: Is there a second level of meaning to these pagan myths? If so, are the subsequent interpretations valid? Also, are not the original intentions of the author applicable above subsequent interpretations, particularly given that the author could not have known about the Christ-event and therefore the similarity? Is this doctrine of Christological prefigurement simply a coincidence, and are we projecting our own considerations and conclusions onto ancient texts? Is there a connection between the human mind and intimations of revelation? If so, what role do the faculties of reason and/or imagination have to play in generating second or subsequent meanings?

Lewis was not alone in subscribing second or subsequent meanings to religious myths. Sir James George Frazer and other academics recognized the coincidences in these of stories of incarnate gods/idols, and dying and reviving gods.[2] Frazer, a late nineteenth-century colonial religionist and social anthropologist, provided a catalogue of these ancient pagan myths, and the similarities both among them and to the incarnation-resurrection narrative. Frazer grounded all these myths in the human psyche. Many of his followers were rooted in a Feuerbachian-Freudian interpretation of a Darwinian model of human cultural development/evolution, which classified religion as a tribal human construct within a hostile world. Frazer's supporters used these conclusions as ammunition against Christianity and the church. The young apostate and atheist C. S. Lewis read Frazer and concluded that the gospel account of Jesus'

---

2   Frazer, *The Golden Bough* (1911–15). Initially published in two volumes in 1890, the work grew to the final 12-volume 3rd edition, published 1911–15: Vol 1–2, Part I, *The Magic Art*; Vol 3, Part II, *Taboo and the Perils of the Soul*; Vol 4, Part III, *The Dying God*; Vol 5–6, Part IV, *Adonis, Attis, Osiris Studies in the History of Oriental Religion*; Vol 7–8, Part V, *Spirits of the Corn and of the Wild*; Vol 9, Part VI, *The Scapegoat*; Vol 10–11, Part VII, *Balder the Beautiful, the Fire-Festivals of Europe, and the Doctrine of the External Soul*; Vol 12, *Bibliography and General Index*. See also Frazer, *The Golden Bough* (abridged ed.; 1922).

death and resurrection was simply one amongst many similar stories. On the evening of his conversion from theism to Christianity, C. S. Lewis is recorded as having described myths as beautiful and moving, though they were "lies and therefore worthless, even though breathed through silver."[3] At the point of his conversion, in other words, he is dismissive of the Frazer-Feuerbachian position he had subscribed to. Gradually, however, Lewis came to regard these prefigurements as the work of the Holy Spirit—intimations of God's salvific action in Christ. Indeed, in his maturity he was to comment that we should *expect* the similarities to be there, given the cosmic importance of the Christ-event and the fact that God in freedom seeks the redemption of creation. Lewis's understanding of myth was to change radically during his life as a result of his adoption and championing of an orthodox Christian faith. Myth was, and continued to be, very important to him—primarily the Northern European myths, Greek mythology, and Asiatic-Indian (Hindu) religion and myth.

Perhaps the most significant Christological myth, for Lewis, was the myth of Balder the Beautiful. But can Balder be said to be the Christ? Certainly Balder's characteristics are in many ways similar to those of Christ—love, joy, light, beauty, compassion—, and there are also similarities with the *Logos*, the Word.[4] Moreover, the Norse word notably used of Balder, *tivor*, is unquestioningly taken to mean divine, god-like—Balder is the *blaupom tivor*, the bloody victim, the slain god. Similarities can be seen today with the suffering Christ, though perhaps more with the Hebrew concept of the scapegoat than with a specifically Christian idea. Balder does not take on death voluntarily as Jesus did; he fears death from the prophetic dream, yet the action taken to defend him causes his death. His death is caused by the trickery of Loki; Jesus wrestled with his fate in the Garden of Gethsemane, but accepted what was to befall him. What is more, there is the potential for Balder being revived or restored, but this falls short of resurrection: it does not happen in our reality. There is a similar potentiality with the Egyptian god Osiris here, who is tricked into death, like Balder.

3 Quoted by Tolkien in his poem "Mythopoeia," reflecting Lewis's position up to the point of his conversion: see Tolkien, "Mythopoeia" (1978). See also C. S. Lewis to Arthur Greeves, Oct. 18, 1931, in *Collected Letters*, Vol. I (2004), 975–77; also published in Lewis, *They Stand Together* (ed. Hooper; 1979).

4 See, Frazer, *The Golden Bough* (1913), Part VII: *Balder the Beautiful*, Vol I and Vol II (1913) specifically, ch. 3, "The Myth of Balder," 101.

3. Revelation and Second Meanings

But what did the original composer(s) of the Myth of Balder believe? In claiming prefigurement, is not Lewis working against the original setting of the myth, ignoring the intentions of the author and audience, how they were conceived to be read and heard? By doing so, Lewis is claiming a second or hidden meaning. Such a subsequent interpretation and context, Lewis claims, generates suspicion: it "arouses deep distrust in a modern mind, because, as we know, almost anything can be read into any book."[5] So what are the issues to consider?–

- How do myths arise?
- What were the original intention and meaning, the aims and objectives of the author, or authoring community?
- Truth: what truth is there underpinning the text/myth, and does this meaning change with context?
- What aims and objectives, intentions, lie outside of the mind of the author/authoring community?
- How, and in what way, does meaning and truth lie ultimately with God, with divine inspiration?
- What place is there for human freedom in the composition, subject to inspiration?

There is always scope for self-deception because we are human, fallible and fallen. Are we guilty of reassigning meaning and intention? Lewis recounts several examples of prophetic prefigurement, and although he concedes that in some instances these can be explained simply as coincidence, and although it is easily possible for someone to make a comment that can be applied to subsequent events there is, Lewis asserts, something more than a chance happening.

> [It is feasible that] someone says what is truer and more important than he knows; but it does not seem to me that he could have done so by chance. I hasten to add that the alternative to chance which I have in mind is not "prophecy" in the sense of clear prevision, miraculously bestowed.[6]

---

5   Lewis, *Reflections on the Psalms* (1958), 85 (ch. 10, "Second Meanings").

6   Lewis, *Reflections on the Psalms* (1958), 87.

Lewis therefore posits an alternative to both prophecy and coincidence. To *previse* (Lewis's term) or *preview* may be the result of wisdom. Foreseeing, even unselfconsciously, may be caused by wisdom, where wisdom is insight and knowledge, an understanding of how the world works, of what constitutes human existence, which leads to a mature reflection on what is, and what is possible.

Lewis as a classicist places great emphasis on examples that confirm a doctrine of prefigurement from Græco-Roman sources. There are cases where the later truth, after the event, which the author/teller was unaware of, is, however, closely related to the truth, a truth that had in many ways underpinned and motivated the composition. Examples of prefigured truths that can be seen after the event they foretell are manifold in relation to the incarnation-resurrection. The sheer number must, Lewis asserts, deny a theory of chance coincidence (here the Victorian atheistic anthropologists are in agreement with Lewis in claiming a unifying cause, though he dismisses their citing of psychology as a common denominator). Lewis's preferences are for North European pagan myths, but in defending a doctrine of prefigurement he draws on Graeco-Roman examples.

III. PLATO AND THE CHRIST

Perception, insight, and knowledge will lead to wisdom. This is grounded in reason, but, as Lewis notes, "something more sensitive and personal than scientific knowledge is involved—what the writer or speaker was, not only what he knew."[7] Lewis here draws on Plato's *Republic*. Plato argues that righteousness is often praised for its benefits, honor, and popularity, but that if we are truly to understand righteousness, we must see it without these popular worldly attributes and rewards. Lewis continues:

> He [Plato] asks us therefore to imagine a perfectly righteous man treated by all around him as a monster of wickedness. We must picture him, still perfect, while he is bound, scourged, and finally impaled (the Persian equivalent of crucifixion). At this passage a Christian reader starts and rubs his eyes. What is happening? Yet another of these lucky coincidences? But presently he sees that there is something here which cannot be called luck at all.[8]

---

7   Lewis, *Reflections on the Psalms* (1958), 89.
8   Lewis, *Reflections on the Psalms* (1958), 89.

3. Revelation and Second Meanings

This is not a case of someone who is talking about something else which coincidentally resonates with a subsequent event or person. Lewis correctly asserts that Plato is consciously extrapolating about what happens to goodness in this world, a wicked and misunderstanding world. This understanding is not separate or independent from what happened to Jesus of Nazareth, the Christ, the only true and good and sinless person. The Passion, for Lewis, is the supreme example of goodness destroyed by fallen humanity:

> If Plato was in some measure moved to write of it by the recent death—we may almost say the martyrdom—of his master Socrates then that again is not something simply other than the Passion of Christ. The imperfect, yet very venerable, goodness of Socrates led to the easy death of the hemlock, and the perfect goodness of Christ led to the death of the cross, not by chance but for the same reason; because goodness is what it is, and because the fallen world is what it is. If Plato, starting from one example and from his insight into the nature of goodness and the nature of the world, was led on to see the possibility of a perfect example, and thus to depict something extremely like the Passion of Christ, this happened not because he was lucky but because he was wise.[9]

But what exactly did Plato write?

> Now, if we are to form a real judgment of the life of the just and unjust, we must isolate them; there is no other way; and how is the isolation to be effected? I answer: Let the unjust man be entirely unjust, and the just man entirely just; nothing is to be taken away from either of them, and both are to be perfectly furnished for the work of their respective lives. . . . They will tell you that the just man who is thought unjust will be scourged, racked, bound—will have his eyes burnt out; and, at last, after suffering every kind of evil, he will be impaled: then he will understand that he ought to seem only, and not to be, just.[10]

Lewis concludes that Plato's insight is not simply a prevision or preview, a prophecy. For Christians to recognize something here that resonates with the Passion is not simply retro-projection. Plato's insight issues from wisdom. There is a universal truth. But not all examples of prevision are rooted in wisdom. There may be a parallel or comparable perception

---

9   Lewis, *Reflections on the Psalms* (1958), 90.
10 Plato, *The Republic*, Bk II, (trans. M. J. Levett), 1001–2.

which resonates with the ultimate sacrifice of goodness that is the Passion, but still rooted in wisdom. For example, Lewis cites the instance of a poem by the Roman poet Virgil, written not long before the birth of Christ, which extols the new age where the Virgin returns, the reign of Saturn is renewed, and the new child is sent down from high heaven. The poem goes on to describe the paradisal age that this nativity ushers in. Throughout Christian history, Virgil's comments were taken to have been prophetic. The question is, "Is this resemblance to the birth of Christ simply an accident?" It may be argued that knowledge from the Old Testament prophets might have reached Virgil (though whether there is evidence for this is another matter); however, there is a resemblance which, as with Plato, can be explained through a common consciousness grounded in knowledge and understanding of humanity, leading to wisdom. Virgil may well have recognized, through wisdom, what the world needed: "Indeed, Virgil may well have recognized in his wisdom that these were the things the world needed, and trusting in his own gods, believed that they would come."[11] Rooting or grounding prefigurement in a common consciousness leading to wisdom also applies to the numerous examples of prefigurement in pagan myths—whether North European, Asiatic-Indian, Egyptian, or Oceanic.

IV. WISDOM

Lewis therefore concludes that wisdom is at the heart of prefigurement. But this is not just human cleverness and ingenuity. Wisdom involves inspiration, imagination, and reason—it is a bridge between the divine and the human. Wisdom, in the Bible, is often personified to suggest that it is external to the human, proceeding from the Holy Spirit. Lewis commented on several occasions that no good work is done anywhere without the aid of the Father of Lights.[12] This raises once again the question of inspiration and illumination. Lewis writes, "In other words, when we examine things said which take on, in the light of later knowledge, a meaning they could not have had for those who said them, they turn out to be of different sorts."[13] This implies a conception of meaning as, like truth, existing outside of the human, where the original intentions and

---

11   Comment on this research by Brendan N. Wolfe, an Oxford patristics scholar.
12   Lewis, *Reflections on the Psalms*, 95 (ch. 11, "Scripture").
13   Lewis, *Reflections on the Psalms* (1958), 95.

3. Revelation and Second Meanings

aims of the author of the myth, the teller of the tale, are only relative and contribute to a wider meaning and truth that reflects Christ as the way, the truth, and the life. This approach is, to a degree, Platonic, reflecting Lewis's beliefs as a Christian Platonist. So, we may ask, if wisdom is to be equated with light, divine illumination, how does this wisdom relate to revelation?

Wisdom raises the question of prefigurement in the Old Testament in relation to the sayings of Jesus, and the second meanings applied to ancient Hebrew events and stories in the Acts of the Apostles: for example, Stephen's speech before the Sanhedrin and the High Priest, reinterpreting Jewish events and history in the light of the incarnation-cross-resurrection (Acts 7). This is potentially a large area of study; suffice it briefly to see what Lewis made of it. Lewis read and studied the Psalms and was aware of the subtle references which could be seen as applying to Jesus of Nazareth and his Passion.[14] Further, from what is recorded both in his ministry and in his words from the cross, Jesus aligned himself with the suffering servant in Isaiah 53.[15] The resurrection narratives—for example the encounter on the road to Emmaus—have Jesus looking back over the history of the Jews, and the Old Testament, to confirm what has happened.[16] Isaiah 53—referred to explicitly in the Acts of the Apostles—is probably the clearest example of the full meaning of an ancient passage coming out only after an event subsequent to it composition. On the question of second meanings and validity Lewis concludes that

> [when] I read that poem of Virgil's . . . such a reading may after all be a mere coincidence (though I am not sure that it is). I may be reading into Virgil what is wholly irrelevant to all he was, and did, and intended. . . . But when I meditate on the Passion while reading Plato's picture of the Righteous One, or on the Resurrection while reading about Adonis or Balder, the case is altered. There is a real

---

14   Lewis in particular notes Mark 15:34, linked to Psalm 22. See C. S. Lewis, *Reflections on the Psalms* (1958), 102.

15   Lewis in particular notes Acts 8:26–39, Phillip's encounter with the Ethiopian Eunuch over the interpretation of Isaiah 53. See Lewis, *Reflections on the Psalms* (1958), 101–2.

16   Lewis in particular notes Jesus's identity as David's Lord (Mark 12:35–36); the use of words from Ps 91:11–12 in Matt 4:6; the explicit appropriation of Ps 118:22 in Mark 12:10; and the linking of Ps 16:11 to the resurrection. See Lewis, *Reflections on the Psalms* (1958), ch. 11 "Scripture."

connection between what Plato and the myth-makers most deeply were and meant and what I believe to be the truth.[17]

Second meanings are therefore valid precisely because there is a God, and this God seeks to impart to humanity some knowledge of himself and his salvific actions for humanity. This is revelation both in the imparting of understanding, which is relational, and the event or action of the atonement-redemption of humanity. This single event moves ever and onward towards the final fulfilment in the *eschaton*. Therefore, revelation unfolds. Meaning will thus change, or be augmented. It is a contemporary Western concept that protects and holds sacrosanct the aims, objectives, and intentions of the author, leading to the idea that the author is immutable, while other contemporary literary scholarship rejects intention as a fallacy. What was known in part and led to the inspiration of myths hundreds or even thousands of years ago will inevitably develop *in the fullness* of the revelatory event of Jesus of Nazareth, the Christ. Or is it the significance of the myth, rather than what underlies it, that changes, develops? Meaning is therefore teleological and our *grasp* on revelation is tentative, and unfolds towards the final completion in the *eschaton*: only with death and the last judgement will we know as completely as we are known (1 Cor 13).

V. IMAGINATION AND THE THEOLOGICAL TRADITION

If pagan Christs are a foreshadowing or allusion, relating figuratively to the incarnation-resurrection, and if they are rooted in wisdom, where wisdom is more than human cleverness, then how do we assess and judge one interpretation from another? Lewis's mature beliefs about inspiration and imagination must be examined to ascertain what value he placed on prefigurement. It is Lewis's doctrine of the imagination that is fundamental to prefigurement and the developing understanding of the meaning and truth that we can learn from such myths.[18]

An important source for Lewis of a doctrine of the imagination is the Scottish author, poet, and Christian minister George MacDonald

---

17   Lewis, *Reflections on the Psalms* (1958), 92.

18   For Lewis on imagination see Schakel, *Reason and Imagination in C. S. Lewis* (1984), as well as Lewis, "Psycho-Analysis and Literary Criticism" (1962). See also Swinburne, *The Concept of Miracle* (1970), and Swinburne, *Revelation* (1992).

3. Revelation and Second Meanings

(1824–1905)—Lewis's acknowledged master and teacher.[19] According to MacDonald, it is not necessarily our cognitive faculties that identify truth, but our imagination: God uses people's imagination to get through to them. Through MacDonald, Lewis viewed imagination and the intellect as given by the Holy Spirit; however, the reception of intimations, and our subsequent actions are governed by free will, and consequently also by the effects of original sin: humanity is free to reject or accept God on a conscious level, even though God may be pressing on each and every one in their, to a degree, sub-conscious minds. What is important here is a baptized imagination: "It is not surprising that for MacDonald the closer one is to Christ the Creator, the more faithful and vibrant the imagination will be."[20]

If, to summarize, the imagination is the capacity (or, in many ways, the gift) to create mental images, the ability to spontaneously generate illustrations, pictures, or images in the mind, which give meaning to our experience of reality, then the imagination helps us to understand and make sense of the world. The imagination is therefore of fundamental importance if we are going to learn, particularly if we accept the idea of revelation as *unfolding*. Storytelling is the key to both imaginative creating and to listening and learning. This is, of course, distinct from the manner in which our cognitive mental processes work: thoughts appear to arise from an often-unidentifiable source, and are therefore creative. Lewis and MacDonald therefore, in this context, saw how the imagination should, must, be pneumatologically governed—i.e., under the influence and persuasion of the Holy Spirit.

Walter Hooper[21] notes the importance for Lewis of a distinction between fantasy and imagination: Lewis argued that Freud was incorrect in asserting that all creative art issues from day-dreams, fantasies, and wish-fulfilments generated by the sub-conscious mind. Instead, Lewis the literary critic asserted that there are two modes or activities of the imagination: one free, and the other enslaved to the will. This will-enslaved imagination conjures up images and ideas primarily, in Lewis's words, to provide imaginary gratifications. Both may be the genesis for creativity, for art: "The former or 'free' activity continues in the works it

19   See Lewis, *The Great Divorce* (1945), 66–67. See also Lewis, "Introduction," in George McDonald, Phantastes (2000), v–xii.

20   Dearborn, *Baptized Imagination* (2006), 81.

21   Hooper, *C.S. Lewis: A Companion and Guide* (1996), 565.

produces and passes from the status of a dream to that of art by a process which may legitimately be called 'elaboration': it is a motive power which starts the activity and is withdrawn when once the engine is running, or a scaffolding which is knocked away when the building is complete."[22]

If imagination is rooted in creativity, then we may ask, "Where do ideas come from?" Imagination has had a troubled standing in Western philosophy and theology. In the Reformed tradition, imagination is considered suspect. Calvin asserted that God rejects without exception all shapes, pictures, and other symbols by which the superstitious believe they can bring him near to them:

> For we know that the Persians worshiped the sun; all the stars they saw in the heavens the stupid pagans also fashioned into gods for themselves. There was almost no animal that for the Egyptians was not the figure of a god. Indeed, the Greeks seemed to be wise above the rest, because they worshiped God in human form. But God does not compare these images with one another, as if one were more suitable, another less so; but without exception he repudiates all likenesses, pictures, and other signs by which the superstitious have thought he will be near them.[23]

Calvin was writing in the context of humanity's proclivity for creating idols out of stone and wood, for worshipping the sun, the moon, and so forth, or for inventing gods in humanity's own image. However, his comments in this chapter of *The Institutes*[24] have detrimentally affected the understanding of imagination and its relation to God and God's revelation. Calvin quite correctly emphasized the condemnation of idols and idolatry enshrined in the Ten Commandments; however, there is more to the human faculty of imagination than idolatry. In the Reformed tradition, this suspicion of imagination and images has influenced not only architecture and decoration, but also created a highly conceptualized form of articulation which sought to reduce image-based thinking amongst theologians. The Lewis family's religious roots were

---

22 Lewis, "Psycho-Analysis and Literary Criticism" (1962), first delivered at Westfield College in 1941 to a Literary Society, published by The English Association in Essays and Studies XXVII; subsequently published in Lewis, *They Asked for a Paper* (1962), 120–38 (quotation 125).

23 Calvin, *Institutes of the Christian Religion* (2006 [1960]), Bk 1, ch. 11, 1, 100.

24 Calvin, *Institutes of the Christian Religion* (2006 [1960]), Bk 1, ch. 11, "It is Unlawful to Attribute a Visible Form to God, and Generally Whoever Sets Up Idols Revolts Against God," 99–116.

3. Revelation and Second Meanings

in the Reformed tradition of Ulster Presbyterianism, though his parents and grandparents were religiously of the Anglican tradition, and he was educated in the English public school system. When he embraced Christianity it was as an Anglican. In sharp contrast to the negative view of imagination in the Reformed tradition (and for that matter amongst Freudian skeptics), Lewis represented a much more positive approach. Lewis's initial contact with this approach was through J. R. R. Tolkien, and his understanding was then proximately built upon the writings of two theologians/philosophers: Samuel Taylor Coleridge and George MacDonald.

VI. COLERIDGE, SCHELLING, AND KANT'S CATEGORICAL IMPERATIVE

The English and continental romantics from the late eighteenth and early nineteenth centuries, such as Samuel Taylor Coleridge and F. W. J. Schelling, regarded a form of imagination derived from Immanuel Kant's aesthetic idealism as important. For Coleridge, in particular, imagination was to be equated with creation. Imagination here is fused with passion; this is a romantic concept of the imagination. Coleridge did not see all imaginings as of equal value. Coleridge saw imagination as a three-part faculty: he identified two elements to the imagination, and a third element that related to the imagination but not holding the same creative relationship with the divine. Therefore, as poet, philosopher, and theologian, Coleridge distinguished between "primary imagination," "secondary imagination," and "fancy." Drawing very much on the continental philosopher Schelling, and through him on Kant's transcendental philosophy, Coleridge in his doctrine of the imagination noted how the mind appeared to work. Within the mind, a reflective element often seemed to make sense *reflectively* of what was being observed by creating images and models. Coleridge commented on the mind's ability to self-reflect, but also—crucially—to self-experience in the very act of thinking:

> There are evidently two powers at work, which relatively to each other are active and passive; and this is not possible without an intermediate faculty, which is at once both active and passive. In

philosophical language, we must denominate this intermediate faculty in all its degrees and determinations, the IMAGINATION.²⁵

According to Kant's transcendental philosophy, particularly in Coleridge's interpretation and application of it, the central role of the imagination is validated through an autonomous principle of the will—Kant's categorical imperative.²⁶ Contrary to much modern sociological and psychological consideration, the will in its purest form is not habituated, changed, or subject to external influence or cultural conditioning. Therefore, Schelling (drawing on Kant), whose writings Coleridge studied and valued, could look into the human mind and on reflection deduce something of the transcendental nature of reality: we can see that there is more to reality and to life than what is immediately perceivable and derivable from sense perception, and our actions are not always governed by self-preservation and self-love.

These ideas are evident in Lewis's own account of his philosophical development as a student and young don. In *Surprised by Joy*, Lewis acknowledges that the will can be influenced, indeed tainted, by external events and people, but also writes that as the point of conversion came close, it was as if he was offered a pure moment of free will, untainted. He recounts how, while on a bus travelling up Headington Hill, he was being presented with a choice—without words or images—in which he was not moved by desire. He saw this as a decisive moment, when he appeared as close as it is possible to being a free agent.²⁷

Coleridge and Schelling's theories complement the voluntary basis of human behavior, and consequently Christian ethics: we are responsible

---

25   Coleridge, *Biographia Literaria* (1997 [1817]), 77 (Coleridge's emphasis and capitalization). The *Biographia Literaria* is a discursive philosophical and literary autobiography with important essays on philosophy and aesthetics, and as such draws on continental philosophy in the form of Kant and Schelling.

26   The categorical imperative implies a transcendent reality and that morals and ethics that affect and appear to issue from our will, are grounded in this transcendent reality. From Immanuel Kant's *Groundwork for the Metaphysics of Morals* (1785) the categorical imperative is the standard of rationality on which all moral requirements are based; it is a fundamental philosophical concept in Kant's moral philosophy. Morality is derived from an imperative, a commandment grounded in reason. A categorical imperative is an unconditional requirement, it is absolute. Kant so defined the categorical imperative that we should act only according to that maxim whereby we can simultaneously resolve that it should become a universal law—see Kant, *Grounding for the Metaphysics of Morals* (trans. Ellington; 1993), 30.

27   Lewis, *Surprised by Joy* (1955), 217.

3. Revelation and Second Meanings

for our decisions and actions, and universal laws and values exist. However much we may consider that we are the product of our nurture and environment, of the culture we grow up in, God will grant us moments of what is closest to perfect freedom, close to the human condition prior to the fall. Human freedom, free choice, is no longer innately possible after the fall, because of the way we are buffeted to and fro on the winds of fashion, fashion: desire, fear, influenced by all around us. Having taken decision-making onto ourselves (Gen 3), we are the product of forces outside of us and not of a free-will decision. But God will still, through grace, grant us moments closest to, as Lewis termed it, being a free agent, where we may choose God's way or not (John 3). Art—poetry and stories (fact or fiction does not enter into it)—is pre-eminent in the relationship of the human mind to the transcendent. However much our choices are conditioned from without, freedom is the basis of any philosophical consideration of the human in relation to the transcendent. A key proposition here, indeed the fundamental key to Lewis's work, is a doctrine of transposition: Lewis proposed what he called a doctrine of transposition, which was heavily reliant upon George Berkeley and Plato, but also on the patristic theologian and philosopher Augustine of Hippo.[28] Just how far, for Lewis, will reason take us in our understanding of God and eternity, rooted as we are in the shadowlands? Those who champion reason above revelation must, perhaps, acknowledge transposition. This is how Lewis saw revelation mediated to humanity by Christ: transposed, changed, altered, a diminution without one-to-one correspondence. Lewis's doctrine of transposition is designed to explain how revelation works, how revelation is communicated, or, more pertinently, how revelation can never be fully imparted—therefore meaning and truth will always be open to interpretation, re-interpretation.

---

28   Lewis, "Transposition" (1962), a sermon given in Mansfield College, Oxford on Whit Sunday, May 28, 1944; published in *Transposition and Other Addresses* (1949), 9–20. A reworked and extended edition of the sermon as an academic paper was published in Lewis, *They Asked for a Paper* (1962), 166–182 (quotation from 181). For an account of and systematic analysis of Lewis's doctrine of transposition, see Brazier, "C. S. Lewis: A Doctrine of Transposition" (2009).

VII. PRIMARY AND SECONDARY IMAGINATION

Coleridge wrote of the objective basis of his doctrine of the imagination that "it implies an act, and it follows therefore that intelligence or self-consciousness is impossible, except by and in a will. The self-conscious spirit therefore is a will; and freedom must be assumed as a GROUND of philosophy, and can never he deduced from it."[29] Without this freedom of will, philosophy and science are impossible, and art and poetry are just fanciful yearnings. Coleridge laid out his doctrine of the imagination systematically at the end of the first volume of the *Biographia Literatia*:

> The IMAGINATION then I consider either as primary, or secondary. The primary IMAGINATION I hold to be the living power and prime Agent of all human perception, and as a repetition in the finite mind of the eternal act of creation in the infinite I AM. The secondary imagination I consider as an echo of the former, coexisting with the conscious will, yet still as identical with the primary in the *kind* of its agency, and differing only in *degree*, and in the *mode* of its operation. It dissolves, diffuses, dissipates, in order to re-create; or where this process is rendered impossible, yet still at all events it struggles to idealize and to unify. It is essentially *vital*, even as all objects (as objects) are essentially fixed and dead.
>
> FANCY, on the contrary, has no other counters to play with but fixities and definites. The fancy is indeed no other than a mode of memory emancipated from the order of time and space; and blended with, and modified by that empirical phenomenon of the will which we express by the word CHOICE. But equally with the ordinary memory it must receive all its materials ready-made from the law of association. [Coleridge's emphasis/capitalization][30]

---

29   Coleridge, *Biographia Literaria* (1997 [1817]), ch. 12, thesis 7, 160–61 (Coleridge's emphasis/capitalization). See also Coleridge's comments in Thesis 9: "This *principium commune essendi et cognoscendi* [common principle of being and knowing], as subsisting in a WILL, or primary ACT of self-duplication, is the mediate or indirect principle of every science; but it is the immediate and direct principle of the ultimate science alone, i.e. of transcendental philosophy alone. For it must be remembered, that all these theses refer solely to one of the two polar sciences, namely, to that which commences with and rigidly confines itself within the subjective, leaving the objective (as far as it is exclusively objective) to natural philosophy, which is its opposite pole. In its very idea therefore as a systematic knowledge of our collective KNOWING (*scientia scientiae*) it involves the necessity of someone highest principle of knowing..." (161–62; Coleridge's emphasis and capitalization).

30   Coleridge, *Biographia Literaria* (1997 [1817]), ch. 13, 175. See also Barfield, *What Coleridge Thought* (1972).

3. Revelation and Second Meanings

Coleridge's account of the primary imagination is of paramount importance. It states that the living power of God is the primary cause of *all* human perception. This relates to the *imago Dei*, the image of God in humanity (Gen 1:26–27): Through the imagination, men and women are made in the image of God, reproducing—though not always—elements of the mind of God in miniature. It is this which separates us from all other animals, which raises us above nature, though our feet are still embedded in clay. The primary imagination is therefore an echo, a reproduction, in the human mind of the eternal I AM. The secondary imagination, which dominates and occupies the human mind most of the time, is similar; indeed it is as much an echo etched in our minds, differing, for Coleridge, only in the degree or mode of its operation. The third level—fancy—can be mistaken for primary or secondary imagination, but does not relate to the *imago Dei* or directly to God, for it is, for Coleridge, only a mode of memory emancipated from the order of time and space: for a fleeting moment we think we have originality, but this is an illusion. Coleridge's doctrine of the imagination was a profound influence on Lewis. He cites these ideas obliquely as instrumental in his intellectual and religious development on a number of occasions in his spiritual autobiography.[31]

VIII. MACDONALD ON COLERIDGE

The source of Lewis's contact with Coleridge's doctrine of imagination was George MacDonald. Ever the master of Lewis's understanding of myth, saga, and story, MacDonald wrote a full exposition of Coleridge's ideas in two essays.[32] There, he writes that the word "imagination" means an "imaging," that is, the making of likenesses. Therefore, the imagination is a faculty which gives form to thought:

> Not necessarily uttered form, but form capable of being uttered in shape or in sound, or in any mode upon which the senses can lay hold. It is, therefore, that faculty in man which is likest to the

---

31 Lewis, *Surprised by Joy* (1955), 10–11, 25–26, 63, 130, 132, 140, 153, 158, and 164.

32 MacDonald, "The Imagination: Its Functions and Its Culture" (1895 [1867]) and "The Fantastic Imagination" (1895 [1867]). In relation to Lewis, see also the account of MacDonald and Coleridge's doctrine of the imagination in Barfield, *Poetic Diction* (1973).

prime operation of the power of God, and has, therefore, been called the creative faculty, and its exercise creation.[33]

Thus, drawing on Coleridge's concept of the primary imagination, MacDonald asserts that the imagination in its creativity is analogous to the prime operation of the power of God. In this context, for both MacDonald and Lewis, the role of the poet is as maker, creator—as sub-creator, in Tolkien's terminology. If Coleridge, and MacDonald and Lewis, are correct, then the potential of an unbaptized imagination for corruption and its scope for evil is demonically awesome. The implication of what MacDonald is saying is that the poet or sage, like the prophet, drawing on wisdom in and through the imagination, must be seen as standing aside from society. This is essential, but it does not make the poet divine. MacDonald continues that we must not forget the unsurpassable gulf between creator and poet. This gulf is "teeming with infinite revelations"; but it is by default a vast space that the poet cannot pass over: "no man can pass to find out God, although God needs not to pass over it to find man."[34] The chasm or abyss is between that which calls (God), and that which is thus called into being (humanity), where humanity is made in God's image. Therefore, all sub-creation can only be in the context of the primary creation of God: God calls across the gulf, the chasm, and if we respond through the faculty of the imagination, our creative impulse will, to take this beyond Coleridge, echo back to God in love.

MacDonald can see how Coleridge did not divorce the creativity of the poet's imagination from analytic or scientific knowledge and investigation. Imagination complements intellectual truth—it clothes truth in beauty.[35] Therefore, MacDonald asserts, "Coleridge says that no one but a poet will make any further great discoveries in mathematics; and Bacon says that 'wonder,' that faculty of the mind especially attendant on the child-like imagination, 'is the seed of knowledge.'"[36] Therefore, the scientific imagination is essential for truth and reality. The scientific mind is influenced by the poetic; indeed, without the faculty of the imagination scientific mental models could not be constructed. This is most so in

---

[33]   MacDonald, "The Imagination: Its Functions and Its Culture" (1895 [1867]), 11.

[34]   MacDonald, "The Imagination: Its Functions and Its Culture" (1895 [1867]), 11–12.

[35]   MacDonald, "The Imagination: Its Functions and Its Culture" (1895 [1867]), 13–14.

[36]   MacDonald, "The Imagination: Its Functions and Its Culture" (1895 [1867]), 14.

the construction of an invisible whole, a model of reality and greater reality, from the intimations given by the visible world: the shadows of this world are guides "to a multiplex harmony, completeness, and end, which is the whole."[37] It is MacDonald's understanding of Coleridge that is almost certainly Lewis's point of contact with these concepts. For Lewis and MacDonald, and Coleridge before them, the imagination is the medium by which we enquire into God's creation; hence, it is both scientific and poetic.[38] Imagination therefore occupies a central place in enquiry, in hypothesizing, in creating mental-images (for example, mental model-making and conceptualization as practiced by historians, mathematicians, and theologians, as well as scientists).[39] Methodologically, from the perspective of the philosophy of theology, David Kelsey writes, "At the root of any theological position, there is an imaginative act in which a theologian tries to catch up in a single metaphorical judgment or model the full complexity of God's presence."[40] In this respect, it may be valid to consider that those who composed (or imagined) the stories of dying and reviving gods, myths of prefigurement, are methodologically operating in a similar way to contemporary theologians. It has been argued that theologians of whatever denomination always undertake acts of the imagination. They select from the knowledge base of the culture and tradition within which they operate those structures that are to form the system behind a theological position. (By comparison Calvin Seerveld, writing from the viewpoint of a biblical, Reformed tradition, distinguishes between imagining that is perceptual error and imagining that is an oracle of truth.[41])

---

37   MacDonald, "The Imagination: Its Functions and Its Culture" (1895 [1867]), 14.

38   MacDonald, "The Imagination: Its Functions and Its Culture" (1895 [1867]), 203–8.

39   For the role of imagination in a thinker representative of the time when C. S. Lewis was at the peak of his creative writing, see Collinwood, *The Idea of History* (1946) and Kroner, *The Religious Function of Imagination* (1941). In the field of philosophy of science, see Black, *Models and Metaphors* (1962); also indicative of the understanding around the time of Lewis's intellectual formation is Lewes, *Comte's Philosophy of the Sciences* (1904).

40   Kelsey, *The Use of Scripture in Recent Theology* (1975), 163.

41   See Seerveld, "Imaginativity" (1987), 43–58.

IX. CONCLUSION

Lewis absorbed MacDonald and Coleridge's theorizing about the imagination (grounded essentially in the philosophical idealism of Schelling, Kant's categorical imperative, and aesthetic idealism) in relation to God's revelation, and therefore in relation to the manner in which theology is formulated; this allowed him to justify re-interpreting the ancient pagan myths Christologically, identifying a second, fuller, subsequent, meaning *a posteriori*—after the Christ-event. Lewis wrote, "I think that all things reflect heavenly truth, the imagination not least."[42] Lewis acknowledges that the mind is illuminated by the divine, and that this leads to a degree of understanding—theological activity is not solely the result of human striving and searching. The imagination can, under certain circumstances, be an oracle of truth where general cognitive activities fail. Therefore, for Lewis, there is still the possibility of prevenient grace engendering inspiration and intimation, although such revelatory reception is still subject to the effects of the fall. Lewis asserted that God has used this fallen human imagination, images, and mental pictures/models, to communicate some sort of intimation of God's salvific actions: the prefiguring images/myths were for Lewis pneumatologically given, gifted by the Holy Spirit, not humanly invented.

> The Divine light, we are told, "lighteneth every man." We should, therefore, expect to find in the imagination of great Pagan teachers and myth-makers some glimpse of that theme which we believe to be the very plot of the whole cosmic story—the theme of incarnation, death and rebirth. And the differences between the Pagan Christs (Balder, Osiris, etc.) and the Christ Himself is much what we should expect to find.[43]

Therefore, there will be second, or subsequent, meanings to identify and interpret. Given that meaning and truth relate to that which is of most importance to humanity—our salvation—and given that such meaning is communicated in stories and images, through the faculty of the imagination, the relationship between any given individual and the Holy Spirit is to be paramount: a baptized imagination is the litmus test of any

---

42 Lewis, *Surprised by Joy* (1955), 167.
43 Lewis, "Is Theology Poetry?" (1962 [1944]), a paper read to the Socratic Club in Oxford and first published in The Socratic Digest (1944); republished in Lewis, *They Asked for a Paper* (1962 [1944]).

3. Revelation and Second Meanings

"author" or "hearer" of such Christological prefigurements—intimations will be subject to second and subsequent meanings. Truth and meaning are therefore, as we have established, teleological: all meaning and truth relates to a greater or lesser degree to the central event in cosmic human history—the incarnation-cross-resurrection.[44]

---

44   This was Lewis's view; and neither modernism nor postmodernism—which questions such a doctrine of Christological prefigurement—can accommodate such a proposition.

4

A Doctrine of Transposition: Towards a Philosophy of the Incarnation

SYNOPSIS

This paper examines Lewis's doctrine of transposition, referred to by him as a contribution to the philosophy of the incarnation. We show how it is rooted in Lewis's Platonism, in his reading of the works of Henry More and Bishop Berkeley, and how it discloses his understanding of Scripture, revelation, and reason. In taking the analysis beyond the limited number of theologians who have attempted to unravel what Lewis's proto-doctrine was in this field, we describe Lewis's view of revelation as *supra-theological*. Lewis's doctrine of transposition is designed to explain how revelation works, how revelation is communicated, or, more pertinently, how revelation can never be fully imparted; this we conclude relates to the *communicatio idiomatum* (the communication of attributes), the knowability of God (which is both a veiling and an unveiling), and how human fallibility can lead us to misread what is communicated to us. Therefore we may conclude that the key to Lewis's work is in a doctrine of "flawed" transposition (a doctrine whereby revelation is itself transposed; likewise our codified understanding that we may label doctrinal, is also incomplete and flawed). How does Lewis's "flawed" doctrine of transposed revelation come together? The value he accords to reason, indeed the symbiotic relation between revelation and reason he subscribes to, his understanding of the witness that Scripture gives to and as revelation, likewise the importance he gives to church tradition (the role of and for the "mere" core), also his philosophy of the incarnation, this is all epitomized by the transposed movement of God towards humanity, descending into the incarnation to draw humanity out of sin and up into the divine life. Therefore the modes of revelation in Lewis's doctrine of transposition move teleologically, lead ever towards eternity; this movement is dialectical, but a supplementary dialectic, in the sense that creation will be subsumed into eternity. Lewis's doctrine of transposition is key to all of Lewis's work (literary, apologetic, and philosophical).

IN THE HIGHEST DEGREE

I. INTRODUCTION

A trained philosopher, a *literatus*, and Professor of Medieval and Renaissance Literature, C. S. Lewis was awarded an honorary Doctor of Divinity degree by the University of St. Andrews in 1946 in recognition of his work in theology and apologetics. Although he had no formal training in theology his intellect was confirmed in that he was awarded, as a young man three first-class honors degrees within four years from the University of Oxford: in Greats (Greek and Roman Literature), in classical philosophy, and in English. Lewis's training in classical philosophy was similar to, and as an apologist places him with, Justin Martyr. Though often classified as such, Lewis was no amateur, yet he had, in effect, erected an elaborate smokescreen to separate himself from a clerical elite in the Church of England of his day. Why?—because his self-claimed opponents were "modern" and/or theologically "liberal," as he saw them.[1] It is important to remember that Lewis was not a systematic theologian in the sense that Karl Barth or Paul Tillich were; however, their work was incomplete upon their deaths. It is perhaps the case that no theologian or philosopher has managed to pin down and produce a coherent and complete *summa*, integrated and flawless. Perhaps Lewis realized this was not possible, that all theology is in effect reactionary and contextual—hence his work in apologetics and the comparison with Justin Martyr. However, there is one area where his work was as insightful and reflective as, or even surpassed, the average academic theologian: his philosophical theology. The aim of this paper is to examine Lewis's doctrine of transposition, which he referred to as his contribution to the philosophy of the incarnation.[2] In so doing we will examine not only what he proposed and how it is rooted in Platonism, but consider Lewis's understanding of Scripture, revelation, and reason. Our conclusion will be that a doctrine of transposition is actually the key to all of Lewis's work.

    1   The word modern is often confusing in its multiple meanings and uses; the word liberal may often be seen as contentious or problematic, often it appears to generate an emotional response, may be considered pejorative, and may also be invoked in an equally subjective manner. Lewis's disillusionment with "modernism" and theological "liberalism" was similar in many ways to that of the young Karl Barth. All subsequent uses of "modern" and "liberal" will be in inverted commas to signify Lewis's use.

    2   Lewis, "Transposition," an essay first given as a sermon in Mansfield College, Oxford, on Whit-Sunday—no year is recorded—then published in, *Transposition and Other Addresses* (1949), 9–20. A second, expanded, edition was published in Lewis, *They Asked for a Paper* (1962), 166–82. All subsequent references are to this second edition.

4. A Doctrine of Transposition: Towards a Philosophy of the Incarnation

II. PLATONIC IDEALISM

What was Lewis's background as a philosopher? We need to briefly recap. Lewis's understanding of revelation is informed by his philosophical idealism, specifically the Cambridge Platonism of the seventeenth century and in Lewis's deeply held respect for the idealism of Bishop George Berkeley. Lewis as a philosopher and logician valued reason, he saw it as the organ of truth; further, he believed that Christianity was inherently rational, that truth was real, objective, and available for us to perceive and understand.[3] The depth, sharpness, and piercing logic of Lewis's intellect were primarily the result of "The Great Knock"—William T. Kirkpatrick, who, though a self-confessed atheist, had a passionate love of truth. Lewis's education and development as a philosopher at Oxford in the early 1920s did not take place in isolation; he may have been something of a loner, but his philosophical development mirrored that of the establishment at Oxford and Cambridge. In the years immediately after the First World War Oxbridge was still dominated by the English Idealism of T. H. Green, rooted arguably in continental Hegelianism; however, a brutal positivism, as we have seen, was in the ascendant. As he commenced teaching at Oxford, however, Lewis, the promising young positivistic realist that Oxford philosophers had begun to respect, started to become religious: Lewis first became a theist, then a Christian. For Lewis, it was important, however, to avoid the vague indeterminate spiritualism that in the 1920s appeared to be the only alternative to this brutal realistic positivism: according to Lewis's understanding of his peers, Christianity was by and large repudiated by academics in favor of a variety of intellectual religious cults, which were considered superior and more advanced than the ancient religions. This was in part the chronological-intellectual proposition that Lewis talks about escaping from as he developed towards becoming a Christian: "the uncritical acceptance of the intellectual climate of our own age and the assumption that whatever has gone out of date is on that count discredited."[4] Lewis's chronological-intellectual proposition (snobbery, in

---

3   For Lewis's comments on skepticism and the objectivity of truth see Lewis, "De Futilitae" (1967), 60–63. Also see Lewis, "The Poison of Subjectivism" (1967).

4   See Lewis, *Surprised by Joy* (1955), ch. 13, specifically 206–8, quotation, 207. Along with Owen Barfield and J. R. R Tolkien, Lewis would then raise the question of why did a particular thought system cease to be fashionable, and whether it was ever refuted, and if so, how. See also Lewis, *Mere Christianity* (1952), ch. 7; also, the first volume of *The Space Trilogy*, Lewis, *Out of the Silent Planet* (1938), where the anti-heroes,

Lewis's terminology) was expressed thus: if one argues that A implies B, and if A implying B is an old argument from the times when people also believed C, then A implying B is false because C was found to be untrue. This is, arguably, flawed logic built on the assumption that humanity progresses from crude ignorance, year on year, and today we are superior to all that has gone before. Identifying the arrogance of this flawed "modernist" argument helped Lewis extract himself from a plethora of philosophies and belief systems in the 1920s. But it was the inverse of this chronological-intellectual argument that, as we have established, provided a ground to his Christian apologetics: anything "modern" was to be mistrusted because it was contemporary and must first be measured against the established wisdom. Lewis mistrusted "modern" philosophy and theology, and through his training in classical philosophy he drew from Plato, essentially avoiding the continental Cartesian and Kantian schools and their derivative thought systems. Parallel to his development towards becoming a Christian, therefore, was this development in idealism (essentially a pre"modern" idealism) as a philosophical basis, along with his understanding of and the value accorded to reason. Idealism was, for Lewis, contrary to the closed-universe positivistic realism that dominated Oxford by the mid-1920s.

The seventeenth-century English philosopher Henry More, a leading Cambridge Platonist, gave Lewis the subject for his doctoral research. More also contrasted with the continental Cartesian school, which thereby assisted Lewis in his own intellectual development. James Patrick writes, "What Lewis found in More was an anti-Cartesian rationalist, someone who understood reason not as an abstract, analytic faculty presiding over an indeterminate field of extension, but as the consubstantial light joining the intellect to reality."[5] Unlike Karl Barth who spent his career as a theologian trying to work within a Kantian framework, Lewis simply went back before "modern" philosophy, starting with Henry More, and working back to Plato; once he was a Christian this extended to the patristic theologians and Neo-Platonists, then also medieval scholasticism and seventeenth-century Protestants and Reformed scholastics: "More's thought ... pointed beyond the merely rational and merely material, and in him Lewis found an idealist who believed in God, in reason as a living

---

Devine and Weston, assume all ideas that have gone before are inferior and flawed, even in relation to alien species on another planet.

5   Patrick, "C. S. Lewis and Idealism" (1998), 160.

4. A Doctrine of Transposition: Towards a Philosophy of the Incarnation

principle, in nature as alive with *Logos*."[6] Patrick, again commenting here, shows how Lewis the philosopher was brought to maturity by his study of More and the seventeenth-century Platonists, and how this philosophical framework remained constant during the rest of his life, his work, and his academic career. In addition, Patrick shows how Lewis's philosophical method extended often to the use of *reductio ad absurdum*: Lewis the philosophical apologist often attempted to defeat his opponents by exposing the irrationality of their arguments through the existence of basic, as he saw them, logically self-evident truths. This relates closely to Lewis's respect for the objectivity of truth, that there is no simultaneity to truth and falsehood; we are forced to weigh up the options and decide— hence Lewis's famous *trilemma*.[7]

Lewis's graduate studies exposed him to the Irish philosopher George Berkeley, Bishop of Cloyne, and to a lesser extent Hegel (who is probably the only continental modern to exert any influence over Lewis, and that influence was itself muted, given Hegel's status as a modern thinker), but this is all rooted in Plato. Hence Lewis's foundational respect for the forms, his assertion as a Christian Platonist that the real, the truly real, lay beyond what we take for reality in these shadowlands (Lewis and J. R. R. Tolkien's term). He borrowed from Berkeley his use of a theory of immaterialism, or subjective idealism, encapsulated in the dictum, *esse est percipi* (to be is to be perceived); the young Lewis drank in the theory that we only know sensations or ideas of objects. Of equal importance as he began to become first a theist and then a confessing Christian was Alexander's *Space, Time and Deity*, where he discovered the proposition that we cannot simultaneously experience and contemplate an object.[8]

---

6   Patrick, "C. S. Lewis and Idealism" (1998), 161.

7   That Jesus was either mad, bad, or who he said he was, who he revealed himself to be: God incarnate. See Lewis, *Mere Christianity* (1952), see Bk. 2, ch. 3. This is sometimes referred to as Lewis's triumvirate, that Jesus was either a lunatic, a liar, or Lord.

8   Alexander, *Space, Time and Deity* (1920). Lewis makes much of this theory in *Surprised by Joy* (1955), how it was something of a watershed, a eureka moment, which allowed him to see how he had taken intimations from the Holy Spirit as objects in themselves, therefore responding idolatrously.

III. REASON AND IMAGINATION

For Lewis, the world was imbued with the good and the true and hence beauty; these transcendentals were real and not merely subjective. Reason without imagination was without meaning, however, because it is through the imagination that we discern meaning. Revelation is therefore the intuiting of absolute truth, in varying degrees, from eternity, from ultimate or absolute reality: imagination and reason operate, to a degree, symbiotically. All truth comes from this spiritual realm; it *translates* into our world. There may appear to be a sharp divide between this world and eternity, but there are intimations and, yes, for Lewis, a breaking-in by God for to us to be drawn out. Lewis's emphasis is Platonic in that he sees the ideal eternal world as the real world, and that it is through reason and imagination that we get glimpses and intimations that begin to draw us out through Christ's Holy Spirit. If God is incarnated in Christ, if he descends to raise us up, then all true or valid intimations of this eternal realm are from Christ, who reconciles and imparts understanding and knowledge both when on earth and as the universal Christ. Lewis is at his most reliant upon the philosophy of Bishop Berkeley when he espouses a cautious denial of a realistic account of matter, because ideas and the imagination give us a clearer account. What is important is that we perceive the world, objects, not because of any correlation between the perceptions of our senses, but because God wills it to be so; hence Berkeley's argument that we can only know sensations and ideas of objects. Andrew Walker notes how,

> Lewis in *Prayer: Letters to Malcolm*, says "Matter enters our experience only by becoming sensation (when we perceive it) or conception (when we understand it)" this could have been lifted out of Berkeley's *A Treatise concerning the Principles of Human Knowledge*. In Berkeley's philosophy humankind could perceive reality directly from the mind of God, and indeed was sustained by it.[9]

The framework for this was established in the young Lewis in his twenties at Oxford; the synthesis of his beliefs came for the mature apologetic Lewis, however, from Augustine's doctrine of illumination. The faculties of reason and imagination symbiotically give rise to understanding through illumination by the divine light; we cannot perceive and derive

---

9   Walker, "Scripture, Revelation and Platonism in C. S. Lewis," (2002), 27.

4. A Doctrine of Transposition: Towards a Philosophy of the Incarnation

truth from our senses alone.[10] For Lewis, therefore, God reveals of God's-self and God's purposes for humanity in many subtle ways that are revealings—like the planting of seeds—through sensations and ideas in our minds, sourced through the divine light, which we reflect on, and thereby come to understand something of what was given. All these hints and intimations, though disparate and diverse, general and incomplete, and seemingly contradictory to our human minds, work together towards the one concrete and particular perfect self-revelation in Jesus Christ.

IV. A PROTO DOCTRINE OF SCRIPTURE

To understand what Lewis proposed was happening in God's revealedness, we first need to examine how he understood Scripture. Scripture, for Lewis, bears witness to revelation, but in ways that separate it from revelation; Scripture is divinely inspired but humanely generated, and thus complements revelation. Scripture, or more pertinently Lewis's proto-doctrine of Scripture, illustrates his understanding of revelation, and thereby how transposition works. The belief in the objectivity of reason and truth was central to his understanding of Scripture. From an acknowledgement of God's infallibility Lewis could see that if creation was to be, it could then exist only in freedom. The writers of Scripture were divinely inspired, but each was a fallen and fallible human, characterized by a degree of free will. Biblical inspiration can therefore be described as the dove whispering into the ear, the illumination of the Holy Spirit imparting intimations to the human mind, though the mind is free to make of these intimations what it will: this is the divine presence behind the Bible. This is where Lewis's understanding of the humanity of Scripture comes into play. In the context of the Book of the Psalms, for example, Lewis speaks of the human qualities—naivety, error, contradiction, cursing, and wickedness—which are not excluded:[11]

> The total result is not "the Word of God" in the sense that every passage, in itself, gives impeccable science or history. It carries the Word of God; and we (under grace, with attention to tradition and to interpreters wiser than ourselves, and with the use of such intelligence and learning as we may have) receive that Word

---

10   *Saint Augustine Confessions* (trans. Chadwick; 1991). See, Bk. IV.xv.25, 67–68; Bk. V.vi.10, 77–78; Bk. X.ii.2, 179; Bk. X.xl.65, 217–18; Bk. XII.xxv.35, 265.

11   Lewis, *Reflections on the Psalms* (1958), 96.

> from it not by using it as an encyclopedia or an encyclical but by steeping ourselves in its tone or temper and so learning its overall message.[12]

The humanity of Scripture presents us with a Bible that is—as Lewis termed it—an untidy and leaky vehicle; we no doubt would have preferred absolute truth systematically presented, unrefracted illuminating light which we could have contained and quantified in an encyclopedic fashion.[13] However, this is not what has been given. Lewis does not approach the Bible with the fundamentalist mindset characteristic of certain Evangelicals. The humanity that shines through the Old Testament, and indeed Paul's Epistles, is there also in the sayings of Jesus. Lewis notes how Jesus preached rather than lectured in an academically impartial manner; his responses to questions and the demands placed on him are couched in paradox and proverb, exaggeration, parable, and irony: Scripture is steeped in humanness. Lewis comments, "Yet it is, perhaps, idle to speak here of spirit and letter. There is almost no 'letter' in the words of Jesus. Taken by a literalist, he will always prove the most elusive of teachers. Systems cannot keep up with that darting illumination. No net less wide than a man's whole heart, nor less fine of mesh than love, will hold the sacred Fish."[14]

Lewis shared a proposition relating to the inspiration and authorship of Scripture with Tolkien, that God creates in freedom enabling the world and humanity to be sub-creators: creation creates, it brings forth. A baptized imagination (Lewis and Tolkien's term) in the mind of a faithful writer would seek to be as true to the revelation as possible, though here Lewis's Platonism wields in: any revelation from on high given to fallen humanity in these shadowlands will be a diminution, will be in effect watered-down, changed: this we will see is at the heart of transposition. For Lewis, therefore, the writer of Scripture is inspired to write; the content is given and constructed through the faculty of imagination and reflected on through reason. As a consequence, the human element filters, because the human is egotistical, flawed, and fallen. There is something of a dialectic in Lewis's understanding of Scripture between the God-given freedom to make of the inspiration what the writer will, and the emphasis

---

12   Lewis, *Reflections on the Psalms* (1958), 96.
13   Lewis, *Reflections on the Psalms* (1958), 97, 100.
14   Lewis, *Reflections on the Psalms* (1958), 102–3.

4. A Doctrine of Transposition: Towards a Philosophy of the Incarnation

he places on the importance of a *baptized* imagination: we are created in freedom, yet the Holy Spirit presses on us, influences our decisions.

As a lecturer in literature, Lewis knew genre in ways that most New Testament scholars often did not; this led to one of his severest criticisms of the mid-twentieth-century Bultmannian demythologizing trend in the academy.[15] If through the humanity of Scripture grace inspires and illumines rather than dictates, then the resulting work will have importance and authority, but there will be inconsistencies—usually on extraneous details. If the books and chapters of the Bible are not all of the same type of genre, then contradictions over the historicity of details in the books of the Old Testament, or even between the Gospels, do not necessarily undermine the veracity of the overarching claims of the New Testament. For example, Lewis regarded the Book of Jonah as sacred fiction, but gave a greater respect to its mythical qualities than many would. Michael J. Christensen, quoting from Lewis's, *The Problem of Pain*, comments:

> The Adam and Eve tale, for instance, may express poetically the reality of man's fall from perfection better than any strictly historical account possibly could. Was the forbidden fruit symbolic, then? "For all I can see, it might have concerned the literal eating of a fruit," says Lewis, "but the question is of no consequence." Clyde S. Kilby, an acknowledged authority on C. S. Lewis, states that "Lewis's frequent discussions of the Garden of Eden make it apparent that it means a hundred times more to him as myth than it does to most Christians as history."[16]

The story of the fall meant more to Lewis as the truth about humanity's predicament, its fall from perfection, presented as myth than if it were argued as historical and scientific fact. On the relation of the historicity of Scripture to revelation, Andrew Walker comments that:

> What we can say with some certainty about Lewis is that he did not subscribe to the view—still widely held in the American Bible-belt—that Scripture is itself God's revelation to humankind.

---

15 See Lewis, "Modern Theology and Biblical Criticism" (1967), a paper read at Westcott House, Cambridge, 11th May 1959. (Note that in later volumes of essays the title of this paper is changed to "Fern-Seed Elephants.")

16 Christensen, C. S. Lewis on Scripture (1980), 34–35. Christensen is quoting from Lewis, *The Problem of Pain* (1940), 68; and Kilby, *The Christian World of C. S. Lewis* (1964), 153.

> I know of nowhere that Lewis denies that the Bible in some sense reveals something of God's intentions for the world, but neither do I know of anywhere where he talks of revelation in terms of propositional truth, or of isomorphic pairings between biblical words and God's utterances.[17]

If Lewis refused to subscribe to a fundamentalist view of Scripture that ignored the contradictions and inconsistencies self-evident in the books of the Bible, the philosopher Lewis could see that there was no direct isomorphic coupling, no one-to-one correspondence, between God's speech-act and what is written down by humanity.

Michael J. Christensen, writing on Lewis's understanding of Scripture, notes how many people press the Bible to give more of itself than there is: Lewis did not demand an infallible authority, universal and absolute, eternal yet manifest.[18] We err if we desire to replace the aseity of God with a book. This also raises questions about the dangers of a doctrine of Scripture, if such a doctrine attempts to tie-up everything systematically in neatly defined propositions: "To demand this of Scripture is to fail to recognize that God's infinite wisdom exceeds man's ability to conceptualize it, . . . the divine light is obscured by the medium through which it shines."[19] The key term for Lewis, and also for Tolkien, as we have seen in the context of Christological prefigurement, was "refraction": the light of revelation was refracted—splintered truths, and limited by our *fallen* short-sightedness, even blindness. We make demands on the historicity of Scripture that it will not sustain, precisely because it is not the product of an ordinary academic discipline: it is both human and divine in origin. Lewis commented that some of his critics argued that he was a fundamentalist for not dismissing the miraculous and the historic in the Old Testament out of hand; others criticized him if he did not accept every event recorded, every sentence in the Bible, as historic and scientific truth: "The reason why I can accept as historical a story in which a miracle occurs is that I have never found any philosophical grounds for the universal negative proposition that miracles do not happen."[20] For Lewis, the Book of Job appears unhistorical simply because the events

---

17   Walker, "Scripture, Revelation and Platonism in C. S. Lewis" (2002), 19.
18   Christensen, *C. S. Lewis on Scripture* (1980), 94–95.
19   Christensen, *C. S. Lewis on Scripture* (1980), 94.
20   Lewis, *Reflections on the Psalms* (1958), 94–95.

4. A Doctrine of Transposition: Towards a Philosophy of the Incarnation

recorded do not fit in with the historical tradition of ancient Israel. Lewis classifies the material in the Old Testament as chronicle, poetry, moral and political diatribe, romances and myths, and some material that is unclassifiable to our contemporary conceptions of types of literature.[21] He explains that the poet who wrote the Song of Songs did not in all probability conceive the work for anything other than what he terms "a secular purpose." The problem is compounded when a passage is taken in isolation; any contradictions are then ignored: we cannot assume that if one event written in the Bible is true, then all accounts are without flaw—"that the numbers of Old Testament armies (which in view of the size of the country, if true, involves continuous miracle) are statistically correct because the story of the Resurrection is historically correct."[22]

V. THE WORD OF GOD AND THE WORD OF GOD

There is therefore God-given space between divine inspiration on the one hand and our reception and transmission of the content of revelation through words on a page. For Lewis, however, the graceful inspiration of the Holy Spirit in the reader will elevate their value and meaning; as these words are read the text is imbued with an authority above mere common books and words. For Lewis, the act of reading (usually dcripture) is in itself revelatory, but the knowledge of God given in Scripture is partial and incomplete; there is as much withheld as there is revealed of God, but it does have a perfection to it within the confines of this reality. Andrew Walker notes how there is no evidence that Lewis subscribed to the doctrine of *sola scriptura*.[23] In some ways this relativizes the Bible, though it is still, through its status, an inspired sacred text. Lewis asserted that the Holy Spirit may also be behind the inspiration of many other works—including myths and works of great literature from a variety of cultures and civilizations.[24] In the context of the effect North European pagan myths have on us, Lewis regarded them as perlocutionary, in the sense that reading (or hearing, as in an oral tradition) about Christ's

21   Lewis, *Reflections on the Psalms* (1958), 96.
22   C. S. Lewis to Clyde S. Kilby, May 7, 1959, in *Collected Letters*, Vol. III (2007), 1046.
23   Walker, "Scripture, Revelation and Platonism in C. S. Lewis" (2002), 23.
24   I have dealt with the question of Lewis's profound respect for pagan myths as revelation in depth elsewhere: see Brazier, "C. S. Lewis Christological Prefigurement" (2007), which in many ways complements this article.

atoning sacrifice through a pagan myth changed us, moved us closer to God's salvific actions:[25] this is even more so with Scripture. In the context of the letter to Clyde Kilby, his comment, quoting James 1:17, is pertinent: "If every good and perfect gift comes from the Father of Lights then all true and edifying writings, whether in Scripture or not, must be in some sense inspired."[26] The Bible, however, is ordered to God's revelation to humankind in Jesus Christ: it is Christ who is the Word of God, as the prologue to John's Gospel puts it. The Word became flesh; it did not become a book: Christ is the Word of God, not the Bible. Lewis, writing to a Mrs. Johnson in 1952 commented:

> It is Christ himself, not the Bible, who is the true word of God. The Bible, read in the right spirit and with the guidance of good teachers, will bring us to him. When it becomes really necessary (i.e. for our spiritual life, not for controversy or curiosity) to know whether a particular passage is rightly translated or is myth (but of course myth specially chosen by God from among countless myths to carry a spiritual truth) or history, we shall no doubt be guided to the right answer. But we must not use the Bible (our fathers too often did) as a sort of Encyclopedia out of which texts (isolated from their context and not read with attention to the whole nature and purport of the books in which they occur) can be taken for use as weapons.[27]

Writing to a Mr. Lee Turner in 1958 on the question of inspiration in relation to genre, Lewis went to the heart of the matter by asserting that the main problem is what exactly we mean by saying that something is inspired. He notes how many people in the past believed that "the Holy Spirit either just replaced the minds of the authors (like the supposed "control" in automatic writing) or at least dictated to them as to secretaries."[28] In this context, Lewis cites Paul's comments that, "Scripture itself refutes these ideas. St Paul distinguishes between what 'the Lord' says and what he says 'of himself'—yet both are 'Scripture'" (1 Cor 7:8–10). In addition, much that is now Scripture was not written with the sort of audience in mind which it is now exposed to: ". . . in Scripture, a mass of human legend, history, moral teaching etc., are taken up and made the

25 Brazier, "C. S. Lewis Christological Prefigurement" (2007), 761 and 770.
26 C. S. Lewis to Clyde S. Kilby, May 7, 1959," in *Collected Letters*, Vol. III (2007), 1045.
27 C. S. Lewis to Mrs Johnson, Nov. 8, 1952, in *Collected Letters*, Vol. III (2007), 246.
28 C. S. Lewis to Lee Turner, July 19, 1958, in *Collected Letters*, Vol. III (2007), 960.

4. A Doctrine of Transposition: Towards a Philosophy of the Incarnation

vehicle of God's Word. Errors of minor fact are permitted to remain. (Was our Lord himself incapable, qua man, of such errors? Would it be a real human Incarnation if He was?)."[29]

VI. MODES OF REVELATION

The Bible is, for Lewis, revelatory, though it is not the primary form of God's revelation. This does not deny or repudiate the Bible, or the importance of Scripture as inspired and revealed; the Bible has a unique place in the world, especially in relation to human affairs. This sets the priorities, however: the revelation of God is a person, a unique act in history—the incarnation; this therefore has universal and cosmic implications. As words written, Scripture recognizes and bears witness to the incarnation. Scripture becomes the Word through inspired reading; it is essentially self-referential.

It will help us to consider the views of two theologians on how to understand Lewis's categorization of revelation. To this purpose Michael J. Christensen identified six modes of revelation.[30] Andrew Walker goes a step further by separating them into two groups: five that are general and incomplete, partial and relative; and a sixth, which is particular and perfect. A fundamental principle to Lewis's understanding of revelation is that there are different modes of God's revealedness, different ways in which God communicates to humankind. Such communication is possible because of the relationship between our reality and the supernatural realm—eternity. The ordering here is taken from Michael J. Christensen's work, *C. S. Lewis and Scripture*.[31]

First, the experience of the numinous, God's holiness: the human capacity to experience awe or fear; but it is also more than these intimations. The numinous is a brush with the holiness of God as Lord, that instils in us a right understanding, a right relationship. It can be argued that there is nothing specifically Christian in such mystical intimations, that they are not restricted to self-confessed Christians. This is precisely the point: they emanate from the *universal* Christ; they are part of the work of

---

29 C. S. Lewis to Lee Turner, July 19, 1958, 960–61.

30 See Christensen, *C. S. Lewis on Scripture* (1980); and Walker, "Scripture, Revelation and Platonism in C. S. Lewis" (2002).

31 Christensen, *C. S. Lewis on Scripture* (1980), 68–77.

Christ and should not be thought of solely in terms of human religiosity, or denominational/religious boundaries.

Second, the universal ought, or moral responsibility: conscience is a precursor and manifestation of the revelation of God, a universal given. Some people may deny their conscience, smother it and create their own morality—history is replete with individuals who raze whole cities, slaughter millions, and then sleep soundly at night—but there are universal moral laws that can be known by our minds. The universal is defended by Lewis in that, however different morals and ethics are in different cultures and civilizations, "they all have a moral sense that we ought to do some things rather than others."[32]

Third, *Sehnsucht*: the fleeting, piercing, conscience-troubling stab, that after his conversion Lewis saw had been prompted by the Holy Spirit, an encounter with the divine will, an unnamed desire, that longing for heaven which only God can satisfy. Lewis's conception of *Sehnsucht* was as a God-given revelation of longing, an unrequited love, a non-rational yearning for ultimate reality, that disappeared as soon as it had stabbed and had disabled him.

Fourth, election, Israel, and the law: God reveals of God's self and simultaneously God's desire and will for humanity, through a chosen people, Israel, and through covenant and law (though Lewis is reticent to talk in terms of election). For Lewis, this process of revealing to a chosen group of people is not an end in itself, however; it lays the groundwork, it prepares for a concrete, particular, and perfect revelation.

Fifth, good dreams, pagan premonitions of Christ: outside of Israel humanity is not bereft of revelation. Lewis makes much in his theological apologetics and in his symbolic narratives (*The Chronicles of Narnia*, *The Space Trilogy*, etc.) of premonitions and intimations of Christ to pagan people.[33] This of course reflects a deep love Lewis had all his life of such myths—especially those North European in origin. Lewis balances, almost dialectically, the rules and election of the Jews with the pictures infused into the minds of the pagans. Both are modes of imperfect revelation, general and incomplete. Pagan premonitions of Christ's incarnation and resurrection relate to the numinous and also to *Sehnsucht*, but they

---

[32] Walker, "Scripture, Revelation and Platonism in C. S. Lewis" (2002), 31, referring to Lewis, *The Problem of Pain* (1940), 4–13, specifically 10; and Lewis, *Mere Christianity* (1952), Bk. 1, ch. 1, 3–9.

[33] Brazier, "C. S. Lewis Christological Prefigurement" (2007), 745–52.

4. A Doctrine of Transposition: Towards a Philosophy of the Incarnation

contain pictures given to the imagination that have generated words/stories/myths, and hence give meaning and direction, whereas *Sehnsucht* is more an instantaneous encounter with the Holy Spirit.

Sixth, incarnation, the Word of God revealed: the fullest revelation possible for humanity to comprehend comes with the incarnation of the universal Christ in human form: Jesus of Nazareth, Son of God and Son of Man. The revelation of the incarnation is concrete and real, no nebulous intimation, no lawgiver—except for the law of love and forgiveness. In a comment that reflects Lewis's understanding of the concrete reality of the incarnation, Andrew Walker comments that "the veil of myth is parted and God steps into the full glare of historical reality, and yet, being God, remains forever veiled and mysterious—always unknown, even in his revealedness."[34]

VII. A HIERARCHY OF REVELATION

Andrew Walker correctly separates the mode of revelation that is the incarnation as belonging to a different realm—as particular and perfect—from the partial, incomplete, and general nature of Lewis's other modes of revelation. These modes exclude Scripture, however, and Lewis's respect for the way the natural world reveals God's beauty. We must consider the natural world as part of the general and incomplete modes, but we must invoke a third category for Scripture. So:

The Particular and Perfect:
Christ Incarnate

The General and Particular:
Scripture

The General and Incomplete:
Israel, pagan premonitions, ethics,
the numinous, *Sehnsucht*,
and the natural world, etc.

In addition, there is an implied hierarchy—the general-incomplete is superseded by the particular and perfect. That is, Lewis was wise enough not to deny the ongoing validity of the revelation to and election of the Jews, even if he seldom mentions it. If we are to integrate Scripture into

---

34   Walker, "Scripture, Revelation and Platonism in C. S. Lewis" (2002), 30.

these modes and look at them hierarchically, therefore, we must elevate the incarnation and place it as the final and fullest revelation. Scripture is ambiguous, because on the one hand it is a human product; it is divinely inspired, however; it lays witness to revelation, but is not the Word of God (Christ). Yet for Lewis, it becomes the Word of God when read by a baptized imagination: Christ is in and with the reader. We must therefore take Lewis's understanding of revelation beyond what Christensen and Walker have identified, and acknowledge—from Lewis's writings—three levels, three hierarchies, of revelation in Lewis's theology and apologetics. Primarily there is the full self-revelation of God in Christ incarnate, remembering that the second (Scripture, the general and particular) and third (general and incomplete intimations) issue from and bear witness to Christ, whether explicitly or implicitly.

Why elevate Scripture above the general modes of revelation, but hierarchically below the incarnation? As Lewis asserted when writing to Mrs Johnson in 1952 "It is Christ Himself, not the Bible, who is the true word of God. The Bible, read in the right spirit and with the guidance of good teachers, will bring us to him."[35] Writing to Clyde Kilby in 1959, Lewis, commenting on whether or not a passage of Scripture was historical or not, asserted that "it would still act on me as the word of God if it weren't, so far as I can see. All holy Scripture is written for our learning."[36] In this context, Lewis sees Scripture as subjective and relative to the action of the comforter, the advocate of truth (John 14:16–17 and 26). Hence the comparative position of the general and particular (Scripture) just below the particular and perfect (Christ)—in the table above.

Within the five modes of general and incomplete revelation, we must add a sixth—the natural world, creation itself, which for Lewis imparts knowledge that there is a creator God; but more than that, the sense of the numinous and *Sehnsucht* is often related to and triggered by the beauty inherent in creation that sings of the glory of God. Of these six modes of general and incomplete revelation, we must surely rank them in relation to the incarnation (as in the table above, the left column). Therefore, we must rank first (A) the election of Israel and the revelation to the Jews as superior to the other general modes—simply because they were the preparation for the incarnation, and Jesus the Jew was from the

35 C. S. Lewis to Mrs Johnson, Nov. 8, 1952," in *Collected Letters*, Vol. III (2007), 246.
36 C. S. Lewis to Clyde S. Kilby, May 7, 1959," in *Collected Letters*, Vol. III (2007), 1044–45.

4. A Doctrine of Transposition: Towards a Philosophy of the Incarnation

chosen people of God. We may rank next (B) the pagan premonitions of Christ's incarnation, cross, and resurrection because, though not concrete and particular, these intimations communicate, to a degree, what is at the heart of revelation, even though many of these visions-myths were misinterpreted. The next three are in the form of general religious modes that impart little in the way of explicit knowledge directly related to the incarnation, but have the ability to move the creature towards God: (Ci), the sense of a universal moral impulse; (Cii), the experience of the numinous, and (Ciii) *Sehnsucht*. These are then followed by (D) the natural world, because the sense of the numinous and *Sehnsucht* is prior to the perception of God as creator; indeed, without the numinous and *Sehnsucht* it is possible to conclude that creation is an accident, that there is no God: the natural world can lead to atheism as much as theism. These general and incomplete modes may convince people that there is a God, that there are demands on them, and these modes are important in moving people towards the love of Christ; but equally they may not. They are relatively minor modes of revelation compared to the others.

VIII. MODES OF REVELATION AS *SUPRA-THEOLOGICAL* CATEGORIES

How do these modes of revelation come together for Lewis? In *Mere Christianity*, he comments about humanity's perception of such intimations as were available through the numinous or *Sehnsucht*, but also of humanity's failure to turn to God:

> And what did God do? First of all he left us conscience, the sense of right and wrong: and all through history there have been people trying (some of them very hard) to obey it. None of them ever quite succeeded. Secondly, he sent the human race what I call good dreams: I mean those queer stories scattered all through the heathen religions about a god who dies and comes to life again and, by his death, has somehow given new life to men. Thirdly, he selected one particular people and spent several centuries hammering into their heads the sort of God he was—that there was only one of him and that he cared about right conduct. Those people were the Jews, and the Old Testament gives an account of the hammering process. Then comes the real shock. Among these Jews there suddenly turns up a man who goes about talking as if he

was God. He claims to forgive sins. He says he has always existed. He says he is coming to judge the world at the end of time.[37]

According to traditional theological categorization some of the modes listed above would not be regarded as revelation. According to Lewis, some may indeed be stronger, more temporal and actual, than others, but they are still revealings from God (the sense of the numinous is less concrete than the incarnation but has its place in God's plan of salvation, and through the numinous God reveals intimations, engendering fear, and awe in the presence of holiness). Lewis's understanding of revelation is not confined to conventional "modern" theological categories: his understanding is in effect *supra-theological*—that is, *supra-theological* modes grounded in God's unknowable *aseity*. Most professional theologians will argue that Lewis did not have a systematic doctrine of revelation. It can be argued that no theologian has ever managed to produce a fully worked out and tightly contained doctrine of revelation—for if they did, it would exclude God's freedom to act in the world and towards humanity as God saw fit. For Lewis, these modes of revelation are not comprehensive or exclusive. In effect, the general and incomplete modes are all related to and manifestations of the particular and perfect, because they all emanate from God in Christ: the, to our perceptions, nebulous becomes the concrete and particular. Therefore, all revelation perceivable by humanity comes from Christ. If we exclude the numinous, *Sehnsucht*, and pagan dreams/myths, we exclude the work of God in Christ speaking in a hidden mode, through a veil, to humanity.

IX. A DOCTRINE OF TRANSPOSITION

Lewis shares an understanding that the Christian faith was essentially supernatural or preternatural with many, but not all, "modern" theologians and philosophers, but where he departs from them is in the relation between these two realities: for Lewis we are not closed-off from eternity. Lewis's teleologically conceived Christology is clearly framed in such terms, for Christ is not Christ because of a value we accord him, he is not the product of human status. Christ is fully human but equally more than human: ontologically he is of the Trinity and therefore God incarnate—God descending, entering into our reality in human form to raise us up. Therefore, revelation proceeds eschatologically, from eternity

---

37   Lewis, *Mere Christianity* (1952), Bk. 2, ch. 3, 50–51.

4. A Doctrine of Transposition: Towards a Philosophy of the Incarnation

and into our reality; this is primarily in the form of the incarnation, but secondarily in the modes of general and incomplete revelation. Reality, for Lewis, was simply a veil through which we might glimpse the source of this greater reality: eternity, heaven. But this is on God's terms and proceeds from eternity, drawing our gaze back to eternity. God initiates, the grace initiates, always: the *fall* means we can initiate none of this for ourselves, we cannot (in the Augustinian anti-Pelagian sense for Lewis) pull ourselves up by our boot laces.[38] And that greater reality will affect us, press on us, and influence us: grace draws us up. This other reality is at the heart of Lewis's Platonic idealism. But how does he see the two realities relating? And where is Scripture in this?

Lewis is at his most philosophically theological in invoking the concept of transposition to explain how revelation operates, how God communicates and mediates truth and God's salvific intentions to us through these various modes—from the general and incomplete to the particular and perfect. A doctrine of transposition is set out in a paper given initially at Mansfield College, Oxford, and first published in 1949.[39] Transposition is inevitably framed in Platonic terms. Lewis, like Berkeley and other idealists and Platonists, saw that we can only understand the world around us through its relationship to a higher spiritual reality. The key words here are higher, superior, and richer; but this is not to denigrate the inherent biblically-asserted goodness of creation. Intimations of the higher realm—eternity—will inevitably be translated, transposed—hence Lewis's term. But transposed revelation is more than a mere dilution, more than a watered-down version of the *real* thing. Revelation will give us intimations; the imagination then will conjure up images that help explain and draw us up to where we should be: eternity. The Bible, particularly the New Testament and specifically the parables of Jesus, are therefore couched in allegorical, symbolic—transpositional—language; more pertinently they are for Lewis analogical. There is no one-to-one correlation because this is simply not possible, in the same way that lines drawn on paper, in a drawing, are a diminution of a solid object

---

38 Revelation would have to come from God even if there were no fall. God, eternity, does not necessarily take the initiative in revelation because of the fall. Rather, that is simply the grammar of reality, of creation. God has no need to reveal to us, it is simply an act of love. However, the character of revelation and the means of communication is changed by the fall.

39 Lewis, "Transposition" (1962), 166–82.

because they cannot be the real thing: they represent for us a fluid three-dimensional reality in an artificial two-dimensionality. Lewis cites many examples in his essay entitled "Transposition" to explain this. He gives us the idea of a drawing, also the complexity of a composition for full orchestra in the form of musical notation (especially a piece for full orchestra rescored on paper for a piano alone). In *The Last Battle*, in *The Chronicles of Narnia*, he waxed Platonic and Berkeleyian. After the apocalyptically-charged end of the world in Narnia, Digory, having died and been raised in eternity, comments that:

> "Of course it is different; as different as a real thing is from a shadow or as waking life is from a dream." His voice stirred everyone like a trumpet as he spoke these words: but when he added under his breath "It's all in Plato, all in Plato: bless me, what do they teach them at these schools!", the older ones laughed.[40]

In the same book Lewis explains further by using an image, a picture:

> You may have been in a room in which there was a window that looked out on a lovely bay of the sea or a green valley that wound away among mountains. And in the wall of that room opposite to the window there may have been a mirror. And as you turned away from the window you suddenly caught sight of that sea or that valley, all over again, in the looking glass. And the sea in the mirror, or the valley in the mirror, were in one sense just the same as the real ones: yet at the same time they were somehow different—deeper, more wonderful, more like places in a story: in a story you have never heard but very much want to know.[41]

These two realities are intimately connected and inform each other; but our reality will be drawn up into the spiritual, eternal, realm, and will be subsumed. Lewis establishes two principles for the relationship between the higher realm and the lower: first, that the lower can only be understood in terms of the higher (a proposition essentially from Berkeley); second, that the word symbolism is inadequate to explain the relationship between the higher and lower realms, the transposition of the higher into the lower. Analogy is a better term.

The problem that Lewis identifies is that we are forced to resort to images and concepts from *this* world to explain the world to come, the

---

40   Lewis, *The Chronicles of Narnia—The Last Battle* (1956), 159–60.
41   Lewis, *The Chronicles of Narnia—The Last Battle* (1956), 160.

4. A Doctrine of Transposition: Towards a Philosophy of the Incarnation

truly real world: in the case of the drawing analogy, Lewis comments that all images of this world, which are three-dimensional, solid, ever shifting, are offered as two-dimensional shapes recognizable as belonging to a drawn world. Skeptics could therefore doubt the existence of a three-dimensional world in much the same way that flat-earthers refused to believe the world was round: "your vaunted other world, so far from being the archetype, is a dream which borrows all its elements from this one," writes Lewis.[42] This is the problem with transposition when applied to revelation. In *The Silver Chair*, in *The Chronicles of Narnia*, he presents such skepticism in symbolic narrative. Jill and Eustace are trapped deep underground amongst people who have always lived there, people who have never seen the sun or the sky. A witch has ensnared them along with Prince Rilian, whom they have come to rescue. The witch beguiles them with sweet music, perfume, and charms in an attempt to convince them that the world above, with the sky and the sun, does not exist. Prince Rilian, fighting off the soporific effects of the magic, tries to explain that the sun is real; he likens it to a lamp, only greater, much greater, that it hangs in the sky. The witch answers:

> "Hangeth from what, my lord?" asked the Witch; and then, while they were all still thinking how to answer her, she added, with another of her soft, silver laughs: "You see? When you try to think out clearly what this sun must be, you cannot tell me. You can only tell me it is like the lamp. Your sun is a dream; and there is nothing in that dream that was not copied from the lamp. The lamp is the real thing; the sun is but a tale, a children's story."[43]

When Jill and Eustace try to explain who Aslan is, her argument and logic is the same—they say he is like a cat because he is just a large cat in their imaginations—

> The Witch shook her head. "I see," she said, "that we should do no better with your lion, as you call it, than we did with your sun. You have seen lamps, and so you imagined a bigger and better lamp and called it the sun. You've seen cats, and now you want a bigger and better cat, and it's to be called a lion. Well, 'tis a pretty make believe, though, to say truth, it would suit you all better if you were younger. And look how you can put nothing into your

---

42 Lewis, "Transposition" (1962), 172.
43 Lewis, *The Chronicles of Narnia—The Silver Chair* (1953), 142–43.

make-believe without copying it from the real world, this world of mine, which is the only world."[44]

They are almost beguiled by the witch's arguments because she is inverting all that they know to conform to her own personal kingdom, which is her own personal hell. This is reminiscent of the arguments of skeptics who turn around the images that have been transposed by the will of God from eternity, transposed into our minds, the skeptics then claim they are imaginings from below (i.e., of human generation), not from above (from God).

There will inevitably be a diminution. This is why Lewis invokes the term transposition. Can we see an example of this independent of Lewis? If Scripture by witnessing to revelation is more than revelation, what do we find? In the Acts of the Apostles, Peter has a vision of something like a large sheet being lowered by its four corners; in it were all kinds of creatures, reptiles and birds. Peter is commanded to get up, kill, and eat. This happens three times. Only when Peter receives a visit from three men whom the Spirit commands him to go with does the vision make sense. Peter had been on the roof, famished, dozing off. His vision is in the imagery of this world, affected by his hunger. The vision was really a reassurance and a command to go with the men and convert the gentile Cornelius who had sent the men. Peter therefore exclaims:

> I truly understand that God shows no partiality, but in every nation anyone who fears him and does what is right is acceptable to him. You know the message he sent to the people of Israel, preaching peace by Jesus Christ—he is Lord of all. (Acts 10:34b-36.)

The image Peter has in his vision is therefore a transposition, a translated diminution, effected by his fatigue and his hunger; only in the context of the visit of Cornelius's men shortly after the vision does it make sense: preach the gospel to the gentiles, baptize them, not only the Jews. As intimations of Christ, such prophetic dream visions relate to the numinous and to *Sehnsucht*, and are to be seen as part of the general and incomplete modes of revelation. Such transposed visions have occurred throughout history, and continue to occur today, but they may not always be part of a divine commissioning. They may instead be part of the dynamics of the

---

44   Lewis, *The Chronicles of Narnia—The Silver Chair* (1953), 142-43.

4. A Doctrine of Transposition: Towards a Philosophy of the Incarnation

eschatological relationship between the two realities, the persistent and consistent consubstantial illumination.

X. INCARNATIONAL TRANSPOSITION

Transposition does not only occur as revelation between eternity and the human mind; Lewis is not a gnostic dualist, he does not believe the world of matter is evil and to be repudiated; no, transposition occurs between spirit and nature, and, importantly for our salvation, between God and humanity. Here the mediation of Christ is essential.

> I am not going to maintain that what I call Transposition is the only possible mode whereby a poorer medium can respond to a richer: but I claim that it is very hard to imagine any other. It is therefore, at the very least, not improbable that Transposition occurs whenever the higher reproduces itself in the lower.[45]

The lower, because of its diminution, can therefore exist with meaning only in relation to the higher. But what is this meaning? It is sacramental. Lewis explains how the sun and sunlight in a picture only make sense as signs because the real sun shines on them; in the context of the real sun the picture makes sense:

> It is a sign, but also something more than a sign: and only a sign because it is also more than a sign, because in it the thing signified is really in a certain mode present. If I had to name the relation I should call it not symbolical but sacramental.[46]

So through transposition the spiritual can be known within the natural world as sacrament. Symbolism and allegory may help, but they are subject to the problem cited above—symbols and allegory borrow their elements from *this* world. By contrast, a sacrament as a thing of mysterious or sacred significance is on one level a religious symbol; the symbol or sign is sacramental because it is the real participation between the two realms, the higher and lower, but emanating from the higher to draw up the lower. On another level, it is the reflection in the shadows of eternity. As signs, they are sacramental because they are in reality the coinherence, the participation, of the natural and supra-natural realms: this participation

---

45   Lewis, "Transposition" (1962), 173.
46   Lewis, "Transposition" (1962), 173.

makes of them something more than signs or symbols. The revelation is changed, transposed, *within* the sacrament: there is something in the here and now which was not in the here and now before. If grace is the action of God imparting a mysterious communion with God though Christ, the signs/images intimated through this general revelation are the mode whereby grace draws us up. These revelatory signs are as sacramental as Baptism and the Eucharist, because they are an outward sign from Christ conveying an inward grace imparting salvific knowledge, though Lewis probably would have placed them hierarchically. Lewis held to a high doctrine of the Eucharist, that it is also experiential: it is the highest form of this spiritual drawing-up, the transformation of the material into the eternal. Therefore, he subscribed to a doctrine of transubstantiation, which we can see influenced his doctrine of transposition; however, he was also critical of traditional Thomist transubstantiation because it made what was happening too concrete and too objective within *this* reality. Transposition must be viewed with a degree of apophatic space between the two realms. For Lewis the material world is too insubstantial; it is a diminution of the spiritual world but is not thereby debased or repudiated dualistically. What is more, eternity is not thin and ethereal, wisp-like: rather it is more real, tangible, supra-real, as in the Book of Revelation. Through Christ's incarnation, *this* reality is drawn up into eternity, or begins to be drawn up following Christ's resurrection. This is at the heart of the incarnation: the spiritual in the form of Christ, the *Logos*, descends to rise again, to draw humanity into eternity, a humanity rendered insubstantial through sin. Transposition is therefore at its most profound, at its most complete and highest in the incarnation. Andrew Walker comments, "Transposition of nature into higher reality works not by bringing the higher down to earth, as it were, but by allowing spiritual life to draw nature into itself."[47] Athanasius in his treatise on the incarnation, echoing Ignatius of Antioch and Irenaeus of Lyons, states this explicitly, that God became man so we might become God:

> He, indeed, assumed humanity that we might become God. He manifested Himself by means of a body in order that we might perceive the mind of the unseen Father. He endured shame from men that we might inherit immortality. He himself was unhurt by this, for he is impassable and incorruptible; but by his own

---

[47] Walker, "Scripture, Revelation and Platonism in C. S. Lewis" (2002), 29.

4. A Doctrine of Transposition: Towards a Philosophy of the Incarnation

> impassability he kept and healed the suffering men on whose account he thus endured.[48]

Lewis also notes this:

> I venture to suggest, though with great doubt and in the most provisional way, that the concept of Transposition may have some contribution to make to the theology—or at least to the philosophy—of the Incarnation. For we are told in one of the creeds that the Incarnation worked not by conversion of the Godhead into flesh, but by taking of the Manhood into God. And it seems to me that there is a real analogy between this and what I have called Transposition: that humanity, still remaining itself, is not merely counted as, but veritably drawn into, Deity.[49]

As God is incorruptible and immortal, the incarnation is therefore essential for atonement, a uniting of God with humanity whereby we are drawn into God through God's graceful action in Christ. The incarnation is the most concrete and complete, the most particular form of God's self-revelation. In relation to Lewis's doctrine of transposition we may ask, Is the incarnation a transpositional diminution? Well, cautiously, we must answer yes, for three reasons:

First, because of the *communicatio idiomatum*: within an attempt to account for the relationship between the divine and human natures in the one person, Christ Jesus, how do the properties of the Word of God and the human nature coexist? That God is love, further that God is Trinitarian, transcendent, eternal, uncreated, omnipotent, omniscient, or omnipresent is given us, to a degree, through revelation, that when we see Jesus we see God; but is God more than Jesus because God is triune? What is revealed is therefore *mediated* through Jesus Christ—but not *everything* of God is communicated in Jesus Christ. In the incarnation we have a transposition into human flesh of the second person of the Trinity: God divested Godself of some of his attributes. Jesus of Nazareth was not all-powerful, all-knowing or simultaneously everywhere, because he was human. This was a diminution, but was voluntarily enacted by God out of love for humanity, not out of any need or weakness in God. Jesus was the humble servant, lowly, submitting himself to his destiny: therefore, the

---

48 Athanasius, *The Incarnation of the Word* (trans. Penelope, intro. Lewis; 1944), ch. 8, §. 54, 93.

49 Lewis, "Transposition" (1962), 178.

communication of attributes is characterized by restraint and self-denial by God (we see this in particular in the figure of the Aslan-Christ). In terms of the *communicatio idiomatum*, there is a self-emptying, a restraint of the divine attributes, for the sake of the incarnation (Phil 2:5–8); this restraint leads to a degree of transposition.

Second, veiling-unveiling, the knowability of God: all revealings are in some form a veiling. Many writers, including Andrew Walker, note this in Lewis's work. Colin Gunton summarizes this well from Karl Barth's work:

> The point here is that in Jesus Christ we see the limits, the possibilities of the knowability of God. God the Father represents the limits of this. The Holy Spirit imparts this to human beings: veiling-unveiling, knowability-unknowability, revelation-hiddenness. God is revealed but at the same time he is a hidden God. Even as he reveals himself he is hidden, . . . as he reveals himself he is hidden. After all, when you see Jesus Christ it is a hidden God, it is not obviously God is it, it's just a man wandering around teaching. God is hidden and unless the Spirit reveals him then he remains hidden. God is revealed but also remains in himself unknowable. In the end you have only got paradox. For example, Irenaeus says that the impassable becomes passable, the eternal becomes temporal.[50]

This is so even within relations between people: however long we live with and know someone there will always be something of them we don't know, and how that person chooses to reveal themselves to us is personal and subjective, and our perception of them may vary. There will always be something unknown; we can never fully "know" another person; we can never fully know eternity even in its transposed diminution.

Third, human fallibility: a misreading of the transposition. All ideas transposed from eternity will inevitably be framed in concepts, imaginings, and reasonings from our experience. How is it possible to explain frost, ice, and snow to children living in equatorial Africa? It is not really possible without transposing the idea into language and concepts the children will be familiar with. In science fiction films and programs (which Lewis would surely have enjoyed), aliens which are supposed to be beyond our imagining and different from anything we perceive of reality in our world are always presented in terms of reference from what

---

50   Gunton, *The Barth Lectures* (2007), 80.

4. A Doctrine of Transposition: Towards a Philosophy of the Incarnation

we perceive of reality in our world: therefore they are not truly alien, for they are only imaginings constructed from what we perceive. But are they intimations of the possibility of the truly alien, of the wonders of creation? They should be.

Applied to revelation this merely confirms our human epistemic limitation. For example, in the essay "Transposition" Lewis uses a picture, a story, to explain our flawed perception of transposition. He imagines a woman incarcerated in a dungeon who gives birth to a son; she raises this child as best she can, but the son can never see the outside world. The mother draws pictures—pencil lines on paper—good pictures, artistic representations, to try to explain the real world outside to her son. However, there comes a point where the transposition of the real countryside, sky, sun, and world, fails, because of the limits in the son's perception and the concepts he uses in his mind. The son appears to be getting on well with his education until he says something that causes his mother to realize she has failed:

> Finally it dawns on her that he has, all these years, lived under a misconception.
> "But", she gasps, "you didn't think that the real world was full of lines drawn in lead pencil?"
> "What?" says the boy, "No pencil-marks there?"
> And instantly his whole notion of the outer world becomes a blank. For the lines, by which alone he was imagining it, have now been denied of it. He has no idea of that which will exclude and dispense with the lines, that of which the lines were merely a transposition—the waving tree-tops, the light dancing on the weir, the colored three-dimensional realities which are not enclosed in lines but define their own shapes at every moment with a delicacy and multiplicity which no drawing could ever achieve.[51]

In Lewis's story, the child is convinced that the outside world is therefore less than the visible world of the prison cell in which he is incarcerated. The real world is without "lines" because it is *more* visible, *more* real, but the child, like all of us humans, falls for the realism of the pictures, the drawn lines, and takes it for all there is (which in psychological terms is idolatrous, if we try to root our ideas about God utterly in this world).

The passable and finite, the temporality of the incarnation with all the suffering involved, is in a sense a diminution, yes, voluntarily taken

---

51   Lewis, "Transposition" (1962), 180.

on by God, but it is nonetheless a transposition: primarily on the cross, but then in the work of the Holy Spirit drawing us upwards and onwards through intimations transposed. At his most profound and Platonic Lewis commented in a sermon given in St Mary the Virgin Church in Oxford on Sunday 8th June 1941,

> We discern the freshness and purity of morning, but they do not make us fresh and pure. We cannot mingle with the splendors we see. But all the leaves of the New Testament are rustling with the rumor that it will not always be so. Someday, God willing, we shall get in.[52]

The New Testament specifically, the Bible generally, becomes revelation when we read it, though a baptized imagination is paramount here; thereby the New Testament becomes sacramental in revelatory terms when we read it. The divine light illuminates: there are intimations, transpositions, from eternity in our perception of the freshness and purity of morning, we perceive but cannot fully be with the splendors we perceive. The New Testament is crucial here and is therefore superior to the general revelation, the numinous, *Sehnsucht*, et al., for within its pages there is the rumor, as Lewis terms it, more pertinently the promise, that we shall get in, we will be fully drawn into eternity.

XI. THE KEY

What value is there to a doctrine of transposition? Transposition lies at the heart of Lewis's understanding of revelation and is the key to his theology and apologetics: it permeates all of his work, theological, philosophical, literary, and apologetic, even the symbolic narratives. Whether conceiving of revelation in transpositional modes, or in being inspired to write analogically on the Christ, Lewis's work is like the Bible, an untidy and leaky vehicle, perhaps intentionally unsystematic, the object of fragmented, refracted consubstantial light. Lewis saw his role as reasserting a mere orthodox core, developed through the patristic era. There was therefore a core of belief and faith that existed outside of human perception; doctrine was not humanely created—truth was revealed and given. This is to evoke a Platonic otherness: eternally created truth that we

---

[52] Lewis, "The Weight of Glory," first published in, *Transposition and other Addresses* (1949), 21-33. Republished in *They Asked for a Paper* (1962), 208-9, and subsequent volumes.

4. A Doctrine of Transposition: Towards a Philosophy of the Incarnation

can perceive, truth we can realize the veracity of with the human faculty of reason and whose meaning we can intimate through the imagination. This is Lewis's idealism: ideas are truer than the reality of the shadowlands. Transposition allows us to glean intimations of eternity and God's loving purposes for us, but we will invariably get it wrong: we will misconstrue what is being revealed. Our human sinful desires and needs will get in the way. Peter's hunger affected the vision of the vocation to extend the gospel to gentiles; the boy in Lewis' story wants to hold on to the idea of drawn lines rather than use his imagination to intimate what the real world is like. It is always possible to regard these revelatory intimations as nothing more than something of *this* world, because they are transposed in the language and concepts of this world. In *The Voyage of the Dawn Treader*, in *The Chronicles of Narnia*, Eustace is in conversation with a resting star, who in appearance has the verisimilitude of a human being; he foolishly gets into conversation about what a star is in our reality:

> "In our world," said Eustace, "a star is a huge ball of flaming gas."
> "Even in your world, my son, that is not what a star is but only what it is made of."[53]

Therefore, what lies behind all reality is more than we perceive of reality. What we perceive is a transposition; reductionalist, nominalistic, scientific concepts will only tell us what things are made of, not what they *are*. What is important, therefore, is what Jesus Christ *is*, not only what we take him to be: Lewis's Christology is rooted in ontology, not status.

A doctrine of transposition, transposed eternal truth, will inevitably be an inadequate doctrine of how revelation is mediated/communicated to humanity: if we truly understand what Lewis is asserting then the doctrine itself will be inadequate because the idea of the doctrine comes from eternity and is transposed for our understanding, but will inevitably be incomplete, a diminution, a translation. It is not incomplete in eternity but it is in our perception. Lewis's understanding was profound; he knew that our knowledge and understanding would be incomplete this side of eternity. A doctrine of transposition asserts this to be so, even as the doctrine of transposition itself is flawed and incomplete, inadequate and partial: our heavenward gaze must in humility be characterized by a degree of apophatic agnosticism with regard to the human ability to

---

53   Lewis, *The Chronicles of Narnia—The Voyage of the Dawn Treader* (1952), 159.

know; but neither is it impossible for us to know, to accept something of God's revealedness.

A "flawed" doctrine of transposition therefore applies to Lewis's understanding of Scripture. This is why there are no hard-and-fast systematic propositional truths in every passage of Scripture. The Bible was for Lewis, as we saw, an untidy and leaky vehicle; transpositional diminution meant we do not have the absolute truth systematically presented from an unrefracted light which we could contain or quantify in an encyclopedic fashion. In a late work, *Reflections on the Psalms*, Lewis notes how there is nothing self-evident; our hold on revelation is precarious, as through the incarnation we are drawn into God's eternity:

> Because the lower nature, in being taken up and loaded with a new burden and advanced to a new privilege remains, and is not annihilated, it will always be possible to ignore the up-grading and see nothing but the lower. Thus men can read the life of Our Lord (because it is a human life) as nothing but a human life. Many, perhaps most, modern philosophies read human life merely as an animal life of unusual complexity. The Cartesians read animal life as mechanism. Just in the same way Scripture can be read as merely human literature. No new discovery, no new method, will ever give a final victory to either interpretation.[54]

What Scripture gives us, albeit dimmed through transposition, is a certain insight, how to get the focus right. We can ignore that focus, that insight; we can concentrate only on the lower level. Peter could have interpreted his vision in Acts as a license to hold a feast, a party, for the other disciples and apostles, with no dietary laws or limitations. But he did not, and was not meant to.[55] Lewis asserts therefore that the Old Testament as literature is taken up to be the medium of something more than the merely human; can we set any limit beforehand to the multiplicity or gravity of meaning that is laid upon it by God?

---

54   Lewis, *Reflections on the Psalms* (1958), 100.
55   Acts 10 is not about abrogating the Hebrew food laws: is is about the relationship between the Christ, the Jews and the rest of humanity—the gentiles, the pagans, the heathens . . . !

4. A Doctrine of Transposition: Towards a Philosophy of the Incarnation

XII. CONCLUSION

An intentionally "flawed" doctrine of transposition, itself platonically transposed, is formulated to explain how revelation works, how revelation is communicated, and, paradoxically, how revelation is never fully imparted; this we conclude relates to the *communicatio idiomatum*, Trinitarian ontology, and human epistemic limitation. This transpositional key applies to how God is revealed, how revelation is in modes, but it also illustrates how Lewis's mind was illuminated and inspired to write, to construct his apologetics and his stories. It could be argued that there is an element of circularity of argument here: that claiming the flaw at the heart of transposition simply covers a badly worked out philosophy. Not so. We are the object, not the subject; God is the verb. God initiates, God is the source and origin, the author of all revelation, and thus sets the terms; Moses knew it was impossible to approach God face to face in this world because of our fallen nature. The triune consubstantial light, though refracted through the shadows of this world, allows us to perceive reality along with the supra-real; it is inevitable that revelation will be communicated in diminuted, translated, transposed modes. Reason is at the heart of this doctrine for Lewis, but he knows its limits: reason is not simply an abstract faculty presiding over an indeterminate field, analyzing at its will. We are not God; nor is our kingdom of reason God.

We may surmise there is a greater degree of transposition in the general and incomplete modes of revelation than in the concrete and complete, but diminution and transposition there will be, and there will be a multiplicity of interpretations by humanity because of the freedom given to creation. There will therefore be a *translation* more than a *dilution*. Ironically the more concrete revelation is (i.e., the incarnation), the greater the risk of misinterpretation; but this is balanced by the perfection of the incarnate Christ as the fullest self-revelation. The balance that Lewis held to between the freedom of God to inspire yet allow creation to be, whilst intimating to humanity the truth of eternity as our final home, built on and from the mediation of Christ, is what lies at the heart of his doctrine of transposition, which in turn makes sense of his understanding of Scripture, revelation, and reason: this balance between *aseity* and creation moves all the modes of revelation in Lewis's work teleologically towards the final and full revelation in the incarnation, and eventually in the parousia. This movement is dialectical, but a supplementary dialectic, because creation will be subsumed into eternity. In conclusion, what value is there to Lewis's doctrine of transposition? Does it cohere with his understanding of Scripture and revelation? Yes, but if it is deemed inadequate and flawed, this is because only in eternity will we know as we are known (1 Cor 13).

5

The Actuality of the Incarnation: Triune Simultaneity and the Will of God— Lewis . . . and Shakespeare

SYNOPSIS:
C. S. Lewis eschewed the multifarious and apparently contradictory atonement theories, yet he implicitly promulgated specifically "debt" and "ransom" models. Within his understanding of the cross as the central mechanism of atonement Lewis tackled the paradox of incarnation through a proposition, almost a motif, of analogical narrative in which he sought to explain the actuality of the incarnation: how God could be made in human flesh (John 1:14a), grounded in Triune simultaneity—how God could be both eternal and actual. After examining the "why" and "how" of revelation, we can analyze Lewis's statement: "if Shakespeare and Hamlet could ever meet, it must be Shakespeare's doing." Lewis's proposition raises questions about temporality, and modernist objections to theistic belief, but essentially about the will of the Triune God.

I. INTRODUCTION

The understanding of atonement and salvation in the writings of C. S. Lewis has become more and more respected in recent years, particularly by philosophers of religion. What did Lewis have to say about humanity in relation to God? What was Lewis's understanding of atonement—specifically how salvation through the cross works? Lewis is publically neutral towards all the multifarious and often seemingly contradictory doctrines of atonement and theories about the cross. For Lewis, differing or competing theories of atonement are not necessarily to be seen as a flaw; Christians are not committed to one single way of understanding the cross, because looking at the cross as God's love and forgiveness is sufficient at the beginning of the Christian pilgrimage.[1] Given that for Lewis the church must by default be missionary, given his belief that it exists for those outside of it, he saw atonement theories as a minefield so that a full and complete understanding of how atonement works is probably beyond humanity's comprehension—this side of the *eschaton*. Lewis may try to keep the multiple and seemingly contradictory atonement theories at an arm's length—he initially adopts an essentially neutral position in his *summa* of the faith, *Mere Christianity*[2]—however, he does endorse, often implicitly, a "debt" model in his apologetics,[3] and a "ransom" model in *The Chronicles of Narnia*.[4] (Lewis's "debt" model is derived, in many ways, from his reading of Gustav Aulen's *Christus Victor*.[5])

Despite his orthodoxy Lewis was no fundamentalist or exclusivist: intimations of God's salvific actions to humanity could be found in North European pagan myths, and in Indian and Oceanic religions, and despite his assertion that we are saved by no other name than Jesus,[6] Lewis could see how many people outside the religion of Christianity were acceptable to Christ in judgement and were saved.[7] But neither was Lewis an inclusive universalist: he was a relatively lone figure in arguing the actuality of hell amongst many of his liberal Anglican Oxford colleagues, and his

---

1   Lewis explains that theories about Christ's death are not Christianity in itself, but are explanations about how the cross works: "The thing itself is infinitely more important than any explanations that theologians have produced, . . . no explanation will ever be quite adequate to the reality, . . . a man can accept what Christ has done without knowing how it works. We are told that Christ was killed for us, that his death has washed out our sins, and that by dying he disabled death itself. That's the formula. That's Christianity. That's what has to be believed." Lewis, *Broadcast Talks* (1942), Part Two, "What Christians Believe," 52–53.

2   Lewis, *Mere Christianity* (1952), see II.4, specifically, 45.

3   See Lewis, *Broadcast Talks* (1942), Part Two, 54–55.

4   Lewis, *The Chronicles of Narnia—The Lion, the Witch and the Wardrobe* (1950), ch. 14. See also: Taliaferro, "A Narnian Theory of the Atonement" (1988), 75–92.

5   C. S. Lewis to Corbin Scott Carnell, Oct. 13, 1958, in *Collected Letters*, Vol. III (2007).

6   "The truth is God hasn't told us what his arrangements about the other people are. We do know that no man can be saved except through Christ; we don't know that only those who know him can be saved through him." Lewis, *Broadcast Talks* (1942), Part Two, 60.

7   Lewis, *The Chronicles of Narnia—The Last Battle*, 154–55. Lewis also placed great eschatological and soteriological value on Matthew 25.

5. The Actuality of the Incarnation: Triune Simultaneity and the Will of God

doctrine of infernal voluntarism[8] is gaining more and more creditability with theologians and philosophers of religion as an explanation of God's loving purposes where hell is self-generated, and we *choose* hell above salvation: "All get what they want; they do not always like it."[9] Lewis's understanding of atonement therefore reflects an Arminian doctrine of election grounded in *faith*: all are called into salvation, many exclude themselves; grace is resistible, judgment is final—there is no election outside of faith.

II. INCARNATION-ATONEMENT-SALVATION

At the center of Lewis's atonement theory is God incarnate in Jesus of Nazareth, the Christ, crucified, resurrected, and ascended, sitting (in the legal sense) in judgment. Incarnation is an essential: we are judged not necessarily by some dispassionate distant and unknowable mono-"god" of human invention, but by God-incarnate, God descended to earth incarnated in human form. Incarnation is central to judgment: if Lewis's invocation, through his reading of Athanasius, of God descending to reascend (cf. Eph 4:7–10) is the essential mechanism for atonement, achieved through the incarnation-cross-resurrection, then God's actual presence is essential. What does God-in-human-form mean? How does incarnation work, for Lewis? The aim of this paper is to analyze one analogical description that purports to answer this question. Lewis tackles the simultaneous nature and relationship between God the Father and God the Son, in God the Holy Spirit. God is both without and within creation, as Lewis's analogy furnishes, but because of the Triune nature God is not panentheistically tied into creation.

III. HOW DOES THE INCARNATION WORK?

Atonement is through the cross; atonement is built upon incarnation. Incarnation is Triune and involves an ontological relationship. Lewis is adamant: it is no good arguing human frailty in the face of divine

---

8   Lewis himself does not invoke the term "infernal voluntarism"; it has been coined in recent years to apply to his theory of judgement, whereby many prefer the *post mortem* hell of their own making to heaven, and we lock ourselves into hell. God's judgement is expressed in that God in Christ passes judgement in the declaration to us, "Your will be done." See Bunting (ed.), *The Problem of Hell* (2010), ch. 11, 163f.

9   Lewis, *The Chronicles of Narnia—The Magician's Nephew*, 162.

perfection: we cannot wash our hands of the responsibility for this, neither dare we shy away from facing God's justifying and forgiving judgment, but God has been there before us—in Christ. God's *actual presence* in the world and in human form is essential for atonement. However, and this is a key question, what does God-in-human-form mean?

If the "why" of revelation is not necessarily the imparting of knowledge about God but the need for an antidote for original sin, to restore humanity, and if the "how" is achieved through the incarnation then we can ask how incarnation is possible, what it means, and what it tells us about God. For Lewis, any answer is typically couched in analogical language. Atonement theories are typically about how the cross-sacrifice works; Lewis took this further and attempted to defuse the arguments and contradictions between competing atonement theories by focusing on how the incarnation happened.

IV. TRIUNE SIMULTANEITY

The key to atonement-redemption is in the incarnation: God descended in human form—not a visiting spirit, not an avatar safely distant yet involved—but actually here limited in flesh and blood with all the risks involved in conscious humanity. God is therefore at one and the same time in heaven and on earth. This is triune simultaneity, in the incarnate relation and within the holy Trinity, between the three persons. As the relation between two events assumed to be happening at the same time in a frame of reference simultaneity, or more pertinently *theological simultaneity*, relates closely to Einstein's theory of relativity. Simultaneity is not an absolute relation between events; what is simultaneous in one frame of reference will not necessarily be simultaneous in another (thus the co-existence yet independent identity of the three persons of the Trinity; i.e. relativity of simultaneity).[10] But for Lewis, theologoumena insists that we ask how this can be. Lewis draws on a literary model: Hamlet.

---

10   The word derives from the Latin *simul*, at the same time with *-taneous*, from spontaneous; *simult* implies a coincidence—often *preter-* or *supernatural*—whereby two or more divinely inspired events concur/occur in temporal relativity, linked, associated, correlated in distinct and evident character.

5. The Actuality of the Incarnation: Triune Simultaneity and the Will of God

V. LEWIS, SHAKESPEARE, AND HAMLET

Lewis postulates how William Shakespeare could appear on an equal footing with one of his characters. This gives us some understanding of how the actuality of incarnation happened, and how the essential aim of the Word-became-flesh is reconciling. How does incarnation work for Lewis? The key here is in a word picture, an item of analogical and symbolic narrative, in Lewis's spiritual autobiography, *Surprised by Joy*.[11] The comparison is between an author and the author's creation and how the author relates, controls, and can dictate the ontology of the creation and the author's part in it. Therefore, the author *could* appear on an equal footing with the characters in a play. Lewis is writing in his fifties about a time in his late twenties when he felt the presence and demand of God growing on him on an almost daily basis. Lewis had been a proud apostate atheist, but had succumbed to some sense of the other through Platonism and idealism, and had eventually acknowledged some sort of "spirit," even a "divinity," but not a personal "god," or *the* God, and certainly no idea that God could become one of us, be incarnated as human. Lewis, by the late 1920s, was teaching philosophy and English at Oxford University. His admits that what he terms his "watered-down" Hegelianism was no defense against questions from students in tutorials (he was questioned about what he and other philosophers meant by "absolute" and "person," where Lewis asserted the former but denied the latter). He began to realize that the philosophers of the recent centuries had not really made progress on these questions:

> After all, did Hegel and Bradley and all the rest of them ever do more than add mystifications to the simple, workable, theistic idealism of Berkeley? I thought not. And didn't Berkeley's "God" do all the same work as the Absolute, with the added advantage that we had at least some notion of what we meant by *Him*? I thought *He* did. So I was driven back into something like Berkeleyanism; but Berkeleyanism with a few top-dressings of my own. I distinguished this philosophical "God" very sharply (or so I said) from "the God of popular religion." There was, I explained, no possibility of being in a personal relation with *Him*. For I thought *He* projected us as a dramatist projects his characters, and I could

---

11   Lewis, *Surprised by Joy* (1954), 173.

> no more "meet" *Him*, than Hamlet could meet Shakespeare. I didn't call *Him* "God" either; I called *Him* "Spirit."[12]

Lewis continues to explain how he began, as God drew nearer, to change his mind and see things differently, that there was a possibility of a "meeting."

> Of course I could do nothing—I could not last out one hour—without continual conscious recourse to what I called Spirit. But the fine, philosophical distinction between this and what ordinary people call "prayer to God" breaks down as soon as you start doing it in earnest. Idealism can be talked, and even felt; it cannot be lived. It became patently absurd to go on thinking of "Spirit" as either ignorant of, or passive to, my approaches. Even if my own philosophy were true, how could the initiative lie on my side? My own analogy, as I now first perceived, suggested the opposite: if Shakespeare and Hamlet could ever meet, it must be Shakespeare's doing.[13]

At the end of this last sentence Lewis inserts a note/reference at the foot of the page:

> I.e. Shakespeare could, in principle, make himself appear as author within the play, and write a dialogue between Hamlet and himself. The Shakespeare within the play would of course be at once Shakespeare and one of Shakespeare's creatures. It would bear some analogy to Incarnation.[14]

VI. THE INCARNATION:
1. AN ACTUALITY

What is happening here? What is Lewis asserting? Is this cogent theology? Pertinently, it is important to see whether it concurs with the reality

---

12   Lewis, *Surprised by Joy* (1954), 173. (Lewis's capitalization; my emphasis.)

13   Lewis, *Surprised by Joy* (1954), 176.

14   Shortly after these personal revelations Lewis did kneel down in his rooms at Magdalen College Oxford and confess God's sovereignty and existence, followed later by the oft-cited and momentous conversation with J. R. R Tolkien and Hugo Dyson in Addison Walk, which confirmed his realization, belief, and acceptance that Jesus was the Christ, the unique revelation and salvation of God. This final acceptance then led him to years of deep reading and reflection, eventually to emerge in his popular apologetics, but also the weight of his philosophical theology. See Lewis, *Surprised by Joy* (1955), 181–85.

5. The Actuality of the Incarnation: Triune Simultaneity and the Will of God

of the incarnation. Is this analogical supposition of Lewis's orthodox or heterodox? Lewis's footnote contains the kernel of a doctrine of the incarnation: that God could choose to create God's self as a person in the world, where God could be simultaneously God the creator and one of his human subjects.

First, the analogy works better as a play, that is, *dramatis persona*, rather than as a story, merely words on a page: we can conceive of someone playing the part of Shakespeare on stage, if Shakespeare appeared in a play written by Shakespeare, himself; this character would simultaneously be Shakespeare, according to the creative will of Shakespeare, and a human representing, ontologically, all that Shakespeare is. But does that mean that Jesus was an actor playing the character of God? Not necessarily. Because life is not a play, it is *real* and dangerous and is defined, primarily, ontologically; secondarily, imaginatively: Jesus was very truly man, very truly human, yet was God in human form. If we as sub-creators (Tolkien and Lewis's concept) can write a play and cast ourselves as a character this is a tiny echo of what God does in the incarnation. But are we no more than characters in a story? Well, in one sense, yes, but in another, and because of our finitude and the nature of humanity as created by God, then do we have an ontic independence, and existence which is more than mere characters? But the important thing is that Shakespeare-the-character is the same as the other characters in the play. There is no difference between Hamlet and Reynaldo (Polonius's servant), or between Ophelia and "Shakespeare the character." Some may argue a superiority of breeding or knowledge between the King of Denmark and a servant but they are all absolutely and unconditionally human: this would apply to "Shakespeare the character," indeed the knowledge and understanding this Shakespeare character would have is limited by his existence in the play as Jesus's divine knowledge is restricted.[15] And the will of Shakespeare-the-author ensures that the character is truly Shakespeare, contains and represents all that the author is—subject to voluntary restraint, *kenosis*.

---

15   "No one knows about that day or hour, not even the angels in heaven, nor the Son, but only the Father" (Mark 13:32).

VII. THE INCARNATION:
2. MODALISM AND INDIVIDUATION

There is, however, a danger of modalism in Lewis's wording. Shakespeare is; he is the author writing plays, shopping, talking with friends, walking the streets of London. Then Shakespeare is an idea in his imagination, then a character in his own play on paper, then Shakespeare sees the character incarnated in human form on the stage of the Globe Theatre, walking, and talking and acting out the part he created (does this Shakespeare-the-character have independence of mind—the ability to make his own decisions, even "rebel?" Presumably Lewis saw Shakespeare-the-playwright existing in time simultaneously with the character in the play. It is important to maintain the right balance between unity and individuation—between the three persons of the Trinity, and the unity of God as God. If there is insufficient individuation the model is insufficiently Trinitarian and therefore modalistic. God does not play the role of "God the Father," then choose to be incarnated and play the role of "God the Son," then after the ascension play "God the Holy Spirit." An orthodox Trinitarian doctrine demands three persons *in simultaneity*. But then there are objections, often perceptive modern objections to individuation in too great a degree. If the danger with modalism is that the Trinity is just a way of saying that God appears or does things in three different modes (the Son is only an appearance—or mode—of God) the danger with too great an emphasis on the individual persons is that it can evoke polytheism. Then there is too great a degree of individuality which leads to three separate "gods," making Jesus Christ a lesser "god." It also means that the father "god" brutalizes and kills the son, the lesser "god." Therefore, for the analogy to work in the sense of having some theological cogency Shakespeare-the-character must be *at one and the same time* distinct as a person from Shakespeare-the-author, yet must not be a lesser person or utterly distinct and separate so that that Shakespeare-the-author can brutalizes and sacrifice Shakespeare-the-character for the sins of the characters in the play, and remain aloof from the proceedings! The Father must not be immune from the Son. However, this does raise questions Lewis does not address as to how much God can suffer: is God immune, immutable, and distinct from the sufferings of the Son, Christ, or are we talking about "The Crucified God"?

5. The Actuality of the Incarnation: Triune Simultaneity and the Will of God

VIII. THE INCARNATION:
3. TRINITARIAN ONTOLOGY

What is the ontological relationship between God as creator and God in the human play that is the reality we occupy? Shakespeare creates a character in a play who is Shakespeare. If this is analogous with the relationship between God the Father and God the Son there is a problem: Arianism. The character of Shakespeare does not exist, and then he exists, is created. There was a time, to invoke the language of Arianism, when the character was not. This made Arianism a heresy, because Christ, the second person of the Trinity, is eternally begotten, not created or adopted. God does not create Christ, the universal and eternal second person of the Trinity; but Jesus is created. So the human is created to take the divine, but this is surely more than a mere vessel of flesh and bone. (This raises questions of the *Logos ásarkos–Logos énsarkos*.[16]) The balance between the human and divine is essential here: marginalize the human, and you veer towards docetism and gnosticism. On the other hand, Jesus is no avatar; if you reduce Jesus to a human nominated or possessed or occupied by the divine, then the divine is progressively denied, as in the ebionites or adoptionists, and the full equality of Christ as the second person of the Trinity is lost. Again, if you reduce the very God and very man, then you imperil our salvation. The key is in the ontological status of Jesus as *the* Christ, *he* is not adopted, nominated, elected; *he* pre-exists before all that is created (as he is the agent of creation), he is not created by the Father; he is co-eternal with the Father and the Holy Spirit. If he is written into the human play it is with the merging in incarnation of the divine and the human. Therefore, this exposes a potential weakness in Lewis's analogy: if Shakespeare is putting his entire *self* into the character of Shakespeare in the play, and simultaneously exists as the author of the play, and, if the person of Shakespeare-the-character exists all the time in Shakespeare-the-author, then Arianism is avoided *in the analogy*!

---

16   We do not have scope to explore it here, however. Lewis's original perception reveals a temporal paradox: is incarnation a particularity, or is it acted out in the universal? Lewis's Platonism raises questions about eternity in relation to the particular—"The Lamb that was slain from the creation of the world" (Rev 13:8). Also "Just as he chose us in Christ before the foundation of the world to be holy and blameless before him in love" (Eph 1:4). Also, we cannot escape from eschatological questions: "All inhabitants of the earth will worship the beast—all whose names have not been written in the book of life belonging to the Lamb that was slain from the creation of the world" (Rev 13:8). This raises questions about the *Logos asarkos-Logos ensarkos*.

Whatever the objections, the crucial consideration is the utter equality between Shakespeare-the-character and the other characters, and that Shakespeare-the-author is truly *in* the character. This is then a mark of the incarnation: Jesus the human is absolutely equal and contiguous, at one with the rest of humanity and with *his* Father. If not, it is not religious doctrine that is compromised (though it is, in varying degrees), it is our salvation that is in peril. It was this separation, often by minute degrees in the nature of the God-man as compared to humanity, that characterized heresy in the early and patristic church. Lewis's analogy is good in general terms but perhaps insufficiently precise in its detail, but it does overcome some of the usual religious objection to the incarnation, where people want a "god" that is utterly distant, unknowable, and separate from the world. Lewis's analogy is precisely what it is: an analogous metaphor, not an exact one-to-one description and account of the exactitude of incarnation; analogies are not supposed to be an exact correlation.

IX. THE INCARNATION 4.
COMMUNICATIO IDIOMATUM AND KENOSIS

Any remaining *differences* between Shakespeare-the-author and Shakespeare-the-character (where the difference or distinction between God the Father and God the Son puzzle so many outside the faith) can mainly be explained by invoking Lewis's doctrine of transposition. For Lewis, any revelation is transposed; transposition relates closely to a kenotic Christology (Phil 2:6–11), to the *communicatio idiomatum*, the knowability of God (which is both a veiling and an unveiling), and how human fallibility can lead us to misread what is communicated to us. The hard-and-firm division and separation posited by Platonic idealism, to a degree, between eternity and our reality, between the forms, and the physical world, the shadowlands, is therefore blurred. The relationship between God and humanity in revelation is defined, for Lewis, by transposition. What is *intelligible* is more real than what is *perceivable*; the *intelligible* becomes incarnated, is *transposed*, diminished into the *perceivable* (Jesus): this is a *translation*, as a pen-and-ink drawing relates to the object depicted, it is changed, *diminuted*, yet true to the original and conveys the essence.[17] Transposition changes, translates; the essence

---

17 Lewis, "Transposition," a sermon given in Mansfield College, Oxford on Whit Sunday, May 28, 1944, published (1st ed.) 1949. A reworked and extended 2nd edition of

5. The Actuality of the Incarnation: Triune Simultaneity and the Will of God

is retained but the form changes, is reduced, modified (like, for Lewis, a symphony transposed for solo piano, or a memory compared to the real thing). There will be a diminution, an apparent reduction or disjuncture—hence the usual objection from skeptics that Jesus can't be God because he is just a Jewish holy man, walking around Palestine, or the inaccurate excuse that he is just a good moral teacher. There must be a difference between Shakespeare-the-author and Shakespeare-the-character simply because of the distinction between the two and the relationship, which in Trinitarian terms, can be seen as Father-Son. *Kenosis* allows for the restraining of many of the divine attributes in order to be in the human form: Jesus is the humble, obedient servant. If the analogy holds then, to echo the kenotic hymn (Phil 2:5–11), Shakespeare-the-character is in very nature Shakespeare-the-author but does not consider equality something to be used to his own advantage but humbles himself, being *made* in the form of a character in the play, becoming obedient to death at the hands of the others in the play for their redemption. Therefore, Lewis's doctrine of transposition could explain the difference between God the creator and God-in-human-form, as it does between Shakespeare-the-creator/author and Shakespeare-the-character in one of his plays.

X. WHERE IS GOD?

The Presbyterian minister and theologian Timothy Keller notes, "When a Russian cosmonaut returned from space and reported that he had not found God, C. S. Lewis responded that this was like Hamlet going into the attic of his castle and looking for Shakespeare."[18] There are serious doubts as to whether these are exactly Lewis's words,[19] however, the idea of a character in a play trying to find the author by searching around its environment does point to the inability of humanity to find God under its own efforts. If Hamlet had been real, he was simply looking in the wrong

---

the sermon as an academic paper was published in *They Asked for a Paper* (1962).

18   Keller, *The Reason for God* (2008), 122. Keller gives no reference or credit to where Lewis wrote this.

19   I have drawn a blank at trying to find where Lewis says that this "was like Hamlet going into the attic of his castle and looking for Shakespeare," in his works from 1961–63 (i.e. post Gagarin). However, the phrase credited to Lewis can be found on hundreds of American Christian blogs and tweets (gossip columns). Keller may have gleaned it from a conversation with someone Lewis knew. The phrase is at the least very Lewisian!

place and in the wrong time. Many saw Jesus two thousand years ago and were blind to the God-given truth and reality. Keller is loosely drawing on Lewis's comments from a paper written late in his life.[20] The Russian cosmonaut Yuri Gagarin was the first human to go into space (i.e., into orbit) on April 12, 1961, and is attributed as saying that he could not see God in space therefore God did not exist.[21] In actual truth Gagarin did not say this, but it was attributed to him by Soviet apparatchiks.[22] However, I personally recall the female pilot of the US Space Shuttle echoing Gagarin's supposed comments by commenting on television in the 1990s that she did not see God from the window of the shuttle, only the beauty and wonder of nature, and a scientific perception.

What Lewis does write in "The Seeing Eye" relates closely to Gagarin's supposed comments and to the question of temporality and the incarnation, and what we may term the ontology of God, in relation to atonement:

> The Russians, I am told, report that they have not found God in outer space. On the other hand, a good many people in many different times and countries claim to have found God, or been found by God, here on earth. The conclusion some want us to draw from these data is that God does not exist. As a corollary, those who think they have met Him on earth were suffering from a delusion. But other conclusions might be drawn.[23]

---

20   Lewis, "The Seeing Eye" (1967), first published as "Onward, Christian Spacemen" in the American periodical *Show*, Vol. III (Feb. 1963).

21   It was attributed to Gagarin that he commented during the flight, "I don't see any God up here," however, no such words appear in the verbatim record of his conversations with Earth-based stations during the spaceflight. See: www.cosmoworld.ru, and http://en.wikipedia.org/wiki/Yuri_Gagarin.

22   In a 2006 interview, Gagarin's friend Colonel Valentin Petrov stated that the cosmonaut never said such words, and that the quote originated from the speech given by the Soviet president Nikita Khrushchev at the plenum of the Central Committee of the CPSU on the subject of the Soviet anti-religion campaign a few months after the historic space flight, saying "Gagarin flew into space, but didn't see any 'god' there." Petrov commented that Gagarin had been baptized into the Russian Orthodox Church as a child, and a 2011 *Foma* magazine article quoted the rector of the Orthodox Church in Star City saying, "Gagarin baptized his elder daughter Elena shortly before his space flight; and his family used to celebrate Christmas and Easter and keep icons in the house." See: www.cosmoworld.ru, and http://en.wikipedia.org/wiki/Yuri_Gagarin.

23   Lewis, "The Seeing Eye" (1967), 167.

5. The Actuality of the Incarnation: Triune Simultaneity and the Will of God

Lewis analyses the Soviet objection that as Gagarin skimmed the atmosphere he saw no evidence of God. First, Lewis asserts, it may be argued that we have not yet gone far enough in space: "There had been ships on the Atlantic for a good time before America was discovered."[24] Second, God does exist, but is confined locally to planet earth. Third the Russians did find God in space but did not realize it; they lacked what Lewis terms, "the requisite apparatus for detecting Him."[25] Fourth, God does exist but is not an object in the temporal sense of the word and is not "located in a particular part of space nor diffused, as we once thought 'ether' was, throughout space."[26] Lewis's first point is in effect the apophatic solution—you will never *know* God. His second point is the pantheist-panentheist solution, God is part of the earth, part of the living organism of the planet. He comments that the first two points are irrelevant: "The sort of religion for which they could be a defense would be a religion for savages."[27] Lewis is quite pleased that the astronauts failed to discover such a "god." It is the third and fourth points that Lewis believes are real explanations: "Looking for God—or Heaven—by exploring space is like reading or seeing all Shakespeare's plays in the hope that you will find Shakespeare as one of the characters. . . . Shakespeare is in one sense present at every moment in every play. But he is never present in the same way as Falstaff or Lady Macbeth."[28] To this end, Lewis can see why scientific atheism developed: scientists won't necessarily find the "god" of their dreams in the world, in nature. Lewis is therefore reiterating that God relates to the world as an author relates to a play. Mere movements in space, Lewis notes, won't bring God nearer, or further away. What is pertinent is not how we try to find God but how God has come to us: through incarnation and through the Holy Spirit; and how we then try to avoid God.[29] Therefore, Lewis notes how space travel has nothing to do with the question of God or knowing God:

> To some, God is discoverable everywhere; to others, nowhere. Those who do not find Him on earth are unlikely to find Him in

---

24 Lewis, "The Seeing Eye" (1967), 167.
25 Lewis, "The Seeing Eye" (1967), 167.
26 Lewis, "The Seeing Eye" (1967), 167.
27 Lewis, "The Seeing Eye" (1967), 167.
28 Lewis, "The Seeing Eye" (1967), 167–68.
29 Lewis, "The Seeing Eye" (1967), 168–69.

> space. (Hang it all, we're in space already; every year we go a huge circular tour in space.) But send a saint up in a spaceship and he'll find God in space as he found God on earth. Much depends on the seeing eye."[30]

Here we come to the central argument of Christian revelation, for if Lewis is to argue that God cannot be known as an object within God's creation does this refute the revelation of the Christ? The answer is that this is the starting point and the condition of all religions: God *may* be knowable by Spirit (and even then one cannot be absolutely sure of dark spirits masquerading as the light—2 Cor 11:14), but the *concrete* revelation is in Jesus of Nazareth, the Christ: and then this is not a didactic exercise where God is incarnated so as to "teach" us about God's self. No, this is primarily about *curing* the human condition, forging salvation—a way out for the righteous, *in Christ*.

> When I said a while ago that it was nonsensical to look for God as one item within his own work, the universe, some readers may have wanted to protest. They wanted to say, "But surely, according to Christianity, that is just what did once happen? Surely the central doctrine is that God became man and walked about among other men in Palestine? If that is not appearing as an item in his own work, what is it?" The objection is much to the point. To meet it, I must readjust my old analogy of the play.[31]

Therefore, Lewis's analogical condition that if Hamlet could meet Shakespeare it would be on Shakespeare's terms and through the will of Shakespeare—through Shakespeare writing himself into the creation while simultaneously being without.

> One might imagine a play in which the dramatist introduced himself as a character into his own play.... We have a real instance of this in Dante's *Divine Comedy*. Dante is (1) the muse outside the poem who is inventing the whole thing, and (2) a character inside the poem, whom the other characters meet and with whom they hold conversations. Where the analogy breaks down is that everything the poem contains is merely imaginary, in that the characters have no free will. They (the characters) can say to Dante

---

30   Lewis, "The Seeing Eye" (1967), 171.
31   Lewis, "The Seeing Eye" (1967), 171.

5. The Actuality of the Incarnation: Triune Simultaneity and the Will of God

only what Dante (the poet) has decided to put into their mouths. I do not think we humans are related to God in that way.[32]

Lewis concludes that this is a transposed "suggestion" of what was established by theologians about the nature of Jesus as very God and very man. When he speaks of the union of the two natures in Christ, the divine and human, Lewis is in effect invoking Chalcedon, and the creed the council issued that settled these arguments about the nature of Christ as very God and as very man. However, would there be two persons/natures in Shakespeare-the-character?—or is this simply a union of the author and character? Perhaps the Greek concept and word, *holos/holon*[33] helps us here, which may defuse all of the heterodox arguments the early church councils fought long and hard against. Lewis recalls Dante's invention: the other characters in Dante's *Divine Comedy* do not realize that Dante is the author of their world, further that he exists outside it. Indeed, they are not *created* to perceive this as we are *created* to perceive the world and the intimations from beyond—of God and eternity.[34] Here Lewis notes how Jesus was perceived to be the Christ (a perception that then pointed to *his* divinity) by very few around him (given that Messiahship and divinity are not one and the same): "Perhaps, for a time only by St Peter, who would also, and for the same reason, have found God in space. For Christ said to Peter, 'Flesh and blood have not taught you this.' The methods of science do not discover facts of that order. If you do not at all know God, of course you will not recognize *him*, either in Jesus or in outer space."[35] Because of ignorance and fallenness humanity was regarded by Lewis as unfit to visit other worlds; whether we find an innocent, unfallen, species orbiting a far-flung star, or a demonically stronger one than ourselves, we will corrupt and despoil as we have done here on earth: such is the power

---

32   Lewis, "The Seeing Eye" (1967), 171. Humanity, unlike Shakespeare's or Dante's creation, does have the ability, taken onto itself, to rebel, to set up on its own, to behave *eritis sicut Deus*, and then crucify God, the author and creator incarnated.

33   This reflects a scriptural axiom that the human is a unity of soul and body: a psychosomatic whole (i.e., from the NT Greek—*psychē* and *sōma*). Maximus the Confessor uses the term *eidos holos*, a "complete whole," a "complete entity," or, *ekplerosis*—completeness. The Greek *holos* implies that something is simultaneously a whole and a part.

34   Lewis, "The Seeing Eye" (1967), 172.

35   Lewis, "The Seeing Eye" (1967), 172.

of original sin.[36] Space travel, real inter-stellar space travel—apart from orbiting our own planet, or struggling to the moon and back—will seem an impossibility. Perhaps humanity is subject to a God-given quarantine.[37] And atonement is limited to humanity for, as Lewis speculates, there may well be other sentient species in the universe that are not *fallen*.[38]

XI. CONCLUSION

So often trying to explain the actuality of incarnation systematically can prove difficult; even Barth is not averse to paradox and mystery in these crucial moments and events in the life of Christ. Lewis's ability in analogical narrative, imagery, that evokes a sense of how a concept can be is of value here. Incarnation is like . . .

There are questions remaining, in particular the question of temporality and enfleshment (*Logos ásarkos–Logos énsarkos*) we alluded to earlier. So we return again to atonement through incarnation where God is both without and within creation as Lewis's analogy furnishes: Shakespeare-the-author and Shakespeare-the-character gives us some understanding of how this happens, as does Dante's *Divine Comedy*. This may seem to some to be a logical impossibility and a contradiction of the laws of nature as they perceive them but to ask an unbaptized imagination to comprehend incarnation-atonement is like asking a goldfish to map out in three dimensions and full analytic detail its goldfish bowl, the water it swims in, and the world (the room, the house, the town, etc.) beyond its narrow reality, distorted, like a lens, by the curved glass of the bowl. The goldfish's limitations and the impossibility of this task is why God comes to meet us, not as we skim earth's orbit in a metal box believing we have traversed the universe but in the frail dependent humility of a newborn babe, threatened all his life for what he was and is, with the primary mission to die for our salvation. This is the will of the Triune God. "If

---

36 Lewis, "The Seeing Eye" (1967), 173.

37 "I have wondered before now whether the vast astronomical distances may not be God's quarantine precautions. They prevent the spiritual infection of a fallen species from spreading." See. Lewis, "Religion and Rocketry" (1960), 91. This notion of quarantine is also formulated in the first book of *The Space Trilogy*: *Out of the Silent Planet* (1938).

38 See Lewis, *Perelandra* (1943).

5. The Actuality of the Incarnation: Triune Simultaneity and the Will of God

Shakespeare and Hamlet could ever meet, it must be Shakespeare's doing."[39]

---

39 Lewis, *Surprised by Joy* (1955), ch. XIV "Checkmate," 181.

6

Election and Predestination: Decision, Faith, and Responsibility— Whither Humanity

SYNOPSIS:
What does the Bible tell us about election? What does the tradition tell us, and how is Lewis's philosophy of election influenced by other theologians: Augustine and Calvin, or the sixteenth-century Reformers? Where is universalism—or the potential that all might be saved? For Lewis, the self-determination/determinism that issues from the *fall* (original sin) relates closely to judgment and responsibility. And how important—or possible—is it for us to make sound impartial decisions for ourselves on these key issues? Is humanity now riven by diminished responsibility (many modern/liberal philosophers and theologians would hide from God's judgement in such an assertion)? And yet, for Lewis, we are "decided upon." How do John Calvin and C. S. Lewis compare on these questions?

Election relates closely to predestination and salvation. Lewis's approach to election—and therefore judgment—is essentially and comparably Arminian (i.e., after the Reformation theologian Jacob Arminius): Christ suffered and died for all, not for a specific elect; all are potentially saved, however, some choose to *exclude* themselves, they prefer hell to heaven. Grace is therefore resistible, and there is no election outside of faith. Lewis is orthodox: it is Jesus Christ who is God's elect. Through faith we elect for Christ, for heaven. If grace were not resistible would we still have *fallen*, or was grace withheld so as to test the human creature (a test that the human failed, as it *fell*)?

Therefore Lewis's philosophy of election is that heaven is open to all, but hell is forced segregation. For Lewis, the gates of hell are locked, secured, and triple-bolted, from the inside—by the condemned. Does this weaken God's judgment? God's judgment is, for Lewis, like a king who casts-out a traitor into exile. (Tolkien's word-picture of Sméagol/Gollum is here apposite: banished for his crimes, for what

IN THE HIGHEST DEGREE

he has become: monarchically initiated exclusion: *poreúesthe* (Matt 25), depart, conduct yourself away.

Lewis quotes the Scottish theologian George MacDonald here: "There are only two kinds of people in the end: those who say to God, 'Thy will be done,' and those to whom God says, in the end, 'Thy will be done;'" if the throwing down of its crown is not forthcoming. Hell, therefore, is forced exclusion through what the individual has become. Lewis's approach is essentially through what is today termed *infernal voluntarism*. Can humanity hold out against the will of God? How does this affect election? *The Last Battle* and *The Great Divorce* (*The Chronicles of Narnia*) illustrate Lewis's thinking. It is therefore imperative to consider Lewis's understanding of atonement in relation to the actual nature of heaven and hell. But how does this square with the judgment of God and the temporal paradox of (biblical) predestination-determinism?

I. INTRODUCTION

C. S. Lewis is noted for re-presenting the orthodox/traditional Christian faith in successful and imaginative ways, contrary to the modern/liberal developments from the mid-twentieth century on. However, in recent years, more and more philosophers and theologians, having dug deep into his works, have realized that his soteriology (i.e., theory of salvation, also of atonement and election) is startlingly original, yet cogent with the Bible and with the early church tradition, so that many skeptical philosophers can at last see sense in his scheme of things. This scheme is centered on what has recently been termed "infernal voluntarism"—a term Lewis did not use, but does accurately reflect his doctrinal position.[1] Considering a doctrine of election raises questions about predestination and judgment, decision and faith, and the consequences—eschatologically—of our actions and beliefs, and therefore consideration as to who bears the responsibility for the predicament we find ourselves in, in this life, and in the world to come. Virtually everything in Lewis's theological, philosophical, and apologetic writings is leading to or is dominated by, or is underpinned by, these eschatological considerations.

The aim of this paper is to examine what C. S. Lewis presented in terms of election (with related understanding of salvation and

---

[1] The term was invented in response to Lewis's doctrine of hell by Bradley L. Sickler, in "Infernal Voluntarism and 'The Deep Courtesy of Heaven'" (2010), 163f.

6. Election and Predestination: Decision, Faith, and Responsibility

reconciliation, atonement and justice, decision and responsibility), and how this relates to the Christian eschatological tradition. The objective of this paper is to assess what evidence there is for a formalized doctrine of election in Lewis's writings? How did he regard the Bible and the tradition. How is Lewis influenced by other theologians: Augustine and the sixteenth-century Reformers? Where is universalism—or the potential that all *might* be saved—in Lewis's scheme of things? How important—or possible, *postlapsarian*—is it for us to make sound impartial decisions for ourselves on these key issues? Election relates closely to predestination, salvation, and judgment: and therefore heaven and hell. And, pertinently, in a highly specific manner, how do John Calvin and C. S. Lewis compare on these questions?

II. ATONEMENT AND THE ESCHATON

The word atonement was invented in the sixteenth century and is attributed to the Bible scholar and translator William Tyndale; the word was conceived to reflect the concept in the Hebrew Scriptures of how forgiveness and reconciliation takes place ("at" "one-ment"). In sixteenth-century early-modern English there was no single word that could reflect and explain this Hebrew understanding of the process of pardoning before God, an understanding from which issued the atonement theories of the early church. Christ's sacrifice reconciles as it forgives: therefore, atonement must explain the simultaneous reconciliation of humanity to God, and the remission of sin, taking into account the question or need of propitiation and satisfaction. Atonement theories are therefore more than explanations of reconciliation. Justice—fairness and impartiality, even-handedness, honesty, veracity and integrity, leading to satisfaction—is to be seen as defined by propitiation (that is, to win or regain the favor of, to appease—from Latin *propitiare*, to make favorable), but there are also questions of punishment, debt, as so forth. It is the conflicting and often contradictory propitiatory elements in doctrines of atonement that have been, and still are, the cause of profound disagreements amongst the churches. Sacrifice leads to reconciliation, which leads to determinism,[2] that is election.

---

2   Determinism: the philosophical doctrine that all events and actions are ultimately determined by causes regarded as external to the will.

Lewis is traditional-orthodox: the *eschaton* is the "four last things" (death, judgment, heaven, and hell) not the cheap grace[3] of the "two last things" (death and heaven) we find in some modern/liberal theologies. The *eschaton* is defined by Lewis in a simple aphorism: "All get what they want; they do not always like it."[4] Election is eschatological because it is about our final destination: what we are elected to; election therefore relates to and issues from atonement, in particularly God's desire to save humanity and the means by which this "at-one-ment" is achieved. Lewis's doctrine of atonement is in essence the classic theory or model: the grace Jesus won was costly; it freed us from bondage to personified evil, the fallen angel: Satan. According to the classic model of atonement (codified and rationalized by Gustav Aulén[5]), Christ's sacrifice releases humanity from its servitude to Satan. In a sense, this resets the human condition back to its *prelapsarian* state. It frees humanity to be for God, or against God, our beliefs and actions, our faith, ethics, and morals, give away our loyalty and allegiance: the last judgment decides who we are for. Briefly: the patristic church formulated the classic atonement model,[6] often referred to as the ransom theory, or the *Christus Victor* model: it is eschatological, and is existential in that it lays emphasis on the crisis humanity finds itself in, with the emphasis on the *krisis* of decisions. The fall enslaved all humanity to the devil, to personified evil, through rebellion. Neither Aulén nor Lewis are postulating a dualistic universe: Lucifer was a creature, created good by God as the highest angel of light, who fell, who rose to attempt to be greater than God, to surpass God—*eritis sicut Deus*—and as a result is exiled from heaven and falls, descends, from God's grace. According to the salvation history presented in Genesis, humanity then enslaved itself to

---

3   "Cheap grace is the deadly enemy of the Church.... Cheap grace means the justification of sin without the justification of the sinner. Grace alone does everything, they say, and so everything can remain as it was before.... Cheap grace is not the kind of forgiveness of sin which frees us from the toils of sin. Cheap grace is the grace we bestow on ourselves. Cheap grace is the preaching of forgiveness without requiring repentance, baptism without church discipline, Communion without confession, absolution without personal confession. Cheap grace is grace without discipleship, grace without the cross, grace without Jesus Christ, living and incarnate." Bonhoeffer, *The Cost of Discipleship* (1998), 43–45. Originally published as *Nachfolge*, in 1937.

4   Lewis, *The Chronicles of Narnia—The Magician's Nephew* (1955), 162.

5   Aulén, *Christus Victor* (trans. Hebert; 1931), a lecture series given University of Uppsala, March-April 1930.

6   Aulén, *Christus Victor* (trans. Hebert; 1931), 16–60.

6. Election and Predestination: Decision, Faith, and Responsibility

this "alien," who had beguiled and seduced in order to possess the human in part by behavioral association. To redeem humanity, God descends in Jesus of Nazareth, the Christ, as a ransom or bait. Through the cross-resurrection Satan loses the (legal) right to humanity: Christ is the victor! This is a monumental spiritual battle acted out eschatologically: "The work of Christ is first and foremost a victory over the powers which hold mankind in bondage: sin, death, and the devil. . . . [T]he victory of Christ creates a new situation, bringing their rule to an end, and setting men free from their dominion."[7] Atonement becomes a liberation. By reuniting the incarnate Christ into the triune Godhead through the cross the devil is subverted.[8] The liberation component makes sense in a modern concept where a child has been kidnapped and held hostage, and the mother offers herself in place of the child, or more pertinently an elder sibling offers himself—the first-born son—in place of the younger child, with the parent's agreement and anguish: Jesus offers himself to the powers of darkness in the place of fallen humanity. This is, therefore—in reality—a story more than a philosophical, rational account of atonement.[9]

Christ in the *eschaton* merely judges us according to our allegiance and ownership: are we with and for God, or not. To whom are we elected? How does this work out for Lewis? We are not left blind and without knowledge, the human may be corrupt but we can *know* something about the coming judgment, about the nature of heaven and hell, for that matter about election, and something of the nature of the *post mortem* life, about purgation and hell, or about the ecstasy of eternity. This knowledge and understanding *should* generate change in us: repentance and conversion. We should then elect for salvation whether we know Christ or not in terms of religious culture and cognitive knowledge (the Parable of the Sheep

---

7   Aulén, *Christus Victor* (trans. Hebert; 1931, 20).

8   Aulén, *Christus Victor* (trans. Hebert; 1931, 22–28).

9   Irenaeus (130–202 AD) advanced a theory of "recapitulation" whereby Jesus became what we are so that we could become what he is; this was further developed by Athanasius (c. 297–373 AD) in his *de Incarnatione verbi Dei* (*The Incarnation of the Word of God*), which profoundly influenced Lewis and was integrated into Lewis's understanding of atonement through the descend-to-reascend motif: God descends to redeem humanity, in the flesh, dying to be resurrected, then to reascend to heaven with humanity. (The Eastern Orthodox Church has consistently through its history remained wedded to the ransom/recapitulation model—Christ as the victor over Satan and death.) See Athanasius, *The Incarnation of the Word* (trans. Penelope; intro. Lewis; 1944). Lewis draws heavily on Athanasius (c.297–373) in this proposition.

and the Goats confirms that our knowledge may be partial, incomplete, or wrong: that we often don't know what we are doing, and are unaware of the consequences![10]).

III. PREDESTINATION AND ELECTION

To understand C. S. Lewis on election and judgment we need to examine briefly the tradition, then consider who influenced Lewis, and what he promoted as a classical, orthodox understanding of election and salvation, of heaven and hell.

IV. FAITH, ELECTION, AND SCRIPTURE

Is there an elect? Is there, in the mind of God, even before the creation, a specific group of people (humans[11]) predestined to be saved? And if so by what conditions? The classic atonement model indicates that those who have faith in Jesus Christ are saved. Their allegiance is now with God, not with the fallen angel, Lucifer. However, their decision was generated by the Holy Spirit, preveniently; grace initiated the turn to grace. Election is intimately connected with salvation. The Bible asserts that some are chosen, others not (Matt 24:40–41; cf. Mark 13:19–23; Luke 21:5–9); some are saved, others not:

> For he chose us in him before the creation of the world to be holy and blameless in his sight. In love he predestined us for adoption to Sonship through Jesus Christ, in accordance with his pleasure and will. . . . In him we were also chosen, having been predestined according to the plan of him who works out everything in conformity with the purpose of his will, in order that we, who were the first to put our hope in Christ, might be for the praise of his glory.
> (Eph 1:4–5, 11–12)

However, Jesus warns us:

> Not everyone who says to me, "Lord, Lord," will enter the kingdom of heaven, but only the one who does the will of my Father who is in heaven. Many will say to me on that day, "Lord, Lord, did we not prophesy in your name and in your name drive out demons and in

---

10   Matt 25: 31–46.

11   It is important to consider here, though it would not be profitable to pursue the question, of what it is to be human in this context.

6. Election and Predestination: Decision, Faith, and Responsibility

your name perform many miracles?" Then I will tell them plainly, "*I never knew you.* Away from me, you evildoers!" [My emphasis.]

(Matt 7:21-23)

Throughout the Old Testament, election appears to be related to those who do the will of God, who serve God and the developing salvation history among the Jews. Colin E. Gunton saw Jacob and Esau as an example of election in the Old Testament:

> In scripture election is considered much more historically than it is in Augustine or Calvin. In scripture election is classically defined as the distinction in choice between Jacob and Esau: Jacob is loved, Esau is not chosen; not that God hated Esau but that he chose Jacob (Israel) rather than Esau. This is the biblical way of putting it. God chooses one person and that means one nation rather than the other—he chooses Israel rather than Edom. So that it is a historical choice for one group rather than another. It is also to do with the call of individuals; for example the call of Jeremiah. This call is of an individual to be a prophet—but in some ways it is traced back to the beginning of his life. The crucial text in many ways is in Ephesians. Here Paul is saying that God has chosen us (both Jews and Gentiles) as the Church from the beginning of time as part of God's plan that all things should be summed up in Christ.[12]

In most cases, election in Scripture is rooted in eternity. Here we have a temporal paradox: we are in time and appear to be able to make decisions, yet we are told all is decided for us, on us, about us, already. *Israel* is called to be God's chosen people; the prophets are *called* from before they were born;[13] the church is called to be the body of Christ, the redeemed (Eph 1:1-10). Is election about salvation solely, or only partially? Religious election, the role, say, of the prophets, or Jacob, relates secondarily to salvation but the primary role is that these people are *elected* or *commissioned* to preach and bear witness to the ancient Hebrews. Colin Gunton again: "Election seems to me to be to do with how God calls individuals and groups to perform a particular task or

---

12   Gunton, *The Barth Lectures* (2007), 110-11. Referring to Jer 1:4-5 and Eph 1:1-10.

13   "Before I formed you in the womb I knew you, before you were born I set you apart; I appointed you as a prophet to the nations" (Jer 1:5).

function on earth."[14] Arguments have erupted through Christian history as to whether Israel is still elected, or replaced by the church.[15]

V. THE TRADITION

Augustine saw election in less worldly terms: election was about whether people would go to heaven or not—be saved or be damned. The Augustinian tradition is that most are damned; God calls a few though God's grace and mercy, an elect, to be saved.[16] The Augustinian tradition continues into Anselm, and medieval scholasticism: the *eternal fate* of the elect is the concern, rather than an historical calling; the question is not about salvation history, or Israel, but who is to be saved? For Augustine, no one deserves or merits election, and humanity is absolutely powerless before the irresistible impulse that draws them to good or to evil. God eternally chooses the elect through grace; but this decree does not destroy the will of Christ to save all, a salvation realized by the God-given human liberty that bequeaths to the elect full power to fall further and to the non-elect full power to rise to salvation.[17] The Augustinian doctrine of predestination dominated, it may be said, thinking in the Western church for a thousand years, until the Reformation when it was absorbed, in principle, and in varying degrees by some of the Protestant churches. As such, the Augustinian doctrine of predestination gives full prominence to a biblical understanding of sin, while emphasizing the grace of God.

In the sixteenth century, there were differing approaches to election and salvation. To Calvinists, election (more specifically, unconditional election) asserts that God chose some individuals from humanity, chosen from eternity, for salvation. This election is outside of any merit or value, strength or faith on the part of the elect, and may not seem logical or discernible to us, but is in accordance with God's good grace and sovereign purposes. By comparison, Jacob Arminius (1560–1609) disputed the mainstream Calvinist approach; after his death his followers

14   Gunton, *Barth Lectures* (2007), 111.

15   See Romans 9–11; specifically, 11:30–32.

16   See, Augustine, *De Spiritu et litterā* (Latin ed.; 2011), xxxiv. See also Cary, Doody, and Paffenroth, *Augustine and Philosophy* (2010), 79–102.

17   For a detailed explanation of Augustine's foundational doctrine of election see the Roman Catholic website, *New Advent*, specifically the Catholic encyclopedia article on "The Teaching of Augustine": http://www.newadvent.org/cathen/02091a.htm.

drew up five articles of remonstrance, opposing what was considered to be the dominant Calvinist approach. Arminians asserted, "That God, by an eternal, unchangeable purpose in Jesus Christ, his Son, before the foundation of the world, hath determined, out of the fallen, sinful race of men, to save in Christ, for Christ's sake, and through Christ, those who, through the grace of the Holy Spirit, shall believe on this his Son Jesus, and shall persevere in this faith and obedience of faith, through this grace, even to the end."[18] This is supported for the Arminians by Scripture: "Whoever believes in the Son has eternal life; whoever disobeys the Son will not see life, but must endure God's wrath" (John 3:36). A more developed understanding of election and salvation in Arminianism is where *Jesus Christ himself* is God's elect, with all others being elect "in Christ" by their participation in him via their faith. Through Christ's sacrifice God has begun to form an elect "in Christ," a people, a new creation, to be the body of Christ: *this election is freely offered to all*. All who belong to Christ are *identified* with Christ through faith—and this even includes all who display allegiance to the Christ even though they know not the *name* or what the Christ has done for them (Matt 25:31f.). These people, the "sheep," are part of the elect, and are assured salvation. But that can change: if they cease to believe and/or to behave wickedly, they can be deemed unworthy and of no allegiance to Christ: they can lose their salvation if they cease to be *identified* with Christ. Or they may choose to reject Christ and heaven.

VI. POTENTIAL UNIVERSALISM: A GOSPEL CONSIDERATION

The basis of any doctrine of election must be in Jesus Christ and what he reveals:

> Jesus answered, "I am the way and the truth and the life. No one comes to the Father except through me. If you really know me, you will know my Father as well. From now on, you do know him and have seen him." Philip said, "Lord, show us the Father and that will be enough for us." Jesus answered: "Don't you know me, Philip, even after I have been among you such a long time? Anyone who has seen me has seen the Father." (John 14:6–9).

---

18 See: http://www.reformed.org/documents/BelgicConfession.html.

There is no God beyond Jesus; there is no God hidden behind Jesus, a God with a different agenda to the Son, the Christ. Jesus invites all to turn to him and have faith. Some theories of election posit that this applies only to a church elite, others that it applies to those already predestined;[19] however, many see Jesus's words and actions as evidence of the gates of heaven being wide open, the invitation is to all. Whether all take up salvation is a key component in Lewis's understanding of election and atonement, an understanding that displays the potential for all to be saved, or more pertinently, all to be *elected to salvation*. Therefore, there was always a glint of universalism (or potential universalism) in some doctrines of election, which related to God's calling of humanity through the election of Jesus Christ. It is this that the Swiss Reformed theologian Karl Barth focuses on in the mid-twentieth century. Colin E. Gunton commented,

> Calvin's doctrine of election is materially the same as Augustine, Anselm and Aquinas. Calvin is a traditionalist so far, what is different is the use he makes of it. . . . Calvin only introduced discussion of election so as to assure the elect of their salvation. What is meant to be a cure for anxiety only reinforced the disease. You see, Calvin didn't say God has called you; he said he has called some and not others. And according to the standard historical accounts this has led to self-examination in the faithful to see if they were called or not, and so we have a recipe for anxiety. That is Barth's complaint about it: Calvin's God is not really defined by Jesus[;] . . . according to Barth, there is a hidden God for Calvin behind the God who chooses us in Jesus.[20]

We find this *potential* universalism in Lewis's works. God is revealed in Jesus Christ; God's purposes are known in that God loves us and desires our salvation. For Barth, if Jesus elects, so does God the Father: the aims of the two cannot be separated. Jesus is the one human who has been elected. And we are all potentially elected in Jesus and therefore raised

---

19   Is there a theological view of election that restricts it to an elite within the church. The worst-case scenario is that a doctrine of election is restricted to the church, alone. To state that some are predestined implies that there are some who are not yet predestined, but who will be. That seems to undermine the whole notion of predestined. Does God choose from all eternity a specific limited subset of humanity that will be saved? How does this contrast with those who see election as—potentially?—embracing everyone.

20   Gunton, *Barth Lectures* (2007), 112.

6. Election and Predestination: Decision, Faith, and Responsibility

up in Christ, so God has elected the whole human race for a reconciled, atoned, relationship: "The doctrine of election is the sum of the Gospel because of all words that can be said or heard it is the best. That God elects humanity; that God too is the one."[21] Revelation informs us that God elects Jesus, and we through faith can be in Jesus, sharing in his election. We can only know election through *who* and *what* God *is*. If Jesus is fully God and fully man then Jesus Christ is the electing God, and the elected human: this is at the heart of Barth's cosmic scheme of things. For Barth, you cannot go beyond the Triune God, which is his criticism of Calvin; we will see how this can be read from Lewis's writings (though Lewis was relatively unfamiliar with Barth and Calvin). Therefore, all are elected, *in potentia*, in Christ; some, however, are called to bear witness to this election, that is, the church; being called to bear witness is a public duty and constitutes the visible church community.[22] Augustine implicitly sees this as a single sovereign act of God, but he differs from Lewis in regarding who is in (saved) and who is out (damned) and how God decides. For us to try to decide the detail, the list of who is saved, is to attempt to see beyond revelation: "Barth therefore imposes a relentless Christological critique on the tradition."[23] Therefore, the status of humanity is that *all* are elected; however, some are called to bear witness to this election. Importantly, this "calling" does not constitute an election that separates a few from the rest of humanity.

> Christ dies for all! The difference he lays out is in calling and not status. All humans beings have the status of being elected by God: some appear to realize that calling differently. And therefore no one is in principle rejected, except of course, Jesus—and he on behalf of others. Barth: "The rejected man who alone and truly takes and bears away the wrath of God is called Jesus Christ. He is the rejected as and because he is the elect. In view of his election there is no other rejected other than himself."[24]

Barth's approach to election and predestination is to pose a paradox: God has elected humanity in Christ; we must accept that the final count as to who is in and who is out is open. This may point to universalism, in

---

21 Barth, *Church Dogmatics*, II/2, §. 32, 3. See, II/2, §.32, 3.
22 Barth, *Church Dogmatics*, II/2, §. 33–35, 177f.
23 Gunton, *Barth Lectures* (2007), 116.
24 Gunton, *Barth Lectures* (2007), 120. Quoting, Barth, *Church Dogmatics*, II/2, §. 35, 345, 349, and 353.

potential, or does it? Contemporary with Barth, C. S. Lewis was arriving at a similar approach and solution. How so?

VII. ELECTION AND DECISION: GRACE IS RESISTIBLE, JUDGMENT IS FINAL— THERE IS NO ELECTION OUTSIDE OF FAITH

Lewis's background in these matters was Church of Ireland:[25] he was raised an Anglican, but was acutely aware from friends and neighbors of the Ulster Calvinistic/Presbyterian faith and its position on predestination and election. Lewis returned to Anglicanism after his adult conversion. In addition, in the years after his conversion, he absorbed a relatively traditional Roman Catholic position on election, salvation, and damnation through his deep study of Augustine and Aquinas. However, in his middle- and mature-period works he reflects an implicitly Arminian position with regard to election and predestination. That is, there is potential universalism, but not all will be saved; we work out our salvation and therefore our election in this life. This position can be summarized thus: grace is resistible, judgment is final—there is no election outside of faith. However, towards the end of his life, he did discuss the paradox of election: that we can appear to have been called from before any decision we make about these issues. Six months before his death Lewis was interviewed by Sherwood E. Wirt on behalf of the Billy Graham Evangelistic Association, and he was pressed to speak about his conversion.[26] In the context of what Lewis had described in *Surprised by Joy*, Wirt asked whether he believed that he had made a decision at the time of his conversion:

> I would not put it that way. What I wrote in *Surprised by Joy* was that before God closed in on me, I was in fact offered what now appears a moment of wholly free choice. But I feel my decision was

---

25   For those unaware of this important, and some might say foundational, part of Lewis's life, the Church of Ireland (*Eaglais na hÉireann*) does not refer to the Roman Catholic Church but what is in effect the Church of England in Ireland: it is a Christian church in Ireland and an autonomous province of the Anglican Communion; its allegiance is to Canterbury, not to Rome.

26   Conducted in Lewis's rooms in Magdalene College, Cambridge, on Tuesday, May 7, 1963, the interview was initially published in two parts, (Wirt and Lewis, "Heaven, Earth and Outer Space" and "I was Decided Upon") in the American periodical *Decision*, later to be combined posthumously. See, Lewis, "Cross-Examination" (1971).

6. Election and Predestination: Decision, Faith, and Responsibility

not so important. I was the object rather than the subject in this affair. I was decided upon. I was glad afterwards at the way it came out, but at the moment what I heard was God saying, "Put down your gun and we'll talk."[27]

Lewis continued by emphasizing that his response to God was a deeply compelled action, and yet paradoxically it was also in many ways the freest action because no part of him was beyond or outside the response. Lewis would not be drawn away from this dialectical paradox: both appear to contradict the other, yet they are both valid and true. Wirt is pressing Lewis to own that he controlled the situation of his conversion, yet Lewis quite rightly asserts that the initiative lay with God and that although the point of assent was probably the freest moment in his life he could see on reflection that he could not have done anything else, he could not have responded in any other way. Lewis answered further that it was a case of everyone coming to terms with the claims of Jesus Christ upon his or her life; if not, then they would be guilty of inattention or of evasion.

VIII. ELECTION: AN EXISTENTIAL PARADOX

Was this encounter predestined? Was God electing Lewis? Was Lewis singled out for special treatment? Is this what happens to everyone at the most opportune time in their life—if they will listen with their heart and respond to God's prompting through the Holy Spirit? This is existential because it is about decision-making and the crisis of existence, and the awesome responsibility we hold for our fate. If this is about election then this is not necessarily the doctrine of election that we might find in the more traditional Roman Catholic approach or for that matter the more hardline Calvinistic system, where there is to be identified a specific and particular elect. This is more to do with God's election of people raised up to bear witness to what God has done for our salvation in Christ: perhaps there was special treatment in this encounter, whereby Lewis was commissioned to bear witness to God's salvific actions in Jesus, the salvation proffered for humanity that reset the human condition so that all were no longer, by default, in bondage to the personified powers of darkness, the devil? Essentially what we have here is a doctrine of election that asserts that all are elected by, through, and in Christ's death on the

---

27   Lewis, "Cross Examination" (1971), 217.

cross; it is then a question of response, a question of turning to be for Christ, to put down one's gun of intellectual (or lifestyle, or identity politics, or cultural, . . . or religious!) rebellion as Lewis terms it, or the crown of sin, religion, and pride.[28] This implies the potential salvation of all. It also asserts the place for human participation through free will in Lewis's understanding of salvation, which can be interpreted as coming from an Arminian perspective: that Christ died for all and not only for an identifiable elect. Therefore, we can do no good for ourselves, any good in us comes from grace, but we can do an evil—we can refuse God, we can resist. If this is so then the judgment of God in Christ is that we condemn ourselves to hell from the inside. Exchanging correspondence with a woman who had written to him, puzzled at all the talk she came across relating to predestination and election, Lewis grounds his comments in paradox:

> All that Calvinist question—free-will and predestination, is to my mind un-discussable, insoluble. Of course (say us) if a man repents God will accept him. Ah yes, (say they) but the fact of his repenting shows that God has already moved him to do so. This at any rate leaves us with the fact that in any concrete case the question never arrives as a practical one. But I suspect it is really a meaningless question. . . . When we carry it up to relations between God and man, has the distinction perhaps become nonsensical? After all, when we are most free, it is only with a freedom God has given us: and when our will is most influenced by Grace, it is still our will. And if what our will does is not "voluntary," and if "voluntary" does not mean "free," what are we talking about? I'd leave it all alone.[29]

If we make an absolutely unconditional and free decision, what role has the Holy Spirit had in bringing us to the point of decision and in the condition of freedom? The relation between grace and freedom must, after the fall, be characterized by paradox. Lewis notes how the Parable of the Sheep and the Goats tells us nothing about predestination; only how through works some individuals may be deemed acceptable to God in Christ as they come before him in judgment. There is nothing about faith

---

28 " . . . the twenty-four elders fall before the one who is seated on the throne and worship the one who lives forever and ever; they cast their crowns before the throne . . ." (Rev 4:10).

29 C. S. Lewis to Mary Van Deusen, Oct. 20, 1952, in *Collected Letters*, Vol. III (2007), 237–38.

6. Election and Predestination: Decision, Faith, and Responsibility

and predestination in the decisions of the saved or the damned, but there may be prevenient grace working in them to draw them to the good, to undertake often dangerous and self-denying acts of charity, of pure love:

> Whatever St Paul may have meant, we must not reject the parable of the sheep and the goats (Matt XXV.30–46). There, you see there is nothing about Predestination or even about Faith—all depends on works. But how this is to be reconciled with St Paul's teaching, or with other sayings of Our Lord, I frankly confess I don't know. ... The real inter-relation between God's omnipotence and Man's freedom is something we can't find out.[30]

Some may argue, with some justification, that Lewis voiced this paradox of human volition and God's foreknowledge, and the question of election and predestination, through the demonic Screwtape, who comments that if God sees us doing things in creation, in God's "unbounded now," then God is observing our doing, not making us do.[31] Lewis therefore speculates on the relationship between how we perceive of time and how God *is*, and operates in time (essentially the relationship between the economic and immanent Trinity, though Screwtape does not use those terms!). The human projects onto God the past, the present, and the future, confusing time for "an ultimate reality"[32]—this is about the relationship between the created order (all things set in motion from the point of creation), in relation to all the prayers that are directed to God, and how the laws of nature may be suspended, altered temporarily, changed *miraculously*.[33]

IX. JOHN CALVIN AND C. S. LEWIS: RESPONSIBILITY AND FREEDOM

Jordan Ferrier has analyzed some of the complex issues involved in comparing Lewis with a more traditional Calvinistic position.[34] Ferrier highlights and attempts to resolve the differences between C. S. Lewis and John Calvin on issues of omnipotence and responsibility, and how the conclusions relate to election and the will of God. That there are

---

30   C. S. Lewis to Emily McLay, Aug. 3, 1953, in *Collected Letters* Vol III (2007), 354–55.
31   Lewis, *The Screwtape Letters* (1942), 107.
32   Lewis, *The Screwtape Letters* (1942), 106.
33   Lewis, *The Screwtape Letters* (1942), 106f.
34   Ferrier, *Calvin and C. S. Lewis* (2010).

major differences is clear, despite the fact that both Lewis and Calvin start from the same biblically informed position (God's freedom and the fall of humanity), but though Ferrier is unique in comparing the two, the solution to the dilemma, the comparison, appears to be left hanging. Many Calvinists will disagree with Ferrier, and at times Ferrier appears to be reluctant to own that perhaps Calvin was simply wrong. But we cannot avoid tacking that issue.

A problem for Calvinism is that everything seems to end up being directly caused by God and thus God's fault. In the 1970s, politicized revolutionaries and anarchists would comment, when they killed hostages, blew-up a bank, or hi-jacked an airliner, that "you" made me do it, "you" are responsible: the "you" being the political establishment, the people they disagreed with. Does the "you" of human rebellion ultimately go back to God because God created us? (This begins to relate to questions of theodicy.)

The problem is essentially that for C. S. Lewis God willed that humanity knew the risks (Gen 2:16–17) and was free to choose, humanity was not coerced into choosing one way or the other. Therefore, God did not author evil, or the fall. For Lewis, humanity before the fall had unconditional freedom to choose, unbiased and dispassionate, a freedom that was lost after the fall, once humanity was in bondage. Also, for Lewis, God did author the creation, which had free will to choose, and God took the responsibility for undoing the fall onto God's self (on the cross). The traditional, some might say stereotypical, position attributed to Calvinists is that God knew all of this and willed the fall to happen, therefore all is predestined. If Calvinists believe that everything that happens is the will of God, then the fall can, for some Calvinists, be attributed to the will of God. Lewis would say not: God created the conditions of freedom that characterized the creature, and waited for the creature to love and turn to God in freedom. Lewis exemplifies this in *Perelandra*, where the Green Lady is free to obey or not to obey; God does not control her but waits for her and observes her response, which in Lewis's *Perelandra* is paradise retained. Some Calvinists deny that humanity can know any good; others regard humanity as capable of perceiving accurately something of the good. Is there one unique position to Calvinism?—Probably not. If God could have prevented the fall, but chose not to, is God responsible? This is a position some Calvinists will raise but most Catholics, Anglicans, and many Protestants see the question as irrelevant: we simply no longer

6. Election and Predestination: Decision, Faith, and Responsibility

know the full conditions of our original creation. Furthermore, God created good and evil, the moral conditions of the creation (natural law), and God is "obedient" to them.[35] But—as Lewis would concur—God can see that bringing good out of the evil of the fall is worth the effort and worth the final result.

X. AN ONTOLOGICAL RIDDLE

Perhaps the answer to the riddle of the Reformation, as Ferrier terms it, is in the very nature of humanity and what we were created for, the answer to the riddle is ontological and not doctrinal. Lewis has the senior demon Screwtape comment on the puzzle, where God is to be perceived, inadvertently, as the "enemy":

> He really does want to fill the universe with a lot of loathsome little replicas of Himself—creatures whose life, on its miniature scale, will be qualitatively like His own, not because He has absorbed them but because their wills freely conform to His. We want cattle who can finally become food; He wants servants who can finally become sons. We want to suck in, He wants to give out. We are empty and would be filled; He is full and flows over. Our war aim is a world in which our father below has drawn all other beings into himself: the Enemy [God] wants a world full of beings united to Him but still distinct....
>
> Merely to override a human will (as his felt presence in any but the faintest and most mitigated degree would certainly do) would be for Him useless. He cannot ravish. He can only woo. For His ignoble idea is to eat the cake and have it; the creatures are to be one with Him, but yet themselves; merely to cancel them, or assimilate them, will not serve.[36]

So are the Calvinists right, is all predestined? Or is Lewis right to claim that the creaturely freedom given to the human does not render God responsible? God is absolved because we accepted the freedom, in freedom of will! Can the protestations of some Calvinists appear, at times, like the convoluted and inverted thinking of Screwtape?

---

35   Lewis often seems to speak of God as lawgiver, not as one under law. In classical theology the natural law is an expression of the divine nature in creation. It is not something external to God to which God must submit; it is simply God being God.

36   Lewis, *The Screwtape Letters* (1942), 30 and 31.

IN THE HIGHEST DEGREE

If Lewis is right, that salvation is open to all but through the accumulation of willful decisions individuals reject their salvation, then do we condemn ourselves to hell. If so, how does this square with the judgment of God and the temporal paradox of predestination-determinism? Given that it is willful independence and autonomy—issuing from original sin—that generates, to a degree, self-determined election and judgment then we must examine the relationship between election and hell. Lewis does focus much more on the self-determination that issues from the fall into original sin and how we are judged by God as personally responsibility for our actions and beliefs, and ultimately our *post mortem status*. This approach is essentially Arminian: Christ suffered and died for all, not for a specific predefined elect—all are *potentially* saved; whether they are *actually* saved depends upon them. As I have asserted, summarizing Lewis's position, *grace is therefore resistible, judgment is final, there is no election outside of faith*:[37] yet we are "decided upon" preveniently.[38] A temporal paradox?

XI. ARMINIANISM: GRACE AND ELECTION

We need to look more closely at the assertion that Lewis's approach to judgment essentially accords with that of the Reformation theologian Jacob Arminius. If Jesus Christ is God's elect, then through faith we choose for Christ, for heaven: if grace were not resistible would we still have fallen, or was grace withheld so as to test the human creature (a test that the human failed, as it fell)?

Lewis comments, in *The Problem of Pain*, on the relation between humanity and God *in election*:

> If He who in Himself can lack nothing chooses to need us, it is because we need to be needed. Before and behind all the relations of God to man, as we now learn them from Christianity, yawns the abyss of a divine act of pure giving—the election of man, from nonentity, to be the beloved of God, and therefore (in some sense)

---

37 How do we see Lewis's concept that judgement is final? If hell is locked from the inside, it is at least theoretically possible that someone in hell would choose salvation in Christ. Once that decision is made then judgement has become final: the saved cannot slip back into hell, once they have cast down their crowns.

38 See, "Cross-Examination" (1971), 215–21.

6. Election and Predestination: Decision, Faith, and Responsibility

the needed and desired of God, who but for that act needs and desires nothing, since He eternally has, and is, all goodness.[39]

God therefore loves in freedom. God desires nothing, God does not need us; we need God. God loves us in freedom and dies on the cross for our salvation. It is the God-man who is elected. We are drawn into that election through grace and through being human, just as Jesus Christ is fully human and fully God.

XII. GRACE-ELECTION-FAITH

A problem with the Reformation is fragmentation: competing and often contradictory theories about election and atonement (but then the medieval Roman Catholic doctrine of atonement is a significant shift away from the classic model common in the patristic churches). Lewis is influenced by Augustine, this we have established, but he steers his own path away from Augustine on predestination and election. Lewis carves out his own position, influenced, to a degree, by his reading of Aulén's *Christus Victor*, though not exactly in accord with Aulén. Based on the classic model of atonement, Lewis's position is in accord with a doctrine of grace and election that underpins the classic model of atonement. As Barth refused to see a God over and beyond and hidden behind Jesus, with a different agenda on election, Lewis refuses to countenance an election outside of faith: through faith we elect ourselves to be for and with Christ. Faith equates with election; there is no (Calvinistic) election independent of faith.[40] This position is coincidentally Arminian. There is no evidence that Lewis read or referred to Jacob Arminius or Arminianism, however, there is a closeness between the two that distinguishes Lewis from Augustine and from Calvin (though ironically Lewis's position is in keeping with most Christians in the pew, so to speak).

---

39   Lewis, *The Problem of Pain* (1940), 44.

40   Both views see election and faith as inseparable; both believe that the elect will have faith. The contrast is that Calvinists see faith as a gift of God given to the elect, a sign of election. Arminians see faith as the means to join God's elect. To Calvinists election precedes faith; to Arminians faith precedes participation in election. (However, in both cases the position on lection is more nuanced.)

XIII. ARMINIANISM: CENTRAL TENETS

A brief reminder:

> Over the centuries, Calvinists have so successfully vilified Arminianism that people who are Arminian are afraid to say so. This is true even though Arminianism is the default theological position of Christian Protestantism; indeed, many people are Arminian and don't even know it, and even deny it. Arminianism is so widespread that even the strongest Calvinist churches are filled with Arminians. It is ironic, then, that people are afraid to say they're Arminian; for example, many Independent and Southern Baptists are typically Arminian, but nonetheless often call themselves Calvinists![41]

There are certain basic principles, tenets, to Arminianism that concern us in relation to Lewis's doctrine of election.

First, that Jesus died for all humanity, every human being, not a predefined elect. *Second*, humanity can do nothing to earn salvation for itself or of its own volition, grace initiates the human response. *Third*, humanity can resist God's grace. *Fourth*, those who believe are born again. *Fifth*, an Arminian position on election is that election is in Christ, anyone who is in Christ is among the elect. Faith is essential to become united with Christ; therefore election is conditioned upon faith.

These are basic principles with which Lewis's writings concur, with the exception of total depravity. Lewis did agree that a human can do nothing towards his or her salvation, but that logic excludes *total depravity*[42] (Lewis argued that if we were totally depraved we would not know that we were[43]). For Lewis, Jesus passion and death was for all, every human being, not a predestined elect; humanity can do nothing to earn

---

41   Society of Evangelical Arminians: http://evangelicalarminians.org/.

42   A doctrine of total depravity is associated to a greater or lesser extent with all Protestant and Reformed churches, who draw it from Calvin's teachings, though it is in essence from Augustine's doctrine of original sin: through the *fall* all are enslaved to sin, therefore it is only through grace we may eventually choose and do the good, to accept salvation. Does Lewis's claim appear to misunderstand total depravity: total depravity means that humans are affected by sin in every area of their humanity (hence, it is total—no area is unaffected). It does not mean that humans are as depraved as they can be. If that is right, then one can recognize genuine good in fallen people, but it will never be undiluted good.

43   Lewis, *The Problem of Pain* (1940), 50.

6. Election and Predestination: Decision, Faith, and Responsibility

or deserve the salvation wrought by Jesus on the cross: grace initiates the change, and also the human response. However, humanity can resist God's grace, humanity can repel the subversive action of the Holy Spirit. Therefore, for Lewis, turning to Christ to believe initiates a new creation: the human is born again. Christ descends, in Lewis' view, to raise up humanity (not an elite or a select few). This is election and election is "in Christ"—anyone who is in Christ is elected. Faith is, therefore, election is conditional upon faith, faith breaks the bondage with the devil, faith that responds to the passion and death, the sacrifice of Jesus. Therefore, some are saved; others are lost: hell is—logically—a voluntary option. Though questions have been raised about the ability and sanity of individuals to actually make such decisions for which they are held responsible for all eternity, these are questions raised as criticisms by many contemporary self-defined liberal/modern theologians and philosophers, but also by traditional and orthodox Christians, also Evangelicals, and even a Roman Catholic doctrine on the question of suicide: was the person in his or her right mind?[44]

XIV. FAITH AND WORKS

Given that these conclusions issue from the rebellion that is original sin we must examine the relationship between election and hell. We noted earlier Lewis's comments about how in the Parable of the Sheep and the Goats salvation is not attributed to predestination or to faith: "all depends on works."[45] Lewis therefore declared that he failed to see how this could

---

44   Marilyn McCord Adams has argued since the 1970s that humanity is characterized by diminished responsibility and psychological flaws, therefore it would be cruel and wrong to send some, condemned, to hell: Adams, "Hell and the God of Justice" (1975); Adams, "*The Problem of Hell*" (1993).

45   C. S. Lewis to Emily McLay, Aug. 3, 1953, in *Collected Letters* Vol III (2007), 354–55. From a contemporary British viewpoint, sheep are very different in appearance to goats: fluffy balls of white cotton-wool, grazers who would attack no one (the product of a thousand years of selective breeding in a mild wet climate), compared to mean-spirited, thin, wiry, grey animals that would eat anything and attack to defend and expand. In the intertestamental period, goats and sheep were mountain animals barely domesticated and looked virtually identical, as can be seen from Iberian and North African sheep today. Jesus's point in his parable is that judging by appearances no one can tell the difference (except for the shepherd, and some discerning livestock workers: the only clue is often in the tail: in most varieties one points up, the other down!); so the same is true with humans: merely looking at someone won't tell you if they are an eschatological sheep or a goat.

be reconciled with the doctrine of the apostle Paul or with Jesus's sayings about the signal importance of faith.[46] How do we reconcile this paradox? If we see faith as a work then this makes sense: faith is something we do; to believe is a verb, an action word. Works—all works of any value before the Lord—flow from this single action of the will: to believe, to have faith. The sheep in the parable care for the sick, the imprisoned, they clothe the naked because this is an *act of faith*: they believe in the poor and the dejected. But the object of the faith is Christ in the guise of the poor, the vulnerable, the naked, and imprisoned: the object of their faith is then Christ—even though they do not realize that this is what they are doing, this is what they are *believing in*! Such works issue from faith, they are an act of faith.

XV. INFERNAL VOLUNTARISM:
1. EXILE AND BANISHMENT

So, in accordance with the rebellion—original sin—generated by free will, do *we* define the conditions of our *post mortem* existence? Lewis will argue that we condemn ourselves to hell, for God seeks the salvation—in love—of all. For Lewis, the gates of heaven are wide open, all are welcome; the gates of hell are locked, secured, and triple-bolted, from the inside *by the inmates*. Does this weaken God's judgment, God's right to judge? God's judgment is, for Lewis, what we can define/name as a form of monarchically initiated exclusion. God segregates. This is like a king or queen sending a traitor into exile, exiling the quisling, the turncoat or criminal, banishing the enemy, to live on its own, by its own wits; outside the protection afforded by the monarch, such exiles ended up living in lawless territory where the strongest and most evil persons dominate: this is hell. Quite literally such a person becomes an out-law (outside the law and without its protection). This is like Lucifer expelled from heaven: the judgment of God on Lucifer was that the fallen angel's arrogance was incompatible with the bliss of heaven, the arrogance of attempting to be God excluded Lucifer from heaven.[47] The necessity to exclude is represented by Lewis in the demonic ramblings of Screwtape when he tries to explain to the junior tempter how Lucifer left heaven, unable

---

46   C. S. Lewis to Emily McLay, Aug. 3, 1953, 354–55.

47   Isa 14:12 (KJV), Rev 12; see also The Book of Enoch.

6. Election and Predestination: Decision, Faith, and Responsibility

to live with God.[48] J. R. R. Tolkien's word-picture of Sméagol/Gollum (*The Hobbit* and *The Lord of the Rings*) is apposite here: banished for his crimes, for what he has become, Sméagol was cast out never to return, he was to live on his own, by his wits, but he was not alone, he was preyed upon: the only company he had was evil.[49] Adam and Eve were banished from the life of paradise (Gen 3:23–24). Cain's punishment for murdering his brother? Not execution, but banishment, exile (Gen 4:10–12). In this context Lewis paraphrases the Scottish theologian George MacDonald:

> There are only two kinds of people in the end: those who say to God, "Thy will be done," and those to whom God says, in the end, "Thy will be done." All that are in Hell, choose it. Without that self-choice there could be no Hell. No soul that seriously and constantly desires joy will ever miss it. Those who seek find. To those who knock it is opened.[50]

Hell, therefore, is voluntary-forced exclusion through what the individual has become (again, a dialectical paradox between setting one's heart's desire on hell as a preference on the one hand, or being judged and condemned on the other; desire or sentence, jump or pushed!).

XVI. INFERNAL VOLUNTARISM:
2. HOW DO WE DEFINE HEAVEN?

But don't we all desire heaven? Often, Lewis notes, the person, the individual in a communal context, develops a belief system and ethic such that he or she can no longer distinguish between heaven and hell as an object of desire, or will in the end desire hell, convincing him- or herself it is heaven. This characterizes many of the damned in hell in Lewis's *The Great Divorce*—an apostate bishop, a self-righteous businessman, an artist desperate for fame and celebrity status, all refuse to leave the hell of their own making and cross over for the joy of heaven, albeit with the pain of purgation, yet with the encouragement of the redeemed. This mistaken focus onto hell is nothing new. For example, the Viking hall of the dead that the Danes, the Norsemen, took to be heaven—where they were to spend all their time, *post mortem*, in feasting and whoring, drunken revelries and

---

48   See, in particular, Lewis, *The Screwtape Letters* (1961), ch. 8.
49   See Tolkien, *The Lord of the Rings* (1954–55). See The Shadow of the Past, 53, 55 and 56, also, Appendix F, 1136.
50   Lewis, *The Great Divorce* (1945), 58.

fighting, mutilating, raping, and killing—is in point of actuality a region in hell! But there were those amongst the Vikings who will love it because feasting, whoring, drinking, sadistic paraphilia, mutilation, and slaughter defined them utterly by the point of their death, to the severe degradation of the *imago Dei* in them. This is about defining God's righteousness in the individual's own image and desiring the consequences. *Eritis sicut Deus*: even in these delusions, are they not still responsible for their beliefs and actions before God, and crucially what they say, what they *will* their hearts and souls to believe? Is what we desire for others what marks out our *post mortem* state? If that desire possesses us, defines us, and takes us over then the nature of that desire will define us—whether we personally call it "heaven" or "hell." This raises the question, just how far do we have to go in demanding that God conforms to our personal religious prejudices? We can look at ecclesial history and with hindsight see individuals who were so involved in promoting their own religious kingdom that they lost track of salvation: retrospection makes such an observation easy. However, recently a senior Anglican cleric (with an impressive record of widely reported "good works"), one who could fairly be described as a religious celebrity, stated publically on a radio chat show that if he arrived at heaven and found God was "homophobic,"[51] he would prefer to go to the other place: hell. And he repeated and stressed this desire. Is this not the sin of Lucifer?[52]—claiming to know better than God? This person yearned for heaven yet refused to lay down her/his crown of religious pride. If someone is so confused, even deluded (one might even consider, deranged), in his/her use of language and simply neither believes or refutes anything they say, then despite what we have noted about people not necessarily being responsible for their sayings and

---

51   The exact broadcast words from the radio program and from the very public address to thousands were: "I would refuse to go to a homophobic heaven. No, I would say sorry, I mean I would much rather go to the other place. I would not worship a God who is homophobic." Quote from a radio interview with the BBC (British Broadcasting Company) 26 July 2013. See: http://www.bbc.co.uk/news/world-africa-23464694. Modesty and respect for this elderly cleric's work and struggle against great political evil prevents me naming, and attributing what was perhaps just playing to the audience. But none-the-less it was said as a public declaration, openly before YHWH the Lord, and heard—witnessed—by thousands.

52   See Ezekiel 28 and Isaiah 14; Sin originated in the free will of Lucifer in which—with full understanding of the issues involved—he chose to rebel against the Creator.

6. Election and Predestination: Decision, Faith, and Responsibility

beliefs, we may ask just how fit for heaven they are? This cleric actually used the word "homophobic," but whatever we think about the merits and demerits of that word, it seems absurd to speak of God having an irrational fear of anything.[53] Despite a lifetime of theological study and discourse at a senior level does this person believe that irrational fears are part of the attributes of God?!?—Or was the meaning, that if God regarded homosexual activity as a sin . . . ? What this person said was questionable, ambiguous and confusing—inaccurate—ultimately meaningless, but it was characterized by spiritual pride, which led him to declare for *infernal voluntarism* . . . even if on reflection he didn't mean it.

How far does this linguistic irresponsibility go, how far does the "well, I didn't really mean it," excuse go, before God must take us seriously in what we say, we believe, we do?[54] With the revival and growth of the theatre in the Renaissance/Reformation, this became an identified problem noted amongst actors: how responsible before the Lord were they for what they said and did on stage? An extreme example of this was in the BBC historical docu-drama *Conspiracy*, detailing the infamous 1942 Wannsee Conference. The SS General Reinhard Heydrich, with Machiavellian skill, plots with his fellow Nazis the final solution (the annihilation of the Jews). The meeting only lasted an hour and a half, sealing the fate of millions of European Jews, Heydrich preached the final solution, persuaded, cajoled, threatened the assorted generals and high-ranking civil servants, a Berlin elite. The actor playing Heydrich used method acting (a range of training and rehearsal techniques that seek to encourage sincere and emotionally

---

53 This use of the word homophobic betrays this contemporary debased use of language in Western liberal democracies to express politicized beliefs/disbeliefs. The word *homo* is from the Greek for "same"; a phobia (from the Greek *Phobos*, the personification of fear) is a psychological reaction to a given situation: an extreme irrational fear of something, accompanied by physical symptoms (sweating and revulsion, even sickness, blushing, changes in heart-lung rate, dilation-dilution of eye pupils, skin rashes, and so forth). So is homophobia a specific psychological reaction (e.g., blushing) to sameness? Wiktionary notes, "In the 1990s, behavioral scientists William O'Donohue and Christine Caselles argued that the term homophobia was pejorative. In 2012, the Associated Press Stylebook was revised to advise against using -phobia words in non-clinical ways." https://en.wiktionary.org/wiki/homophobia#English

54 The German High Command, under General Reinhard Heydrich (SS-Obergruppenführer, Chief of the Reich Security Main Office (RSHA) and Deputy Reichsprotektor of Bohemia and Moravia) was convened under the direct orders of Hitler to draft the procedure for the so-called Final Solution. See: https://en.wikipedia.org/wiki/Conspiracy_(2001_film).

expressive performances, including psychological training to be *in* the role for real; often even outside of rehearsals and filming/performing), he commented afterwards how for days he felt polluted by the part, the acting, as though he had convincingly believed all that Heydrich had been, and it had condemned him. Only after returning to his old Cambridge University college, attending the service of Choral Evensong (including the general confession and absolution), so he commented, did he lose the guilt.

So, how do we define heaven? Simple: we don't. God created heaven and the conditions for being there. Most people have a twisted and distorted concept of heaven whereby they simply get to be and do whatever they feel most comfortable and satisfied doing: but is this not the precise nature of original sin repeated over and over again, *ad infinitum*?

XVII. INFERNAL VOLUNTARISM: 3. "ALL GET WHAT THEY WANT; THEY DO NOT ALWAYS LIKE IT"[55]

Therefore, for Lewis, we work out our salvation in this life. Can humanity hold out against the will of God? How does this affect election? Whatever the truth about election and predestination, death will lead to a judgment that none of us can escape: we will be, for Lewis, "decided upon": heaven or hell. Lewis is orthodox on this, but he reads imaginatively into the tradition some piercing observations, drawing out a profound understanding of how through original sin we hold our fate in our hands, how we create little empires (often religious) that have the potential to cause our damnation; the occupants of these little empires won't leave, can't leave. God's *judgment* on us is then, according to Lewis, to exile the human, leave it to its own willfulness, if it will not submit to forgiveness and the joy of heaven. Even hell itself, for Lewis, is effectively self-generated: humanity—having chosen to live outside of the joy of heaven outside of God, having rejected the forgiveness of Christ—merely projects its own fantasy world to live in: which is hell, and is hellish! The inmates of hell will say that they were "sent"[56] and yet their complaint is not because of forced exclusion but that they were not given a choice, yet hell is what

---

55   Lewis, *The Chronicles of Narnia—The Magician's Nephew* (1955), 162.
56   Lewis, *The Great Divorce* (1945), 8 and 27.

6. Election and Predestination: Decision, Faith, and Responsibility

they desired and represented, what they had become, this tiny irrelevant hell is what they chose.

Lewis's approach is essentially through what is now termed in the early twenty-first century *infernal voluntarism*; that is, those who reside for eternity in hell do so of their own volition, they choose hell rather than heaven. Lewis did not use the term infernal voluntarism, but what he outlines in *The Problem of Pain*, *The Screwtape Letters*, *The Great Divorce*, and many other works, is a form of infernal voluntarism. Central to this is Lewis's axiom, all get what they want, all receive their heart desires, all receive what their life led to, but they may not like the end result of their actions and beliefs: "All get what they want; they do not always like it."[57] Lewis likewise asserts, "For all find what they truly seek."[58] The actual term *infernal voluntarism*—to describe the state of this humanly-willed hell, freely chosen—appears to have been first used by Bradley L. Sickler.[59] Sickler notes how a common assumption among the majority of theologians and philosophers is that no one would choose to go to hell, or elect to stay there. The shared assumption is that people go to hell against their will.

> But what if the occupants of hell are not thrown there by God, but, as it were, they freely jump? That view . . . can be called "infernal voluntarism." Instead of assuming that everyone will want to be in heaven, infernal voluntarism takes the position that there are very many people who would sacrifice the joys of a life lived in submission to God in exchange for something else. Odd as it may sound, infernal voluntarism acknowledges that there is something that people may prefer over true flourishing and happiness— namely, rebellion. If the infernal voluntarist position is right, then hell is chosen by its occupants, not foisted on them against their will. Conversely, heaven would be entered by choice too: no one who seriously desires heaven will be denied it. As we shall see, a corollary to at least one famous infernal voluntarist's position is that Christ has made the way to heaven, and it is only through him that anyone enters—but that does not entail that conscious belief

---

57   Lewis, *The Chronicles of Narnia—The Magician's Nephew* (1955), 162.
58   Lewis, *The Chronicles of Narnia—The Last Battle* (1956), 165.
59   Sickler, "Infernal Voluntarism and 'The Deep Courtesy of Heaven'" (2010), 163–78.

in the person and work of Jesus Christ is a necessary condition for being saved by and through him.[60]

Sickler is in effect referring to Lewis when he refers to "one famous infernal voluntarist's position." Furthermore, Sickler, paraphrasing Lewis, comments, "It is critical to Lewis's soteriology that hell is a place people choose to go. . . . [W]ithout that self-choice there could be no Hell. No soul that seriously and constantly desires joy will ever miss it."[61]

XVIII. INFERNAL VOLUNTARISM: 4. TO DEPART, TO CONDUCT ONE'S OWN LIFE

In the Parable of the Sheep and the Goats (Matt 25:31–46), which combines—indeed sets in opposition—the absolute authority and judgment of God with the will of the sinner, we find a clue to this monarchically initiated exclusion: "Then he will say to those on his left, 'Depart from me, you who are cursed, into the eternal fire prepared for the devil and his angels'" (Matt 25:41). The emphasis here is on the word depart: in the New Testament, *poreuesthe* from, *poreueomai* literally "go," to leave, depart, as an order, "go from me," to travel, to remove (oneself), to journey. *Poreueomai* was also used to mean, to conduct one's own life, therefore to proceed away. Does not Jesus in judgment order the sinner away, to go and conduct his or her own life, to proceed and to leave?[62]

Bradley L. Sickler in defense of what is now seen to be Lewis's doctrine of infernal voluntarism—the deep courtesy of heaven[63]—compares God's judgment on the human of "thy will be done" with a naughty and rebellious child who won't apologize and come back into the family but will happily stay in her room forever, who will hold out in her tantrum and will accept the judgment of the parents to be exiled to her room, a judgment she concurs with:

60   Sickler, "Infernal Voluntarism and 'The Deep Courtesy of Heaven'" (2010), 164.

61   Sickler, "Infernal Voluntarism and 'The Deep Courtesy of Heaven'" (2010), 172, paraphrasing Lewis, *The Great Divorce* (1945), 58.

62   In Greek, (Strong's concordance: 4198) *poreuomai* (from *poros*, passageway), properly to transport, moving something from one destination to another, but when used figuratively, to go or depart, emphasizing the personal meaning which is attached to reaching the particular destination.

63   Sickler, "Infernal Voluntarism and 'The Deep Courtesy of Heaven'" (2010), 163–78.

6. Election and Predestination: Decision, Faith, and Responsibility

The father puts her in her room and closes the door. There is much wailing as the girl "receives in herself the due penalty for her sins," but she persists in her refusal to avail herself of the one way out— repentance and compliance with the will of her father. She chooses rebellion and misery over submission and peace. Is it not true in this scenario that (i) the father has judged and disciplined the girl, and (ii) she has chosen to be confined to her room rather than to enjoy the blessings of liberty? And so it seems that something similar might be said about those who have chosen to live in hell. It is true that they have been judged by God, and equally true that they are only in hell because they choose to be. We often have conflicting desires, but the will can only choose one thing. In the case of the rebel who chooses hell, her desire for happiness conflicts with her desire for self-rule.[64]

Humanity, because of the *fall* is abandoned (Lewis's word) by God; proto-humanity was left to the life it had created, the condition of original sin which it had chosen. God's judgment of "thy will be done" to humanity reflects the original condemnation, the exile from Eden: God's punishment to Adam and Eve is exile, banishment. They wanted to live in a way defined by rebellion against God's word, and this is what they got: they were cast out, exiled from Eden (Gen 3:23–24): "All get what they want; they do not always like it."[65] Because of original sin, the humans are abandoned, this is echoed in the last judgment, when the same condemning exile will be spoken by Christ in judgment to many humans. Augustine notes:

> When God abandons them, for their own life, in virtue of which they are immortal, [they] still persist, in however low degree. But in that last condemnation, although a man does not cease to feel, his feeling is not that of pleasure and delight, nor that of health and tranquility. What he feels is the anguish of punishment, and so his condition is rightly called death rather than life. The second death is so called because it follows the first, in which there is a separation of natures which cohere together, either God and the soul, or the soul and the body.[66]

---

64 Sickler, "Infernal Voluntarism and 'The Deep Courtesy of Heaven'" (2010), 175, invoking, in part, Rom 1:27. This is in many ways an extrapolation of a theme common in Lewis's apologetics, in particular in *The Problem of Pain* (1940).

65 Lewis, *The Chronicles of Narnia—The Magician's Nephew* (1955), 162.

66 Augustine, *The City of God* (trans., Bettenson; 1972). See, Bk. XIII, 510.

IN THE HIGHEST DEGREE

Dig deep enough into Lewis's writings and what may seem questionable from a superficial context does appear orthodox. Many stereotypical fire-breathing evangelists warn that Jesus will condemn you to hell; Lewis, the classics scholar, expert in Greek and Latin, and classical literature, for whom the Parable of the Sheep and the Goats was the touchstone of revelation on God's judgment, knew and understood the meaning of and uses of *poreúemai* so that it complemented his invocation of God uttering to the sinner, "Thy will be done": in other words, leave, depart, go from me, remove yourself, *conduct your own life*, and bear the consequences—which will be hellish! The key to understanding the judgment of God is in the will of God (Matt 7:21–23).

Should grace preveniently convert *all* to accept God's proffered salvation? If yes, and a yes should reflect the omnipotent power of a God of love, then why do some continue to resist? The answer we have considered already. The human will is so corrupt and entrenched in original sin that it can hold out against God's grace. A doctrine of original sin is usually what is missing from many of the critics/philosophers who posit *The Problem of Hell*. Is God's grace sufficient and efficient? If so, then is hell the consequence of a free-will rejection of God's love? Punishment as such is self-generated by the individual's self-exclusion from communion with the God of love.[67] Lewis commented:

> I willingly believe that the damned are, in one sense, successful rebels to the end; that the doors of hell are locked on the *inside*. I do not mean that the ghosts may not *wish* to come out of hell, in the vague fashion wherein an envious man "wishes" to be happy: but they certainly do not will even the first preliminary stages of that self-abandonment through which alone the soul can reach any good. They enjoy forever the horrible freedom they have demanded, and are therefore self-enslaved: just as the blessed, forever submitting to obedience, become through all eternity more and more free.
>
> In the long run, the answer to all those who object to the doctrine of hell is itself a question: "What are you asking God to do?" To wipe out their past sins and, at all costs, to give them a fresh start, smoothing every difficulty and offering every miraculous help? But He has done so, on Calvary. To forgive them? They will

---

67 *Catechism of the Catholic Church* (2006). See, Pt. 1, "The Profession of Faith," 2.1, "The Creeds," Ch. 3 "I Believe in the Holy Spirit," Article 12, "I Believe in Life Everlasting," IV. "Hell," §§. 1033–37, 235–37.

6. Election and Predestination: Decision, Faith, and Responsibility

not be forgiven. To leave them alone? Alas, I am afraid that is what He does.[68]

In keeping with a broadly Arminian position, humanity has taken the power to itself to define right and wrong in its own image, likewise it defines the consequences. Those who reject God's love, those who refuse to repent and submit to God's judgment in Christ, these people simply prefer to reign in hell rather than serve in heaven.[69] Some of the damned may not be that bad, but for Lewis, reflecting something of an orthodox tradition, they insist on holding on to something in their lives, something that they should give up and place before God, at the expense of their eternal damnation. Therefore, Lewis will assert that despite the attraction of universalism, despite the divine sufferance (the cross) in seeking the redemption of *all* humanity, some *will* hold out. And the more they hold out the greater the distance between them and the love of God in Christ so that they become more and more entrenched and less able to turn so that they reach a point where they can no longer turn and their condemnation becomes complete.

> Some will not be redeemed. There is no doctrine which I would more willingly remove from Christianity than this, if it lay in my power. But it has the full support of Scripture and, specially, of Our Lord's own words; it has always been held by Christendom; and it has the support of reason. If a game is played, it must be possible to lose it. If the happiness of a creature lies in self-surrender, no one can make that surrender but himself (though many can help him to make it) and he may refuse. I would pay any price to be able to say truthfully "All will be saved." But my reason retorts "Without their will, or with it?" If I say "Without their will" I at once perceive a contradiction; how can the supreme voluntary act of self-surrender be involuntary? If I say "With their will," my reason replies "How if they will not give in?"[70]

Whatever beliefs we or Lewis hold in relation to election and predestination, the importance of faith, or the ability we have left in us to make decisions before the Lord, we will all go the same way: we cannot

---

68   Lewis, *The Problem of Pain* (1940), 115–16. (My emphasis.)
69   Lewis, *The Great Divorce* (1945), 55.
70   Lewis, *The Problem of Pain* (1940), 96–97.

escape death. The crucial word on grace and justice lies with Lewis: "So much mercy, yet still there is hell."[71]

XIX. CONCLUSION: A TEMPORAL PARADOX?

The Bible attests to predestination. How did Lewis consider this? If election is wide open, dependent upon faith, is there, still, in the mind of God, even before the creation, a specific group of humans predestined to be saved? Likewise if election is open to faith-generated works (Matt 25), where is predestination?[72] And if so, by what conditions? Lewis tackled this thorny question through an imagined conversation, in *The Great Divorce*, theologoumena set out with the nineteenth-century Scottish theologian George MacDonald[73] (who Lewis admits was a profound formative influence on much of the structure of his soteriology).[74] This understanding forms a dialectic between faith and predestination, between time and freedom, and posits a temporal paradox. In answering Lewis's puzzlement, the MacDonald character comments (in keeping with the man's actual philosophical theology):

> If ye put the question from within Time and are asking about possibilities, the answer is certain. The choice of ways is before you. Neither is closed. Any man may choose eternal death . Those who choose it will have it. But if ye are trying to leap on into eternity, if ye are trying to see the final state of all things as it *will* be (for so ye must speak) when there are no more possibilities left but only the Real, then ye ask what cannot be answered to mortal ears. Time is the very lens through which ye see—small and clear, as men see through the wrong end of a telescope—something that would otherwise be too big for ye to see at all. That thing is Freedom: the gift whereby ye most resemble your Maker and are yourselves

---

71   Lewis, *The Problem of Pain* (1940), 98.

72   See, Lewis, *The Great Divorce* (1945), ch. 13.

73   Ironically, McDonald was a universalist, So Lewis must have consciously departed from MacDonald's theology on this issue.

74   Beyond the scope of this paper would be the question, To what extent does nature and nurture, the card dealt to each individual, constitute a form of predestination? How likely through biology and upbringing is each individual "predestined" to move to faith-generated works?

6. Election and Predestination: Decision, Faith, and Responsibility

parts of eternal reality. But ye can see it only through the lens of Time, in a little clear picture, through the inverted telescope.[75]

It is because we are *in* time that we see these issues as irreconcilable, and a puzzle. Outside of time, we may conjecture, these questions have already been resolved, the elect have already been chosen as a result of the faith decisions they made in life (and, yes, it will appear as though it had always been so, that they were the elect). Is this what we see as a temporal paradox?—God in eternity knows all that will happen before it happens on earth? Eternity—beyond time, beyond the temporal order of our universe—already sees the saved as chosen from before the creation and therefore as predestined even though they struggled with personified evil *in this life* leading them to make a decision, a willed decision for Christ! The theologoumena character, MacDonald, continued:

> It is a picture of moments following one another and yourself in each moment making some choice that might have been otherwise. Neither the temporal succession nor the phantom of what ye might have chosen and didn't is itself Freedom. They are a lens. The picture is a symbol: but it's truer than any philosophical theorem (or, perhaps, than any mystic's vision) that claims to go behind it. For every attempt to see the shape of eternity except through the lens of Time destroys your knowledge of Freedom. Witness the doctrine of Predestination which shows (truly enough) that eternal reality is not waiting for a future in which to be real; but at the price of removing Freedom which is the deeper truth of the two.[76]

Hence Lewis's comment about how he "was decided upon"[77] despite the fact that he felt there was a moment of pure free will where he was offered a choice: to convert, or not, to accept Christ's salvation, or not. This relates to Lewis's understanding of purgation: purgatory does not exist—those who appear to be in purgatory and gravitate to heaven were in heaven all along; likewise those who gravitate from purgatory to hell were in hell all along.[78] There is no middle ground, no actual purgatory, and no confusion of realities, and yet purgatory/purgation is seemingly

---

75 Lewis, *The Great Divorce* (1945), 105-6. (My emphasis.)

76 Lewis, *The Great Divorce* (1945), 106.

77 Lewis, "Cross Examination" (1971), 217.

78 Lewis, *The Great Divorce* (1945), ix. See also, ch. 9 for a narrative description of this concept.

IN THE HIGHEST DEGREE

very real to those, *post mortem*, in its sufferance (heaven is very real, super-real; by comparison, and despite the level of suffering in them, hell and purgatory are very nearly nothing[79]). What appears to be purgatory is simply a final honing, a refining (1 Pet 1:7; Zech 13:9; Ps 66:10; Rev 8–9, etc.), and preparation of the person for either heaven, *a heaven they are already in*; or they may simply sink deeper and deeper into an eternal hell of their own generation, but they won't be alone. As Lewis noted, "So much mercy, yet still there is hell."[80] Regardless of questions of time and predestination, purgatory and judgment, genuine *faith* is paramount.

---

79 Lewis, *The Great Divorce* (1945). Lewis expounds this in detail throughout.
80 Lewis, *The Problem of Pain* (1940), 98.

Select Bibliography
"In the Highest Degree" Vol. II

LETTERS BY C. S. LEWIS

———. C. S. Lewis to Anne Jenkins, March 5, 1961." In *Collected Letters, Vol. III: Narnia, Cambridge and Joy 1950-1963*, edited by Walter Hooper, 1244-45. San Francisco: Harper San Francisco, 2007.

———. C. S. Lewis to Arthur Greeves, Dec. 6, 1931. In *Collected Letters, Vol. II: Books, Broadcasts and War 1931-1949*, edited by Walter Hooper, 22-25. San Francisco: Harper San Francisco, 2004.

———. C. S. Lewis to Arthur Greeves from Great Bookham, Oct. 12, 1916. In, *Letters of C. S. Lewis*, edited by Walter Hooper, 52. 2nd ed. New York: Harcourt Brace, 1988 [1966].

———. C. S. Lewis to Arthur Greeves, Oct. 18, 1931." In *Collected Letters, Vol. I: Family Letters 1905-1931*, edited by Walter Hooper, 975-77. San Francisco: Harper San Francisco, 2004.

———. C. S. Lewis to The Church Times, Feb. 8, 1952." In *Collected Letters, Vol. III: Narnia, Cambridge and Joy 1950-1963*, edited by Walter Hooper, 164. San Francisco: Harper San Francisco, 2007.

———. C. S. Lewis to Clyde S. Kilby, May 7, 1959." In *Collected Letters, Vol. III: Narnia, Cambridge and Joy 1950-1963*, edited by Walter Hooper, 1044-46. San Francisco: Harper San Francisco, 2007.

———. C. S. Lewis to Corbin Scott Carnell, Oct. 13, 1958." In *Collected Letters, Vol. III: Narnia, Cambridge and Joy 1950-1963*, edited by Walter Hooper, 978-80. San Francisco: Harper, 2007.

———. C. S. Lewis to Dom Bede Griffiths OSB, April 24, 1936." In *Collected Letters, Vol. II: Books, Broadcasts and War 1931-1949*, edited by Walter Hooper, 187-90. San Francisco: Harper San Francisco, 2004.

———. C. S. Lewis to Dom Bede Griffiths OSB, May 23, 1936." In *Collected Letters, Vol. II: Books, Broadcasts and War 1931-1949*, edited by Walter Hooper, 191-95. San Francisco: Harper San Francisco, 2004.

———. C. S. Lewis to Emily McLay, Aug 3, 1953. In *Collected Letters, Vol. III: Narnia, Cambridge and Joy 1950-1963*, 354-55. San Francisco: Harper San Francisco, 2007.

Bibliography

———. C. S. Lewis to H. Lyman Stebbins, May 8, 1945. In, *Collected Letters, Vol. II: Books, Broadcasts and War 1931-1949*, edited by Walter Hooper, 645-47. San Francisco: Harper San Francisco, 2004.

———. C. S. Lewis to his father, March 28, 1921. In *Collected Letters, Vol. I: Family Letters 1905-1931*, edited by Walter Hooper, 534-35. San Francisco, CA: Harper San Francisco, 2004.

———. C. S. Lewis to Lee Turner, July 19, 1958. In, C.S. Lewis, *Collected Letters, Vol. III: Narnia, Cambridge and Joy 1950-1963*, 960-61. San Francisco, CA: Harper San Francisco, 2007.

———. C. S. Lewis to Mary Van Deusen, Oct. 20, 1952." In *Collected Letters, Vol. III: Narnia, Cambridge and Joy 1950-1963*, 237-38. San Francisco: Harper San Francisco, 2007.

———. C. S. Lewis to Mrs Hook, Dec. 29, 1958." In *Collected Letters, Vol. III: Narnia, Cambridge and Joy 1950-1963*, edited by Walter Hooper, 1004-5. San Francisco: Harper San Francisco, 2007.

———. C. S. Lewis to Mrs Johnson, Nov. 8, 1952." In *Collected Letters, Vol. III: Narnia, Cambridge and Joy 1950-1963*, edited by Walter Hooper, 245-48. San Francisco: Harper San Francisco, 2007.

———. C. S. Lewis to Sister Penelope CSMV, May 15, 1941. In *Collected Letters, Vol. II: Books, Broadcasts and War 1931-1949*, edited by Walter Hooper, 484-85. San Francisco: Harper San Francisco, 2004.

ARTICLES BY C. S. LEWIS

Lewis, C. S. "Cross-Examination." In *Undeceptions: Essays on Theology and Ethics*, 215-21. London: Bles, 1971.

———. "De Futilitae," In *Christian Reflections*, edited by Walter Hooper, 57-71. London: Geoffrey Bles, 1967.

———. "God in the Dock." In *Undeceptions: Essays on Theology and Ethics*, 197-201. London: Bles, 1971.

———. "The Grand Miracle," an expansion on the kernel of material initially presented in 1942 at St Jude on the Hill Church. In *Miracles*, 113-38. London Bles, 1947.

———. "The Grand Miracle." Preached in St Jude on the Hill Church, London. In *Undeceptions: Essays on Theology and Ethics*, 56-63. London: Bles, 1971.

———. "Introduction." In George McDonald, *Phantastes*, v-xii. Reprint. Grand Rapids: Eerdmans, 2000.

———. "Is Theology Poetry?" In *They Asked for a Paper*, 150-65. London: Bles, 1962.

———. "It All Began with a Picture . . . ." *The Radio Times*, Junior Section CXLVIII, July 15, 1960. Reprinted in *Of Other Worlds. Essays and Stories*, edited by Walter Hooper, 42. London: Bles, 1966.

———. "The Kappa Element in Romance (1940)." Published as "On Stories," in *Essays Presented to Charles Williams*, edited by C. S. Lewis, 90-105. London: Oxford University Press, 1947.

———. "Miracles." Preached in St Jude on the Hill Church, London, and appeared in *St Jude's Gazette*, number 73, October 1942, 4-7; a shorter version published in *The Guardian*, Oct. 2, 1942. Later published in C. S. Lewis, *Undeceptions: Essays on Theology and Ethics*, edited by Walter Hooper, 5-16. London: Bles, 1971.

Bibliography

———. "Modern Theology and Biblical Criticism." In *Christian Reflections*, 152–66. London: Bles, 1967.
———. "Myth Became Fact." In *Undeceptions: Essays on Theology and Ethics*, 39–43. London: Bles, 1971.
———. "On Myth." In *An Experiment on Criticism*, 40–49. Cambridge: Cambridge University Press, 1961.
———. "Onward, Christian Spacemen." In *The Show* III (Feb. 1963). Reprinted as, "The Seeing Eye." In *Christian Reflections*, 167–76. London: Bles, 1967.
———. "The Poison of Subjectivism." In *Christian Reflections*, 72–81. London: Bles, 1967.
———. "Preface to the Third Edition." In *The Pilgrim's Regress*, xvii. London: Bles, 1944.
———. "Preface." In *George MacDonald: An Anthology*, edited by C. S. Lewis, xxi–xxxiv. London: Bless, 1946.
———. "Psycho-Analysis and Literary Criticism." In *They Asked for a Paper*: Papers and Addresses, 120–38. London: Bles, 1962.
———. "Religion and Rocketry." In *The World's Last Night and Other Essays*, 83–92. New York: Harcourt, Brace and World, 1960.
———. "Religion without Dogma?" *Phoenix Quarterly* 1.1 (1946) 31–44. Republished in *Undeceptions: Essays on Theology and Ethics* (1971), 99–114.
———. "The Seeing Eye." In *Christian Reflections*, 167–76. London: Bles, 1967.
———. "Sometimes Fairy Stories May Say Best What's to be Said." In *The New York Times Book Review*, Children's Section, Nov. 18, 1956. Reprinted in *Of Other Worlds: Essays and Stories*, edited by Walter Hooper, 35–38. London: Bles, 1966.
———. "Transposition." 1st ed. A sermon given in Mansfield College, Oxford on Whit Sunday, 28 May 1944. In *Transposition and Other Addresses*, 9–20. London: Bless, 1949.
———. "Transposition." 2nd ed. In *They Asked for a Paper*, 166–82. London: Bles, 1962.
———. "The Weight of Glory." In *Transposition and Other Addresses*, 21–33. London: Bles, 1949. Republished in *They Asked for a Paper*, 208–9. London: Bles, 1962.

BOOKS BY C. S. LEWIS

Lewis, C. S. *The Abolition of Man: or, Reflections on Education with Special Reference to the Teaching of English in the Upper Forms of Schools*. University of Durham Riddell Memorial Lectures, fifteenth series. Oxford: Oxford University Press, 1943.
———. *Beyond Personality: The Christian Idea of God*. London: Centenary, 1944.
———. *Broadcast Talks. Reprinted with some alterations from two series of Broadcast Talks "Right and Wrong: A Clue to the Meaning of the Universe" and "What Christians Believe" given in 1941 and 1942*. London: Bles, 1942.
———. *Christian Behaviour*. London: Centenary, 1943.
———. *Chronicles of Narnia—The Horse and His Boy*. London: Bles, 1954.
———. *Chronicles of Narnia—The Last Battle*. London: Bles, 1956.
———. *Chronicles of Narnia—The Lion, the Witch and the Wardrobe*. London: Bles, 1950.
———. *Chronicles of Narnia—The Magician's Nephew*. London: Bles, 1955.
———. *Chronicles of Narnia—Prince Caspian: The Return to Narnia*. London: Bles, 1951.
———. *Chronicles of Narnia—The Silver Chair*. London: Bles, 1953.
———. *Chronicles of Narnia—The Voyage of the Dawn Treader*. London: Bles, 1952.

Bibliography

———. *Collected Letters, Vol. I: Family Letters 1905-1931*. Edited by Walter Hooper. San Francisco: Harper, 2004.
———. *Collected Letters, Vol. II: Books, Broadcasts and War 1931-1949*. Edited by Walter Hooper. San Francisco: Harper, 2004.
———. *Collected Letters, Vol. III: Narnia, Cambridge and Joy 1950-1963*. Edited by Walter Hooper. San Francisco: Harper, 2007.
———. *The Dark Tower and Other Stories*. London: Collins, 1977.
———. *The Discarded Image*. London: Cambridge University Press, 1964.
———. *An Experiment in Criticism*. Cambridge: Cambridge University Press, 1961.
———. *The Four Loves*. London: Bles, 1960.
———. *The Great Divorce*: A Dream. London: Macmillan, 1945.
———. *A Grief Observed* (writing as N. W. Clerk). London: Faber and Faber, 1961.
———. *Letters of C. S. Lewis*. Edited by Walter Hooper, 1st ed. London: Bles, 1966.
———. *Letters of C. S. Lewis*. Edited by Walter Hooper. 2nd ed., revised and enlarged. New York: Harcourt Brace, 1988.
———. *Mere Christianity. A revised and amplified edition, with a new introduction, of the three books Broadcast Talks, Christian Behaviour and Beyond Personality*. London: Bles, 1952.
———. *Miracles A Preliminary Study*. 1st ed. London: Bless, 1947.
———. *Miracles*. 2nd ed. London: Bless, 1960.
———. *Of Other Worlds: Essays and Stories*. Edited by Walter Hooper. London: Bles, 1966.
———. *Out of the Silent Planet*. London: Bodley Head, 1938.
———. *Perelandra*. London: Bodley Head, 1943.
———. *The Pilgrim's Regress: An Allegorical Apology for Christianity, Reason and Romanticism*. 1st ed. London: Dent, 1933.
———. *The Pilgrim's Regress: An Allegorical Apology for Christianity, Reason and Romanticism*. 3rd ed. London: Bles, 1944.
———. *The Problem of Pain*. London: Centenary, 1940.
———. *Reflections on the Psalms*. London: Bles, 1958.
———. *The Screwtape Letters and Screwtape Proposes a Toast*. Combined edition with new Preface/Essay, 1961. London: Bles/Centenary, 1961.
———. *The Screwtape Letters*. London: Bles, 1942.
———. *Surprised by Joy: The Shape of my Early Life*. London: Bles, 1955.
———. *Studies in Mediaeval and Renaissance Literature*. London: Cambridge University Press, 1966.
———. *That Hideous Strength. A Modern Fairytale for Grown-Ups*. London: Bodley Head, 1945.
———. *They Stand Together: The Letters of C. S. Lewis to Arthur Greeves 1914-1963*. Edited by Walter Hooper. New York: Macmillan, 1979.
———. *Till We Have Faces*. London: Bles, 1956.
———. *Transposition and Other Addresses*. London: Bles, 1949.
———. *Undeceptions: Essays on Theology and Ethics*. Edited by Walter Hooper. London: Bles, 1971. Published in the USA as God in the Dock: Essays on Theology and Ethics. Grand Rapids: Eerdmans, 1970.

Bibliography

OTHER BOOKS AND ARTICLES

Adams, Marilyn McCord. "Hell and the God of Justice." *Religious Studies* 11.4 (1975) 433–47.

———. "The Problem of Hell: A Problem of Evil for Christians." In *Reasoned Faith*, edited by Eleanor Stump and Norman Kretzmann, 313–24. Ithaca, NY: Cornell University Press, 1993.

Alexander, Samuel. *Space, Time and Deity—The Gifford Lectures 1910–1918*, Volumes I and II. London: Macmillan, 1920.

Appleyard, Bryan. "The True Face of Art." *The Sunday Times* (London), Feb. 13, 2000, 12.

Athanasius. *The Incarnation of the Word: Being the Treatise of St Athanasius, De incarnatione Verbi Dei*. Translated Sr Penelope CSMV. London: Centenary, 1944.

Augustine of Hippo. *Against the Academicians and the Teacher*. Translated by P. King. Indianapolis, IN: Hackett, 1995.

———. *The City of God (De Civitate Dei Contra Paganos)*. Edited by David Knowles; translated by Henry Bettenson. Harmondsworth, UK: Pelican Classics, 1972.

———. *De Spiritu et litterā*. La Vergne, TN: Lightning Source, 2011.

———. "Letter no 102 to Deogratius . . . ," 409 CE. In *Letters of Saint Augustine*. Translated by Revd J. G. Cunningham. In *The Nicene and Post-Nicene Fathers, first series*, Vol. 1, 820. Edited by Alexander Roberts, James Donaldson, Philip Schaff, Henry Wace, *The Early Church Fathers: Ante-Nicene*. Grand Rapids: Eerdmans, 1979.

———. *On Free Choice of the Will*. Translated and edited by Thomas Williams. Indianapolis, IN: Hackett, 1993.

———. *Saint Augustine Confessions*. Translated by Henry Chadwick. Oxford World's Classics. Oxford: Oxford University Press, 1991.

———. "Sermon No. 185 (Homily 3)." In *Ancient Christian Writers 15. St. Augustine: Sermons for Christmas and Epiphany*, edited by Thomas Comerford, 76–79. Mahwah, NJ: Paulist, 1978.

Aulén, Gustaf. *Christus Victor: An Historical Study of the Three Main Types of the Idea of the Atonement*. Translated by A. G. Hebert. London: SPCK, 1931.

Barfield, Owen. *Poetic Diction: A Study in Meaning*. Middleton, CT: Wesleyan University Press Paperback 1973.

———. *What Coleridge Thought*. London: Oxford University Press, 1972.

Barth, Karl. *The Church Dogmatics*. 14 Vols. Translated and edited G. W. Bromiley and T. F. Torrance. Edinburgh: T. & T. Clark, 1936–77.

Baxter, Richard. "What History is Credible, and What Not." In *Church History of the Government of Bishops and Their Councils*, ix–xviii. London: Simmons, 1680.

Berkhof, Louis. *Systematic Theology*. Grand Rapids: Eerdmans, 1938.

Berkeley, George. *Three Dialogues between Hylas and Philonous, in Opposition to Sceptics and Atheists* (1713). London: Dent, 1910.

———. *A Treatise concerning the Principles of Human Knowledge*. Indianapolis, IN: Hackett, 1982.

Black, Max. *Models and Metaphors: Studies in Language and Philosophy*. Ithaca, NY: Cornell University Press, 1962.

Bonhoeffer, Dietrich. *The Cost of Discipleship* (*Nachfolge*, 1937). London: SCM, 1998.

Bonting, S. L. "Theological Implications of Possible Extraterrestrial Life." *Zygon* 38.3 (2003) 587–602.

Bibliography

Brazier, P. H. *C. S. Lewis—An Annotated Bibliography and Resource. C. S. Lewis: Revelation and the Christ, Book 4*. Eugene, OR: Pickwick, 2012.
———. "C. S. Lewis and the Anscombe Debate: From Analogia Entis to Analogia Fidei." *The Journal of Inklings Studies* 1.2 (2011) 69–123.
———. "C. S. Lewis and Christological Prefigurement." *The Heythrop Journal*, 48.5 (2007) 742–75.
———. "C. S. Lewis's Conversion and Karl Barth's Retraktation—'God is God,' a Realization." Paper presented to the Research Institute in Systematic Theology, King's College London, on July 27, 2004.
———. "C. S. Lewis: A Doctrine of Transposition." *The Heythrop Journal* 50.4 (2009) 669–88.
———. *C. S. Lewis—On the Christ of a Religious Economy. I. Creation and Sub-Creation. C. S. Lewis: Revelation and the Christ, Book 3.1*. Eugene, OR: Pickwick, 2013.
———. *C .S. Lewis—On the Christ of a Religious Economy. II. Knowing Salvation. C. S. Lewis: Revelation and the Christ, Book 3.2*. Eugene, OR: Pickwick, 2014.
———. "C. S. Lewis on Revelation & Second Meanings: A Philosophical & Pneumatological Justification." *The Chronicle of the Oxford University C. S. Lewis Society* 7.1 (2010) 18–35.
———. "C. S. Lewis on Scripture and the Christ, the Word of God: Convergence and Divergence with Karl Barth." *Sehnsucht*, 4 (2010) 89–109.
———. *C.S. Lewis—Revelation, Conversion and Apologetics. C. S. Lewis: Revelation and the Christ, Book 1*. Eugene, OR: Pickwick, 2012.
———. *C.S. Lewis—The Work of Christ Revealed. C. S. Lewis: Revelation and the Christ, Book 2*. Eugene, OR: Pickwick, 2012.
———. "'God . . . or a Bad, or Mad, Man:' C. S. Lewis's Argument for Christ—A Systematic Theological, Historical and Philosophical Analysis of aut Deus aut malus homo." *The Heythrop Journal* 55.1 (2014), 1–30.
———. "The Pittenger-Lewis Debate: Fundamentals of an Ontological Christology." *The Chronicle of the Oxford University C. S. Lewis Society* 6.1 (2009) 7–23.
Bunting, Joel, ed. *The Problem of Hell*. Farnham, UK: Ashgate, 2010.
Calvin, John. *Institutes of the Christian Religion*. Edited by John T. McNeill. Library of Christian Classics. 1960. Reprint. Louisville, KY: Westminster John Knox, 2006.
Campbell, Joseph. "Mythological Themes in Creative Literature and Art." In *Myths, Dreams and Religion*, 138–75. New York: Dutton, 1970.
Campbell, Joseph. *The Hero with a Thousand Faces*. Princeton : Princeton University Press, 1968.
Carpenter, Humphrey. *The Inklings—C. S. Lewis, J. R. R. Tolkien, Charles Williams, and Their friends*. London: Allen and Unwin, 1978.
Cary, Phillip, John Doody, and Kim Paffenroth. *Augustine and Philosophy*. Lanham, MD: Rowman and Littlefield, 2010.
Catechism of the Catholic Church. London: Burns and Oats, 2006.
Christensen, Michael J. *C. S. Lewis on Scripture*. London: Hodder & Stoughton, 1980.
Coleridge, Samuel Taylor. *Biographia Literaria: or, Biographical Sketches of My Literary Life and Opinions*. Edited with an introduction by George Watson. 1817. Reprint. Everyman's library 11. London: Dent, 1997.
Collinwood, R. G. *The Idea of History*. London: Clarendon, 1946.
Dearborn, Kerry. *Baptized Imagination: The Theology of George MacDonald*. Ashgate Studies in Theology, Imagination and the Arts. Aldershot, UK: Ashgate, 2006.

Bibliography

Eusebius of Caesarea. *Proparaskeuē Euangelikē* (*Praeparatio Evangelica*; Preparation for the Gospel, c. 313 and 324 AD). Christian Classics Ethereal Library: Online: http://www.ccel.org/ccel/pearse/morefathers/files/eusebius_pe_00_intro.htm.

Evans, C. Stephen. *The Historical Christ and the Jesus of Faith: The Incarnational Narrative as History*. Oxford: Oxford University Press, 1996.

———. "The Incarnational Narrative as Myth and History." *Christian Scholar's Review* 23.4 (1994) 387–407.

———. "Mis-Using Religious Language: Something about Kierkegaard and the Myth of God Incarnate." *Religious Studies* 15 (1979) 139–57.

Ferrier, Jordan C. *Calvin and C.S. Lewis: Solving the Riddle of the Reformation*. North Charleston, SC: CreateSpace Independent Publishing Platform, 2010. https://www.createspace.com/Help/Rights/TermsOfUse.jsp

Feuerbach, Ludwig. *Das Wesen des Christentums*. Gesammelte Werke, Vol. 5. Berlin: Akademie Verlag, 1973.

Fisher, Christopher L., and David Fergusson. "Karl Rahner and the Extra-Terrestrial Intelligence Question." *The Heythrop Journal* 47.2 (2006) 275–90.

Frazer, Sir James George. *The Golden Bough*. Abridged edition. London: Macmillan, 1922.

———. *The Golden Bough: A Study in Magic and Religion*. 3rd ed. 12 Vols. London: Macmillan, 1911–15.

Geisler, Norman L., and Ronald Brookes. *Chosen But Free: A Balanced View of Divine Election*. Bloomington, MN: Bethany House, 1999.

———. *Come Let Us Reason: An Introduction to Logical Thinking*. Grand Rapids: Baker, 1990.

Gunton, Colin E. *The Barth Lectures*. Transcribed and edited by P. H. Brazier. London: T. & T. Clark, 2007.

———. "A Rose by Any Other Name? From Christian Doctrine to Systematic Theology." *International Journal of Systematic Theology* 1.1 (1999) 4–23.

———. *Revelation and Reason: Prolegomena to Systematic Theology*. Transcribed and edited by P. H. Brazier. London: T. & T. Clark, 2008.

Harries, Richard. *C. S. Lewis: The Man and His God*, London: Fount, 1987.

Healey, Nicholas M. "What Is Systematic Theology?" *International Journal of Systematic Theology*, 11.1 (2009) 24–39.

Hebblethwaite, Brian. "Impossibility of Multiple Incarnations." *Theology* 104.821 (2001) 323–34.

Heck, Joel. "Praeparatio Evangelica." In *C. S. Lewis Light Bearer in the Shadowlands*, edited by Arthur J. L. Menuge, 235–57. Wheaton, IL: Crossway, 1997.

Hick, John. *The Metaphor of God Incarnate*. London: SCM, 1993.

———. "Preface." In *The Myth of God Incarnate*, edited by John Hick, ix. London: SCM, 1977.

Hooper, Walter. *C. S. Lewis A Companion and Guide*. London: Harper & Collins, 1996.

Huttar, Charles A., and Peter J. Schakel. *Word and Story in C. S. Lewis*. Columbia, MO: University of Missouri Press, 1991.

Jenson, Robert. *Systematic Theology*. Oxford: Oxford University Press, 1997.

Johnson, Aaron P. *Ethnicity and Argument in Eusebius' Praeparatio Evangelica*. Oxford: Oxford University Press, 2006.

Kant, Immanuel. *Grounding for the Metaphysics of Morals*. Translated by James W. Ellington. 3rd ed. Indianapolis: Hackett, 1993.

Bibliography

Keller, Timothy. *The Reason for God: Belief in an Age of Skepticism*. New York: Dutton, 2008.
Kelsey, David H. *The Use of Scripture in Recent Theology*. London: SCM, 1975.
Kevern, Peter. "Limping Principles: A Reply to Brian Hebblewaite on the Impossibility of Multiple Incarnations." *Theology* 105.827 (2002) 342–47.
Kierkegaard, Søren. *Philosophical Fragments*. Translated by Howard V. Hong and Edna H. Hong. Princeton: Princeton University Press, 1985.
Kilby, Clyde S. *The Christian World of C.S. Lewis*. Grand Rapids: Eerdmans, 1964.
Kroner, Richard. *The Religious Function of Imagination*. Bedell Lectures delivered at Kenyon College. New Haven, CT: Yale University Press, 1941.
Lewes, George Henry. *Comte's Philosophy of the Sciences*. London: Bell & Sons, 1904
Lock, Walter. *The Gospel according to St John*. In *A New Commentary on Holy Scripture, including the Apocrypha*, edited by Charles Gore, Henry Leighton Goudge, and Alfred Guillame, 240–76. London: SPCK, 1928.
———. "History and Character of the Fourth Gospel." *Interpreter*, July, 1907, 442–50.
———. *The Raising of Lazarus: The Message of the Fourth Gospel for Mourners*. London: SPCK, 1915.
Locke, John. *Essay Concerning Human Understanding*. Edited by R. S. Woolhouse. Harmondsworth, UK: Penguin, 1997.
MacDonald, George. "The Fantastic Imagination." In *A Dish of Orts: Chiefly Papers on the Imagination, and on Shakespeare*, 203–8. 1867. Enlarged ed. London: Sampson, Low, Marston, 1895.
———. "The Imagination: Its Functions and Its Culture." In *A Dish of Orts: Chiefly Papers on the Imagination, and on Shakespeare*, 1–28. 1867. Enlarged ed. London: Sampson, Low, Marston, 1895.
———. *Phantastes, a Faerie Romance*. Grand Rapids: Eerdmans, 2000.
———. *Unspoken Sermons: Series I, II, and III*. Charleston, SC: Biblio Bazar, 2007.
Macquarrie, John. *Jesus Christ in Modern Thought*. London: SCM, 1990.
Patrick, James. "C. S. Lewis and Idealism." In *Rumours of Heaven*, edited by Andrew Walker and James Patrick, 156–73. Guildford, UK: Eagle, 1998.
Plato. "The Republic, Bk. II." In *Plato Complete Works*, edited by John M. Cooper, translated by M. J. Levett, revised by Myles Burnyeat, 1001–2. Indianapolis, IN: Hackett, 1997.
———. "Theaetetus." In *Plato Complete Works*, edited by John M. Cooper, translated by M. J. Levett, revised by Myles Burnyeat, 157–234. Indianapolis, IN: Hackett, 1997.
Schakel, Peter J. *Reason and Imagination in C. S. Lewis: A Study of "Till We Have Faces."* Grand Rapids: Eerdmans, 1984.
Scott, David, and Israel Selvanayagam, eds. *Re-visioning India's Religious Traditions: Essays in Honour of Eric Lott*. Delhi: Published for United Theological College, Bangalore by ISPCK, 1996.
Seerveld, Calvin. "Imaginativity." *Faith and Philosophy* 4 (1987) 43–58.
Sickler, Bradley L. "Infernal Voluntarism and 'The Deep Courtesy of Heaven.'" In *The Problem of Hell: A Philosophical Anthology*, edited by Joel Buenting, 163–78. Farnham, UK: Ashgate, 2010.
Swinburne, Richard. *The Concept of Miracle*. London: Macmillan, 1970.
———. *Revelation: From Metaphor to Analogy*. Oxford: Oxford University Press, 1992.
Tillich, Paul. *Systematic Theology*. 3 vols. Chicago: University of Chicago Press, 1951–63.
Tolkien, J. R. R. *The Lord of the Rings*. 3 vols. London: George Allen & Unwin, 1954–55.

———. "Mythopoeia." In *Tree and Leaf*, edited by Christopher Tolkien, 83–90. London: Allen and Unwin, 1978.

———. "On Fairy Stories." In *Tree and Leaf*, edited by Christopher Tolkien, 1–82. London: Allen and Unwin, 1978.

Toynbee, Polly. *Review of The Lion, the Witch & the Wardrobe* (film review). The Guardian, Dec. 5, 2005.

Vincent of Lérins. *The Commonitory of Vincent of Lérins, for the Antiquity and Universality of the Catholic Faith against the Profane Novelties of all Heresies*. Translated by C. A. Heurtley, edited by Philip Schaff and Henry Wace, 207–60. In *The Nicene & Post-Nicene Fathers, Second Series, Vol. 11, Sulpitius Severus, Vincent of Lerins, John Cassian*. Reprint. Grand Rapids: Eerdmans, 2002.

Walker, Andrew. "Scripture, Revelation and Platonism in C. S. Lewis." *Scottish Journal of Theology* 55.1 (2002) 19–35.

Ward, Keith. *God, Faith & The New Millennium: Christian Belief in an Age of Science*. Oxford: Oneworld, 1998.

Wiles, Maurice. "Myth in Theology." In *The Myth of God Incarnate*, edited by John Hick, Ch. 8, 149–62. London: SCM, 1977.

Wirt, Sherwood E., and C. S. Lewis. "Heaven, Earth and Outer Space." *Decision* II, October 1963.

———. "I was Decided Upon." *Decision* II, September, 1963.

Index of Names

Adonis 36, 41, 44, 75, 81
Alexander, Samuel (1859–1938) 99, 183
Alexandria 15
Anscombe, G. E. M. (Gertrude Elizabeth Margaret) (1919–2001) 3, 27–28, 184
Antioch 59, 118
Aphrodite 44
Aquinas, Thomas (1225–74) 3, 10, 16, 29, 46, 64, 154–56
Aristotle (384–322 BC) 20, 25–26
Arminius, Jacobus (1560–1609) 6, 129, 145, 152, 162–63
Aslan 31, 52, 63–65, 66–70, 74, 115, 120
Athanasius of Alexandria (296–373) 15, 24, 118–19, 129, 149, 183
Augustine of Hippo (354–430) 3, 15–16, 31, 33, 46–47, 51–52, 73, 87, 100–101, 145–47, 151–52, 154–56, 163–64, 173, 183–84
Aulén, Gustaf Emanuel Hildebrand (1879–1977) 16, 148, 149, 163, 183

Balder 36, 39–41, 44–45, 52–53, 59, 75–77, 81, 92
Baldhr 45
Barfield (1898–1997) 13, 48–49, 88–89, 97, 183
Barth, Karl (1886–1968) 11, 29, 42, 56–57, 96–98, 120, 142, 151–52, 154–56, 163, 183–85
Baxter, Richard (1615–91) 4, 9, 17–19, 22–23, 183
BBC (British Broadcasting Company, f. 1922) 27–28, 65, 168–69

Berkeley, Bishop George (1685–1753) 3, 6, 14–15, 87, 95–100, 113–14, 131, 183
Berkhof, Louis (1873–1957) 11, 183
Bonhoeffer, Dietrich (1906–45) 148, 183
Bradley, Francis Herbert, OM (1846–1924) 131, 146, 171–72, 186
Bultmann, Rudolf Karl (1884–1976) 35, 103

Calvin, John (1509–64) 47–50, 54, 84, 91, 145–47, 151–55, 159–60, 163–64, 184–86
Cambridge 3, 14, 35, 38, 97–98, 103, 156, 170, 179–82
Campbell, Joseph John (1904–87) 34, 184
Christensen, Michael J. (b. 1953) 35, 103–4, 107, 110, 184
Coleridge, Samuel Taylor (1772–1834) 31, 33, 48–50, 52–53, 73, 85–86, 88–90–92, 183–184

Damascus 59
Dante (Durante degli Alighieri) (1265–1321) 15, 140–42
Davidman, Joy (1915–60) 28
Dearborn, Kerry 83, 184

Einstein, Albert (1879–1955) 130
England 10, 12, 96, 156
Eusebius of Caesarea (aka. Eusebius Pamphili) (263–339) 17, 185

Indices

Evans, C. Stephen (b. 1948) 33, 34, 44, 185

Ferrier, Jordan 159–61, 185
Feuerbach, Ludwig (1804–1872) 36–37, 75, 185
Frazer, Sir James George (1854–1941) 5, 31, 36–37, 39–41, 43–45, 71, 75–76, 185
Freud, Sigmund (1856–1939) 75, 83
Frigga 45

Gagarin, Yuri Alekseyevich (1934–1968) 137–39
God 1–7, 14–15, 21–28, 31, 32, 34–43, 46, 47, 48, 49, 50–56, 59–67, 69, 70–71, 73–75, 76–77, 82–84, 87, 89–92, 95, 98–113, 116–25, 127–43, 145, 146, 147, 148, 149, 150, 151, 152, 153, 154, 155, 156, 157, 158, 159, 160–87
  Almighty 1, 7
  Christ 4–7, 9, 15–19, 21, 23–28, 31, 33–34, 36–37, 39, 40, 42, 44–47, 50–53, 55–57, 60–61, 63–67, 69–71, 73–76, 78–83, 87, 92, 100–101, 106–12, 116–20, 122, 123–25, 128–30, 132–35, 140–42, 145, 147–55, 157–58, 162–66, 170, 171, 172, 173, 175, 177, 184–86
  Christos/Christus 1, 16, 128, 148–49, 163, 183
  Creator 1, 83, 168
  Deus 1, 26, 141, 148, 168, 184
  El Shaddai 1, 7
  Father 1, 21, 47, 71, 80, 106, 118, 120, 129, 133, 134–37, 150, 153–54
  Godhead 119, 149
  Holy Spirit 1, 4–5, 9, 21, 23, 29, 31, 52–54, 76, 80, 83, 92, 99, 100–101, 103, 105–6, 108–9, 120, 122, 129, 134–35, 139, 150, 153, 157–58, 165, 174
  Jehovah 1
  Jesus 4–5, 7, 10, 18–19, 21, 24, 26, 33–34, 40, 42, 44–45, 51–52, 56, 58, 60–61, 64–65, 70–71, 75–76, 79, 81–82, 99, 101–2, 106, 109–10, 113, 116, 119–20, 123, 128–29, 132–38, 140–41, 145, 148–50, 153–55, 157, 162–66, 172, 174, 185–86
  Jesus of Nazareth 1, 18, 42, 79, 81–82, 109, 119, 129, 140, 149
  Lord 1, 4, 7, 10, 27, 33, 43, 68, 71, 81, 99, 106–7, 116, 124, 150, 153, 159, 166–69, 175, 186
  Messiah 1
  Savior 1
  Trinity 6, 21, 24–25, 29, 34, 65, 71, 75, 112, 119, 130, 134–35, 159
  Yeshua 1
  Yhwh 1, 7
Graham, Billy (William Franklin Jn) (1918–2018) 156
Green T. H. (Thomas Hill) (1836–82) 13, 97, 160
Greeves, Arthur 21, 32, 36–37, 76, 179, 182
Griffiths, Bede (1906–93) 3, 16, 179
Gunton, Colin E. (1941–2003) 11, 29, 120, 151–52, 154–55, 185

Hamlet (*The Tragedy of Hamlet, Prince of Denmark*) 6, 127, 130–33, 137, 140–43
Healey, Nicholas M. 11, 185
Hebblethwaite, Brian (b. 1939) 64
Hegel, G. W. F. (Georg Wilhelm Friedrich) (1770–1831) 14, 99, 131
Herbert, George (1593–1633) 15
Hick, John Harwood (1922–12) 34, 185–87
Hoder 45
Hooker, Richard (1554–1600) 15
Hooper, Walter (b. 1931) 32, 63, 67, 76, 83, 179–82, 185

India 41–42, 61, 186
Israel 27, 105, 108–10, 116, 151–52, 186

Jenson, Robert (1930–2017) 11, 185

Indices

Jerusalem 4, 59
Justin Martyr (100–165) 10–12, 15, 96

Kant, Immanuel (1724–1804) 2, 48, 85–86, 92, 185
Kelsey, David (b. 1932) 49, 91, 186
Kierkegaard, Søren (1813–55) 43–45, 51, 54, 185–86
Kilby, Clyde S. (1902–1986) 103–6, 110, 179, 186
Kirkpatrick, William T. (1848–1921) 12, 97

Lock, Revd Dr Walter (1846–1933) 35, 186
Locke, John (1632–1704) 3, 12, 186
Loki 36, 45, 76

MacDonald, George (1824–1905) 48–49, 54, 73, 82–83, 85, 89–92, 146, 167, 176–77, 181, 184–86
Mary 21, 50, 122, 158, 180
McCord Adams, Marilyn (1943–2017) 165
Miller, Jonathan (b. 1934) 36
Milton, John (1608–1674) 15
More, Henry (1614–87) 3, 6, 14–15, 95, 98–99
Moses (d. 1407 BC) 24, 125

Nygren, Anders (1890–1978) 16

Odin 45
Oedipus 34
Orpheus 35
Osiris 36, 41, 45, 51–53, 75–76, 92
Oxford 1–4, 12, 13–14, 23, 33, 35, 37–39, 50, 53, 80, 87, 92, 96–97, 98, 100, 113, 122, 128, 131–32, 136, 180–81, 183–87

Paul, Apostle (c. 5–64/67) 11, 22, 57, 69, 96, 102, 106, 151, 159, 166, 186
Pelagius (c. 360–420) 113
Persephone 44

Pilate, Pontius (d. 38) 39
Plato (c. 428/427 or 424/423) 2, 5, 14, 20, 33, 73, 78–82, 87, 98–99, 114, 186

Ra 45
Rahner, Karl (1904–84) 64, 185

Satan 148–49
    devil 148–50, 157, 165, 172
    Lucifer 148–50, 166–68
Schelling, Friedrich Wilhelm Joseph (1775–1854) 48, 85–86, 92
Schleiermacher, Friedrich (1768–1834) 11
Seerveld, Calvin (b. 1930) 49, 91, 186
Shakespeare, William (c. 1564–1616) 6, 127, 131–37, 139–43, 186
Sickler, Bradley L. 146, 171–73, 186
Sister Penelope 16, 180
Socrates (d. 399 BC) 5, 73, 79
Solomon (d. 931) 4
Spenser, Edmund 15
St. Andrews (Scotland) 11, 96
Stebbins, Hart Lyman 20, 21, 180

Tertullian, Quintus Septimius Florens (c. 160–220) 4
Tillich, Paul (1886–1965) 11, 96, 186
Tolkien, J. R. R. (John Ronald Reuel) (1892–1973) 13, 15, 32–33, 52–53, 56, 57, 69, 73–74, 76, 85, 90, 97–99, 102, 104, 132–33, 145, 167, 184–87
Traherne, Thomas (1636–74) 15

Vidler, Alexander Roper, "Alec" (1899–1991) 35
Vienna 3
Vincentius (Vincentius—Vincent—of Lérins) (d. 445) 4, 9, 17–18, 22–23

Walker, Andrew G. 14, 100, 103–10, 118, 120, 186, 187
Wirt, Sherwood E. (b. 1911) 156–57, 187
Wittgenstein, Ludwig (1889–1951) 3

Zeus 44

Index of Subjects

absolute 15, 70, 86, 100, 102–4, 124, 130–31, 172
  absolutism 87
abstract 14, 34, 38, 57–58, 98, 125
absurd 25, 132, 169
  absurdity 26
academic 2, 11, 17, 23, 29, 36, 38, 62, 87, 96, 99, 104, 137
  academy 4, 11–12, 15, 29, 103
act of faith 166
actuality 4, 6, 37, 46, 51–54, 56–57, 58, 62, 127–28, 131–32, 142, 168
ad infinitum 170
Agnosticism 38
agrarian 60
aim(s) 5, 10, 15, 28, 32, 45, 62–63, 73–74, 77, 81–82, 96, 129, 131, 146, 154, 161
alien(s) 13, 25, 98, 120–21, 149
allegory 54, 63–64, 117
allegorical 63–64, 113
ambiguity 26, 42
ambiguous 26, 51, 110, 169
analogy 22, 25, 27, 43, 46–48, 115, 119, 129, 132–33, 134–37, 140–42
  analogia entis–analogia fidei 4, 9, 29
  analogia entis 4, 9, 27–29
  analogia fidei 4, 9, 27–29
  analogian tēs pisteōs 22
  analogical 6, 27–28, 113, 127, 129–31, 133, 140–42
  analogies 44, 136
  analogy of faith 22
analysis 6, 10, 40, 48, 74, 87, 95
  analytic 2–3, 14, 90, 98, 142
  analyze(ed) 4, 6, 73, 127, 129
  analyzed 46, 159
Anglican 9–10, 20–21, 46–48, 85, 128, 156, 168
  Anglicanism 156
  Anglo Catholic 10

anthropology 36–37
  anthropologist(s) 5, 31, 36, 75
  anthropologists 43, 78
apologetic(s) 2–3, 6, 10–13, 16–17, 22, 25–27, 29, 32, 95–96, 98, 100, 108, 110, 122, 125, 128, 132, 146, 173
  apologia 16
apophatic 57, 118, 123, 139
apostasy 52
  apostate 14, 36, 52, 71, 75, 131, 167
a posteriori 74, 92
apostles 18–20, 59, 124
argument 7, 13–15, 17, 25–27, 98, 100, 115, 125, 140
Arianism 135
Arminian 6, 129, 145, 156–58, 162–64, 175
  Arminianism 153, 163–64
ascend(ed) 7, 129
aseity 70, 104, 112, 125
atheism 1–2, 13, 46, 111, 139
atheist(s) 1, 12, 14, 16, 36, 71, 75, 97, 131
  atheistic 4–5, 29, 36, 52, 64, 78
atonement 6, 16, 82, 119, 127–30, 138, 142, 146–50, 154, 163, 183
  atone(d) 44, 155
  ransom (theory) 6, 127–28, 148–49
authority 4, 9–10, 18, 23, 42, 65, 103–5, 172
avatar(s) 42, 44, 51–52, 73, 130, 135

baptism 55, 103, 148
  baptize(ed) 5, 31, 50, 54–55, 83, 92, 102–3, 110, 116, 122, 138
Barthian 11, 37, 43, 46
belief(s) 1, 4, 6, 10, 13, 16, 18, 20, 26, 36, 41, 46, 65, 71, 69, 81–82, 98–101, 122, 127–28, 132, 146–48, 162, 167, 171, 175
  believer(s) 11–10

Indices

b/Bible 10, 21, 91, 104, 113, 146, 151–52, 160 (See Scripture, gospel)
  biblical 10, 91, 104, 146, 151–52
  biblically 21, 113, 160
blessed/blessèd 68, 174
  blessedness 69
Brechungen 56

Calvinism 160
  Calvinistic 49, 156–59, 163
  Calvinists 152, 160–61, 163–64
Cartesian 14, 98
categorical imperative 86, 92
c/Catholic 3, 4, 9–10, 12, 17–21, 33, 46, 49, 152, 156–57, 163, 165, 174, 184, 187
Chalcedonian 141
character(s) 2, 35, 65, 113, 130–37, 139–42, 176, 177
choice 48, 86–87, 151, 156, 167, 170–72, 176–77
Christ-event 4–5, 9, 15, 21, 23, 31, 61, 73–76, 92
Christianity 4, 13, 15, 17–22, 28, 32–33, 36–37, 44, 47, 58, 70, 75–76, 85, 97, 99, 108, 111–12, 128, 140, 162, 175, 182
  Christian(s) 1–2, 4, 9–11, 13–19, 22–23, 25–26, 28–29, 31–32, 35–36, 38, 40–44, 47, 50, 54, 58, 60, 62, 64, 70–71, 76, 78–84, 86, 97–99, 103, 107, 112, 127–28, 137, 138–40, 146–47, 152, 156, 163–165, 180–87
  Christocentric 41
Christology 5, 24, 31–34, 39, 42–43, 71, 74, 112, 123, 136, 184
  Christological 5, 31, 37–38, 43, 50, 62, 65, 73–76, 93, 104–6, 108, 155, 184
Christus Victor 16, 128, 148–49, 163, 183
chronological-intellectual position 13, 97, 98

church(es) 4, 9–12, 15–23, 28, 33, 74–75, 95, 128, 136, 141, 146–48, 151–52, 154–56, 163–64
Church of England 10, 12, 96, 156
classical 2–3, 12, 14–15, 96–98, 150, 161, 174
cognitive 50, 52, 54, 56–57, 62–64, 70, 83, 92, 149
communication 24, 55, 95, 107, 113, 120
  communicated 6, 24, 35, 87, 92, 95, 119, 123–25, 136
communicatio idiomatum 6, 24, 95, 119–20, 125, 136
condemn(ed) 145, 158, 162–67, 170, 174
confessiones (Augustine) 16
conjecture 64, 177
conscience 108, 111
conscious 48, 53, 59–60, 64, 83, 88, 130–32, 171
  consciousness 22, 44, 80, 88
conversion 1, 3, 12, 15, 27, 32, 37, 41, 46, 67, 73, 76, 86, 108, 119, 149, 156–57
core 4, 9, 17–23, 95, 122
corpus 3, 10–12, 29
covenant 61, 108
creation 5, 9, 16–17, 27–28, 31, 48–49, 52, 60–64, 69–71, 73–74, 76, 85, 88, 90–91, 95, 101–2, 110–11, 113, 121, 125–26, 129, 131, 135, 140–42, 150, 153, 159–61, 165, 176, 177, 184 (see sub-creators)
  created 16, 47, 56, 64–65, 84, 103, 122, 133–35, 141, 148, 159–61, 170, 173
  create(s) 102, 135, 149
  creative 36, 49, 54, 83, 85, 90–91, 133
  creator 13, 16, 52–53, 90, 110–11, 133, 135–37, 141
  creatures 25, 65, 68, 70, 116, 132, 161
Creed(s) 10–11, 19, 22, 119, 141
crime(s) 145, 167
critical 32, 34, 45, 74, 118, 172
criticism 29, 35, 38, 64, 155
cross 6, 40, 55–56, 70, 74, 79, 81, 93, 111, 122, 127–30, 148–49, 158–60, 163, 165–67, 175

193

Indices

c/Crucified 7, 39, 52, 62, 71, 129, 134
crucifixion 7, 22, 28, 78
crucify 7, 141
cultures 32, 51, 59, 105, 108

damnation 156, 170, 175
  damned 152, 155, 159, 167, 174–75
dark/darkness 41, 45, 57, 68–69, 140, 149, 157
death 12, 28, 32, 44–46, 51, 53, 60, 67, 73, 76, 79, 82, 92, 111, 128, 137, 148–49, 152, 156–57, 164–65, 168, 170, 173, 176
  dying 37–38, 40–41, 44, 45, 46, 49, 54, 60, 74–75, 91, 128, 149
debt 6, 15, 127–28, 147
decision 7, 20, 26–27, 68, 87, 145–47, 150, 156–58, 162, 177, 187
  decide 7, 70, 99, 155
de civitate Dei (Augustine) 3, 16
Deity 63, 99, 119, 183
  deification 41–42
  deified 41
  divine(ly) 7, 24, 27, 33, 41–42, 49, 51–57, 65, 76–77, 80–81, 85, 90, 92, 95, 100–101, 104–5, 108, 110, 116, 119–20, 122, 129–30, 133, 135–37, 141, 161–62, 175
  divinity 11, 96
depraved 164
descend 60, 149
determinism 6, 145–47, 162
determination 6, 145, 162
dialectic 4, 15, 39, 95, 102, 125, 176
  paradox 6, 26, 45, 54, 61, 102, 120, 127, 135, 142, 146, 151, 155–59, 162, 166–67, 176–77
dilemma 57–58, 160
diminution 42, 87, 102, 114, 116–21, 123–25, 137
  diminuted 24, 125, 136
dissent(ed) 20–21
divestment 43
Docetic 42
  Docetism 135

doctrine 5, 6, 10–11, 16–24, 29, 51, 59–60, 73–75, 78, 82, 85, 87–89, 93, 95–96, 100–101, 104–5, 112–13, 118–19, 122–26, 129, 133–34, 136–37, 140, 146–48, 152–53, 154–55, 157, 163–66, 172–75, 177
doctrinal 19, 95, 146, 161
dualist 117

Ebionites 135
echoes 46, 51–54, 61–62, 71
election 6, 108–10, 129, 145–59, 162–63, 164–65, 170, 175–76, 185
  elect(ed) 6, 135, 145, 148–52, 154–55, 157–58, 162–65, 171, 177
empiricism 2
encounter 1, 3, 28, 65–66, 81, 108–9, 157
Enlightenment 4, 9, 34, 46
  enlighten(s) 52, 53
entity 4, 141
epistemology 15
epistemic 6, 55, 121, 125
  epistemological(ly) 44, 46, 51, 55
eschaton 25, 28, 62, 65, 68, 70, 82, 128, 148–49
  eschatological(ly) 67, 74, 113, 117, 128, 135, 146–49, 165
  f/Four last things 9, 17, 148
esse est percipi 15, 99
essence 4, 18, 24, 136, 148, 164
essentia 4
essential(s) 4, 7, 20, 24, 55, 90, 117, 119, 129–31, 135, 164
essentials 4
eternity 21, 24, 55, 87, 95, 100, 107, 112–14, 116–18, 120–26, 135–36, 141, 149, 151–52, 154, 165, 171, 174, 176–77 (see heaven)
  eternal 6, 21, 23–24, 44, 48, 53, 88, 89, 100, 104, 114, 118–20, 123, 127, 135, 152–53, 172, 175–78
Eucharist 118
Evangelical(s) 2, 4, 9, 10–12, 17, 27, 102, 164–65

194

Indices

evangelists 26, 174
exclusion 146, 166–67, 170, 172, 174
    exclude 6, 10, 109, 112, 121, 129, 145, 166
existentialism 2
ex nihilo 62

fable 33 (see story)
fact 5, 12–13, 17, 31, 39, 53, 55, 58, 60, 76, 87, 103, 107, 156, 158–60, 177
factuality 39
faith 1, 2, 4, 6, 9–13, 16–18, 22, 25, 28, 32–34, 38, 40–44, 52, 69, 76, 112, 122, 128–29, 136, 145–46, 148, 150, 152–56, 158–59, 162, 163, 164, 165, 166, 174–78, 183, 185–87
fall, the 6, 9, 16–17, 28, 44, 50–51, 87, 92, 103, 113, 145, 148, 152, 158, 160–62, 164, 173
    fallen 50, 55, 60, 71, 77, 79, 92, 101–2, 104, 125, 142, 145, 148–50, 153, 162–64, 166
    fallenness 26, 54, 57, 141
    falls 43, 45, 76, 121, 148
    free will 7, 83, 86, 101, 140, 158, 160, 166, 168, 177
    free-will 6, 87, 158, 174
    original sin 5–6, 16, 28, 31, 44, 50, 54–55, 83, 130, 142, 145, 162, 164–65, 166, 170, 173–74
    postlapsarian 57, 147
    prelapsarian 148
    rebel 134, 141, 168, 173
    rebellion 148, 158, 160, 165–66, 171, 173
    will 2–3, 6, 19, 21, 25, 29, 33, 38, 40, 44, 46, 48–49, 54–55, 58, 62, 64, 67, 69, 70–71, 78–79, 82–84, 86–88, 90, 92–93, 95–96, 101–8, 110, 112–14, 116, 120–30, 133, 135, 137, 139–42, 146–47, 150–61, 163–64, 166–68, 170–77
    willfulness 170
fallibility 24–26, 95, 120, 136
false 13, 17, 34, 49, 65, 68, 98

fantasy/fantasies 83, 170
Fathers 20, 183, 187
fiction 34, 63–64, 87, 103, 120
fideist 25
flesh 6, 42, 45, 47, 62–63, 106, 119, 127–30, 131, 135, 149
foreshadowing 46, 82
forgiveness 42, 109, 128, 147–48, 170
forms 2, 15, 23–24, 64, 99, 136, 176
foundation 11, 14, 22, 135, 153
foundational 3, 10, 99, 152, 156
freedom 43, 70, 76–77, 87–88, 101–3, 112, 125, 158–61, 163, 174–77
fundamental 2, 14, 40, 82–83, 86–87, 107

glory 43, 67–68, 110, 150
gnostic 117
    g/Gnosticism 117, 135
good(ness) 26, 32, 79–80, 100, 106, 108, 110–11, 113, 121, 129, 136, 137–39, 148, 152, 158–61, 163–64, 168, 174
    good 69, 79, 80, 163
gospel 2, 4, 16–17, 33, 35, 53, 58, 60–64, 75, 103, 116, 123 (*See* Scripture

heaven 6, 28, 38, 43, 53, 58, 68–69, 80, 108, 113, 129–30, 133, 145–50, 152–54, 162, 166–72, 175, 177–78 (see eternity)
Hegelianism 97, 131
hell 6, 28, 69, 116, 128–29, 145–50, 158, 162, 165–68, 170–78
heresy 18, 135–36
    h/Heretical 18
    heterodox 133, 141
Hinduism 32, 41–42, 54
history 10, 19, 21–23, 28–29, 33, 38, 40, 57, 61, 74, 80–81, 93, 101, 103, 106–8, 111, 116, 148–49, 151–52, 168
    historical(ly) 33–40, 44, 46, 49, 54, 57–58, 103–5, 109, 110–52, 154, 169
    historicism 41
    historicity 33, 39, 103–4
    non-historical 33, 35

Indices

human(s) 3–6, 12, 22, 24–26, 28, 31, 34–37, 41–45, 47–48, 50, 52–55, 57, 59, 70–73, 75, 77–78, 80, 82, 84, 86–89, 92–93, 95, 100–2, 104, 106–12, 116–17, 119–25, 127, 129–31, 133–38, 140–41, 145, 148–50, 152, 154–55, 157–64, 165, 170, 172–74, 183, 186
    h/Humanity 7, 13, 22, 27–28, 34, 37, 40, 50, 64, 70–71, 79–80, 82–84, 87, 89, 90, 92, 95, 98, 101–4, 108–9, 111–12, 117–19, 123–25, 127–28, 130, 133, 136–37, 141–42, 145,–49, 152, 154–55, 157, 160–62, 164–65, 170, 173, 175
    humanly 50, 92, 171
humiliation 42–43
humility 19, 42–43, 70, 123, 142

idea(s) 2, 5–6, 13–15, 31, 37, 40–44, 49, 51–55, 59–60, 64, 74, 76, 82–84, 88, 89, 98–101, 106, 114, 120–21, 123, 131, 134, 137, 161 (see thought and understand)
    idealism 2–3, 13–15, 23–24, 46, 48, 58, 85, 92, 97–99, 113, 123, 131–32, 136, 186
    idealists 48, 113
    idealize 48, 88
idol(s) 73, 75, 84
    idolatrous 73, 121
    idolatry 73, 84
illumination 33, 47, 53,–55, 59, 73, 80–81, 100–2, 117
    illuminated 49, 54–55, 92, 125
image(s) 20, 47–51, 53–55, 57, 63, 83–85, 86, 89–92, 113–18, 168, 175
imagination(s) 5, 31–33, 38, 43–44, 46–52, 53, 54, 55–58, 73–75, 80, 82–86, 88–92, 100, 102–3, 109–10, 113–15, 122–23, 134, 142, 184, 186
    imaginary 63–64, 83, 140
    imaginative 36, 49, 53–55, 58, 83, 91, 146
    imaginatively 133, 170

immaterialism 15, 99
immortal 26, 119, 173
immutable 82, 134
impartiality 102, 147
incarnation 5, 6, 9, 17, 22, 24–25, 28, 31–33, 36, 38–46, 49, 51–54, 56–59, 60–62, 64–65, 71, 73,–75, 78, 81, 82, 92–93, 95–96, 107–13, 118–21, 124–25, 127, 129–32, 133, 135–36, 138–39, 142, 142, 149, 183
    incarnate(d) 7, 25, 32, 34, 41, 42, 44, 45, 54, 60, 63, 64, 65, 67, 70, 74, 75, 99–100, 110, 112, 125, 129–31, 134, 136, 140, 141, 148–49
    incarnational 23, 24, 40, 42, 44, 45
infernal voluntarism 6, 129, 146, 169, 171–72
infinite 48, 70, 88, 90, 104
inspiration 2, 33, 46–47, 50, 54, 63, 77, 80–82, 92, 101–6
intellectual(s) 7, 12–14, 36–38, 48–49, 51, 89–91, 97–98, 158
    intelligible 2, 136
interpret 18, 92
    interpretation(s) 2, 5, 18, 20, 31, 52, 55, 73–75, 77, 81–82, 86–87, 124–25
intimation(s) 4–5, 31, 47, 51–53, 55–57, 59–62, 66, 71, 73–76, 83, 91–93, 99, 100–1, 107, 108–10, 11-–13, 116, 12–23, 128, 141
irresponsibility 169

joy 44–45, 76, 167, 170, 172
judgement/judgment 6, 28, 49, 74, 79, 82, 91, 128–30, 145–50, 156, 158, 162, 166, 170, 172–75, 178
Justice 147, 165, 183
justification 16, 71, 148, 159

Kantian 14, 98
kenosis 42–43, 133
    Kenosis 136–137
    kenotic 24, 42, 43, 136, 137
    self-emptying 42–43, 54, 120

Indices

know(s) 15, 19, 23, 24, 39, 55, 57, 58, 67–69, 70, 71, 77, 82, 84, 99, 100, 104, 106, 114, 116, 120, 124–26, 128, 133, 139, 141, 149, 150, 153, 155, 159, 160, 161, 164, 177, 168
    knowledge 22, 24, 36–37, 41, 44, 46, 52, 55, 56, 57, 62, 64–65, 70–71, 73,-74, 78, 80, 82, 88, 90–91, 100, 105, 110–11, 118, 123, 130, 133, 149–50, 177
    knowability 24, 95, 120, 136
    knowing 88, 119, 128, 139
    unknowable 112, 120, 129, 136

language 86, 113, 120–23, 130, 135, 168–69
    linguistic 28, 169
law 16–17, 25–26, 47–48, 63, 86, 88, 108–9, 161, 166
    law of excluded middle 17, 25–26
laws 25, 87, 108, 124, 142, 159
legend 33, 38, 58, 106
l/Liberal 4, 9–10, 12–17, 96, 128, 145–46, 148, 165, 169
lie(s) 20, 32, 53, 71, 76–77, 122–23, 125, 132, 175–76
light 5, 14, 27, 31–33, 41, 44–45, 47, 51–54, 56–57, 62, 67, 73–74, 76, 80–81, 92, 98, 100–102, 104, 121–22, 124–25, 140, 148
literature 1, 12, 15, 32–35, 48, 103, 105, 124, 174
    literary 6, 35, 38, 43, 82, 83, 86, 95, 122, 130
liturgy/liturgical 54–55
logic 1, 13, 25–26, 65, 97–98, 115, 164
    logical 1–4, 7, 13, 16, 26, 29, 142, 152
    logically 1, 99, 165
    logical positivism 2–3, 13
Logos 7, 14, 23–25, 45, 53, 55, 76, 99, 118
logos asarkos–logos ensarkos 135, 142
Lordship 1

love 12, 28, 45, 62, 65, 67–68, 70, 76, 86, 90, 97, 102, 108–9, 111–13, 119, 128, 135, 150, 159–60, 166, 168, 174–75

martyrdom 79
meaning(s) 5, 33, 34, 37, 44, 52–54, 61, 73–75, 77, 80–83, 87, 92–93, 96, 100, 105, 109, 117, 123–24, 169, 172–74
medieval 14–15, 19, 98, 152, 163
mere/meer 4, 9, 19–23, 37, 57, 81, 95, 105, 113, 122, 133, 135
merus 4, 9, 19, 22
messianic 42
metaphysical(ly) 34, 46
method 2–4, 9, 10–12, 17–22, 25, 27, 29, 39, 99, 124, 169
mind 1, 3, 13, 48–49, 51, 53–54, 59, 75–77, 83, 85–90, 92, 100–102, 106, 117–18, 121, 125, 132–34, 150, 158, 165, 176
miracle(s) 28, 37–39, 43, 48–49, 59–61, 82, 104–5, 151, 180, 182, 186
    miraculous(ly) 77, 104, 159, 174
mission(ary) 4, 9, 128, 142
modalism 134
modern 2–3, 12–16, 19, 20–23, 33–34, 38, 77, 86, 96, 98–99, 112, 124, 134, 145–49, 165
    modernism 20, 93, 96
    m/Modernist 4, 6, 9–10, 13, 17, 98, 127
moral 16, 86, 105–106, 108, 111, 137, 161
mortal 26, 176
multiple incarnations 64–65
myth(s) 5, 31, 32–41, 43, 44, 46, 49, 50, 51, 52, 53, 54, 55, 56–59, 60, 61–62, 64, 65, 69, 71, 73, 74, 75, 76, 77, 78, 80–82, 89, 91, 92, 103, 105, 106, 108, 109, 111, 112, 128, 181, 185, 187
    mythopoiia/mythopoios/mythos 33f.
    mythical 35, 38–39, 54, 103
    mythological 33–34, 39, 46
    mythology(ies) 32, 36, 42, 44–45, 52, 54, 62, 76
    mythopoesis 33

Indices

mythopathic 53, 59
m/Mythopoeia 31–33, 52–53, 73, 76, 187
mythopoeic(ally) 5, 31–32, 39, 52–53, 57–58, 59, 62, 71–74

narrative(s) 4–6, 22, 27–28, 31–33, 39–40, 45, 51–52, 54, 57–59, 61–62, 65, 71, 74–75, 81, 108, 115, 122, 127, 131, 142, 177 (see fable & story)
natural theology 5, 31, 33, 36–38, 46–47, 51–52, 54, 61, 73–74 (see philosophy)
nature 2, 7, 10, 14, 17, 38, 41–43, 45, 51–52, 59–61, 64, 79, 86, 89, 99, 106, 109, 117–19, 124–25, 129, 133, 136–39, 141–42, 146, 149, 159, 161, 168, 170, 176
Neoplatonism 2 (see Platonism)
non-historical 33, 35 (see history)
numinous 35, 107–12, 116, 122

objectives 77, 82
omnipotence 41, 159
omniscience 41
ontology 6, 42, 123, 125, 131, 138
    ontological(ly) 7, 42–46, 51, 65, 129, 112, 133, 135, 161
    ontic 7, 133
oral traditions 40
orderly 11
orthodox(y) 3, 5, 9, 11, 15–17, 19–22, 29, 31–33, 39, 76, 122, 128, 133–34, 145–46, 148, 150, 165, 170, 174–75

pagan(s) 17, 32, 39–41, 45, 46, 50–55, 56, 61–65, 66–67, 69, 71, 73–75, 78, 80, 82, 84, 92, 105–6, 108–9, 11–12, 128
pantheist 139
    panentheist 139
pardon/pardoning 147
parousia 125
p/Passion 5, 71, 73, 79–81, 85, 164–65

patristic 2–5, 9–10, 14–19, 22–23, 58, 87, 98, 122, 136, 148, 163
p/Perception 12, 15, 23, 48, 53, 55, 60–62, 78–79, 86, 88–89, 111, 120–23, 135, 138, 141
    perceivable 2, 13, 86, 112, 136
perlocutionary 52, 59, 71, 105
person 21, 24, 39, 55, 65, 71, 79, 107, 119–120, 131, 133–35, 151, 165, 166–69, 172, 178
    persons 47, 130, 134, 141, 166
    personality 41, 57, 133
phenomenology 2
philosophy 1–5, 10–15, 24, 26, 44, 47, 49, 84–86, 88, 91, 95–96, 98, 100, 119, 125, 131–32, 145 (see natural theology)
    p/Philosopher(s) 1–3, 5, 9–11, 13–14, 15–16, 28, 31–33, 46, 48, 73, 85, 87, 96–99, 104, 112, 127–29, 131, 145–46, 165, 171, 174
    p/Philosophical 1–4, 6, 7, 9–17, 26–29, 43, 44, 51, 73–75, 86–87, 92, 95–96, 97–99, 104, 122, 131–32, 146–147, 149, 176–77, 184, 186
piety 36, 41
    pietism 63–64
Platonism 2, 5, 14, 20, 95–97, 100–109, 118, 131, 135, 187
    Neoplatonism 2
    Platonic(ally) 2–4, 9, 20, 24, 29, 33, 46, 52, 56, 58, 61, 69, 81, 97, 100, 113–14, 122, 125, 136
    Platonist(s) 2, 3, 14, 15, 20, 81, 98, 99, 113
pneumatology 5, 31, 32, 74
    pneumatological(ly) 23, 29, 50, 61–62, 68, 71, 75, 83, 92
poem(s) 32, 53, 73, 76, 80–81, 140
    poetry 73, 87–88, 105
poet 31, 33, 48, 73, 80–82, 85, 90, 105, 141
political 2, 13, 41, 105, 160, 168
poreúesthe 146, 172
positivism/positivistic 2, 3, 13–14, 97–98

Possession/possess(ed) 26, 41–42, 135, 149
postmodernist 4, 9 (see modern)
potential 45, 71, 74–76, 90, 135, 145–47, 154, 156–58, 170
praeparatio evangelica 4, 9, 16–17, 27, 185
pragmatism 2
prayer(s) 41, 132, 159
preach(ed) 37–38, 102, 116, 151, 169
  preacher 7
  preaching 4, 116, 148
p/Predestination 6, 145–47, 152, 155–59, 162–63, 165, 170, 175–78
  predestined 150, 154, 157, 160–61, 164, 176–77
prefigurement(s) 5, 31, 33, 37–40, 42–44, 46, 49, 51–52, 54–56, 61, 64, 73–78, 80–82, 91, 93, 104
  prefigure(s)/prefigured 5, 31, 39–40, 43, 46, 51, 69, 74, 78
  prefiguring 5, 31, 50, 71, 92
premonitions 108–9, 111
Presbyterian 137, 156
principle(s) 4, 9, 11–12, 14, 20, 21, 23, 29, 43, 56, 58, 60, 71, 86, 88, 99, 107, 114, 132, 152, 155, 164
professional 11–12, 29, 48, 112
projection 36, 79
proof(s) 2
prophecy 5, 73, 77–79
propitiare 147
propitiation 147
proposition(s) 3, 5, 6, 10–13, 22, 24–27, 33, 38, 39–40, 51, 55, 59, 73, 74, 87, 93, 97–99, 102, 104, 114, 127, 149, 160
Protestant(s) 2, 11, 14, 19–21, 35, 152, 164
  Protestantism 21, 164
psychology 78
  psyche 75
  psychological 1, 34–36, 55, 86, 121, 165, 169–70
  psychologically 46
purgatory 10, 177–178

purgation 10, 149, 167, 177
Puritan 4, 9, 17, 19, 21–22
Puritanism 21

quod ubique, quod semper, quod ab omnibus 18

rational 2, 11, 14, 25, 54–55, 64, 97–98, 108, 149 (see reason)
rationalism 2
rationality 86
read 3, 5, 12, 15–16, 31, 35, 37–39, 46, 52–53, 74–77, 81, 92, 103, 105–6, 110, 122, 124, 155, 163
realism 2, 14, 98, 121
  reality 2–3, 5, 14–15, 24–25, 31, 39–40, 46, 53–55, 58–65, 69, 71, 74, 76, 83, 86, 90–91, 98–100, 103, 105, 107–9, 112–14, 117–18, 120–21, 123, 125, 128, 132, 135–36, 138, 142, 149, 159, 177
reascend 60, 129, 149
reason(s) 3, 6–7, 11, 14, 25–28, 63, 74–75, 78–79, 80, 86–87, 95–98, 100–102, 104, 119, 123, 125, 141, 175 (see rational)
  reasoned 1, 4, 7, 16, 29
  reasoning 1, 4
reconciliation 70, 147
  reconcile 44, 71, 166
  reconciled 70, 155, 159, 166
  reconciling 44, 131
re-create 48, 88
redemption 51–52, 55, 70–71, 76, 82, 130, 137, 175
  redeem(ed) 61, 69, 71, 149, 151, 167, 175
reductio ad absurdum 17, 25–27, 99
Reformation 2, 16, 145, 152, 161–63, 169, 185
  Reformed 2, 11, 47–50, 52, 54–55, 84–85, 91, 98, 154, 164
refractions 56–57, 61–62, 71, 73
regula fidei 22
relativity 130

Indices

religion(s) 10, 13, 16,–19, 36, 41–42, 47, 51, 54, 58, 61–64, 69–70, 75–76, 97, 111, 127–29, 131, 138–40, 158
  religionist 5, 31, 36, 75
  religious 5, 12–13, 31–33, 36, 39, 48, 52, 55, 56–57, 60, 65–67, 70, 73, 75, 84–85, 89, 97, 108, 111, 117, 136, 149, 158, 168, 170
repentance 148–49, 173
responsibility 6, 108, 130, 145–47, 157, 159–60, 162, 165
  responsible 86, 160–61, 165, 168–69
resurrection 5, 9, 17, 22, 28, 31–33, 39–40, 45–46, 51–54, 56–62, 64–65, 68, 71, 73–76, 78, 81–82, 93, 105, 108, 111, 118, 129, 149
  resurrect(ed) 7, 44, 52, 55–56, 71, 129, 149
revelation 2, 6–7, 11, 14, 23–24, 26, 28, 32–33, 37, 42–43, 46, 47–48, 51–52, 55–56, 61, 63, 71, 73–75, 81–84, 87, 92, 95–97, 100–113, 115–27, 130, 132, 136, 140, 155, 174, 184–87
  prevenience/prevenient 33, 50–51, 73, 92, 159
  preview 78–79
  previse 5, 73, 78
  prevision 51, 77–79
  revealed 24, 42–43, 46–47, 99, 105, 107, 109, 119–25, 154
  reveal(s) 43, 51, 101, 104, 108–9, 112, 120, 135, 153
rhetoric 10
  rhetorician(s) 3, 10
righteousness 69, 78, 168
Roman Catholic 3, 10, 20–21, 33, 152, 156–57, 163, 165
rule 18, 22, 60, 149, 173

sacrament(s) 10, 117, 118
  sacramental 117–18, 122
sacred 102–3, 105, 117
sacrifice 16, 64, 69–70, 80, 106, 130, 134, 147–48, 153, 165, 171

salvation 7, 10, 22, 28–29, 56, 65, 71, 92, 112, 117, 127, 129, 132–35, 136, 140–42, 145–46, 147–54, 156–58, 162–66, 168, 170, 174, 177
  salvific 5, 15, 31, 40, 50–51, 55, 59, 66, 71, 74, 76, 82, 92, 106, 113, 118, 128, 157
  saved 47, 69–70, 128, 145, 147, 150–52, 154–56, 159, 162, 165, 172, 175–77
scapegoat 45, 76
scholasticism 14, 98, 152
science-fiction 63–64
scientia/scientiae 88
scientific 34, 78, 90–91, 103–4, 123, 138–39
Scripture 4–6, 9, 14, 17–23, 26, 35, 49, 52, 80–81, 91, 95–96, 100–110, 113, 116, 118, 124–26, 151, 153, 175, 184, 186–87 (*See* Bible, Gospel)
second coming 9, 25, 28
segregation 6, 145
s/Sehnsucht 108–12, 116, 122, 184
  yearnings 88
self 6, 12, 15–16, 25, 36–37, 42–43, 51–52, 54–56, 60, 64, 74, 77, 85–86, 88, 96–97, 99, 101, 104, 107–8, 110, 119–20, 124–25, 129, 133, 135, 140, 145, 154, 159–60, 162, 165, 167, 170, 172–75 (see human)
  self-defined 165
  ego/egotistical 102
  self-determined 162
  self-enslaved 174
  self-righteous 167
shadowlands 15, 87, 99, 102, 123, 136
sheer 4, 9, 19, 21, 22, 43, 78
simul iustus et peccator 55, 71
simultaneity 6, 99, 127, 130, 134
  simultaneous 129–30, 147
  simultaneously 25, 86, 99, 108, 119, 133, 134–35, 140–41
sin(s) 5–6, 16, 23–28, 31, 44, 50, 54–55, 70, 83, 95, 112, 118, 128–30, 134, 142, 145–47, 148–49, 152, 158, 162–66, 168–70, 173–74

Indices

sinful 123, 153
sinless 79
skepticism 97, 115
  skeptical 29, 69, 146
  s/Skeptics 85, 115-16, 137
societies 41, 51, 59, 61, 71
sociological 34, 86
socratic 3
soteriological(ly) 44, 46, 51, 71, 128, 146, 172, 176
spiritual 35, 38, 48, 58, 89, 100, 106, 113-14, 117-18, 131, 142, 149, 169
splintered fragments of the true light 5, 31, 52-53, 56-57, 74
statement 6, 7, 18, 25, 127
story 27, 32-40, 44-46, 49, 51-53, 55, 58-60, 63, 66, 71, 74, 89, 92, 103-5, 114-15, 121, 123, 133, 149 (see fable & narrative)
  stories 4, 34-35, 37, 40-41, 43, 45, 49, 52, 54, 59, 63, 65, 73-6, 81, 87, 91-92, 109, 111, 125
sub-creators 53, 102, 133
subjective 1, 15, 88, 96, 99-100, 110, 120
suffering(s) 45, 63, 76, 79, 81, 119, 121, 134-38, 178
  sufferance 175, 178
Summa theologiae 3, 16, 31, 46
supernaturalists 10, 17, 19
supposal 25, 52, 63-64, 74
supposition 63, 133
syncretism 70
  syncretistic 70
systematic theology 11, 28, 29
  systematic 4, 9-11, 28-29, 32, 56, 87-88, 96, 112, 124
  systematically 11, 46, 88, 102, 104, 124, 142

technique 4, 9-10, 12, 20, 25-27, 29
telos 28 (see *eschaton*)
  teleologically 28, 62, 95, 112, 125
temporal 61-62, 71, 112, 120, 130, 135, 139, 146, 151, 162, 176-77
  temporality 6, 41, 121, 127, 138, 142

theist 13, 97, 99
  theistic 6, 16, 41, 127, 131
theodicy 160
theology 1-5, 7, 9-11, 13, 15-17, 23, 27-29, 31, 33, 34, 36-39, 46-47, 49, 51, 52, 54, 58, 61, 73-74, 84, 91-92, 96, 98, 110, 119, 122, 132, 161, 176
  theologian(s) 1-3, 6, 9-10, 12, 14, 15-17, 22, 29, 31-35, 39, 46, 47-50, 73, 84, 85, 87, 91, 95-98, 107, 112, 128, 129, 137, 141, 145, 146, 147, 154, 162, 165, 171, 176
  theological(ly) 2, 3, 4, 6, 7, 9, 10, 11-12, 15, 16, 22, 25-29, 33, 49, 50, 54, 64, 91, 92, 95-96, 96, 108, 112, 113, 122, 130, 134, 146, 154, 164, 169, 183, 184, 186
  theologoumena 130, 176-77
theophanic 64
theories 2, 6, 32-33, 50, 56-57, 86, 127-28, 130, 147, 154, 163
thought 1-3, 5, 13-14, 25-26, 29, 36, 44, 47-49, 58, 63, 67, 73-74, 79, 84, 89, 97-98, 108, 131, 139 (see ideas and understand)
  think(ing) 2, 4, 11, 45, 47, 49, 58-59, 65, 70, 84-85, 89, 92, 115, 121, 132, 146, 138, 141, 152, 161, 169
t/Time 1, 5, 9, 12, 20, 36, 47-49, 52, 61-63, 66-67, 73, 88-89, 91, 99, 112, 114, 120, 130-31, 134, 135, 138-39, 141, 151, 153, 156-57, 159, 167, 176-78, 183
total depravity 164 (see sin)
tradition 3, 5, 9, 16-17, 21-23, 32, 47-49, 52, 54-55, 59, 64, 84-85, 91, 95, 101, 105, 145-47, 150, 152, 155, 170, 175
  traditions 4, 9, 40, 42
  traditional 3, 10, 29, 112, 118, 146, 148, 156-57, 159-60, 165
transcendent 2, 37, 70, 86-87, 119
  transcendence 42-43
  transcendental philosophy 85-86, 88

201

Indices

transposition(s) 5, 6–7, 23–24, 51, 60, 87, 95–96, 101–2, 113–26, 136–37, 181–82, 184 (see communicated)
  imparted 6, 24, 74, 87, 95, 125
  impartial 102, 145, 147
  translation 123, 125, 136
  transposed 6, 7, 24–25, 87, 95, 113, 116, 118, 120, 122–23, 125, 136–37, 141
  transpositional 113, 119, 122, 124–25
  transubstantiation 21, 118
tribal(al) 41–42, 59, 75
Trinity 21, 24–25, 29, 34, 65, 71, 75, 112, 119, 130, 134–35, 159
  Trinitarian 6, 33, 119, 125, 134, 137
  triune 6, 119, 125, 130, 149 (see name index: God)
truth(s) 3, 10, 12, 16, 18, 21, 23, 25, 26, 34, 49, 50, 51, 52, 53, 54, 56, 57, 58, 62, 68, 70, 77, 78, 79, 80, 81, 82, 83, 87, 90, 91, 92, 93, 97, 99, 100, 101, 102, 103, 104, 106, 110, 113, 116, 122, 123, 124, 125, 128, 138, 153, 170, 177
  true 5, 17, 19–20, 24–26, 31, 37, 39, 43, 47, 52, 53–55, 56–58, 60–61, 67–68, 71–74, 79, 100–106, 110, 132, 136, 157, 164–65, 171–73
  veracity 7, 12, 17, 64, 103, 123, 147

ubique et ab omnibus 18
unconditional 70, 86, 152, 158, 160
understand 24, 35, 60, 70, 78–79, 83, 97, 100–1, 107, 113, 116, 123, 150 (see know)
  understanding 2–3, 5, 6–7, 12, 14, 22–23, 24, 28, 31–33, 35, 37–38, 47, 49, 50–51, 56, 59–60, 64–65, 67, 70, 73, 74, 76, 78–80, 82, 84–85, 87, 89, 91–92, 95–98, 100–102, 104, 107, 109, 110, 112, 122–29, 131, 133, 142, 146, 147, 149–54, 158, 168, 170, 174, 176–77, 186

universal 4, 9, 20–21, 23, 28–29, 55–56, 74, 79, 86, 87, 100, 104, 107–9, 111, 135
  universalism 20, 145, 147, 154–56, 175
  universally 18
unveiling 24, 43, 95, 120, 136

valid 23, 49, 51, 59, 75, 82, 91, 100, 157
validating 23
veiling 24, 43, 95, 120, 136
Viking 167
virginal 40

Weltanschauung 9, 11, 22, 28 (see *zeitgeist*)
wisdom 5, 28, 73, 78–82, 90, 98, 104
witness 10, 17, 26, 43, 95, 101, 107, 110, 151, 155, 157
w/Word 7, 21–23, 32, 45, 62, 64, 76, 101, 106–7, 109, 110, 119, 131, 149, 183–85
work(s) 2–7, 9, 10, 11–12, 14–16, 18–19, 22, 24, 27–29, 31–36, 41, 43, 48, 52, 55, 59, 69, 71, 75–76, 78–80, 83, 85, 118, 87, 95–96, 98–99, 101, 103, 105–7, 112, 120, 122, 124–25, 127, 128, 129–34, 137, 140, 146, 149, 150, 154, 156, 166, 168, 170–76
write 1, 39, 43, 58, 79, 102, 122, 125, 132–33, 138
  linguistic 28, 169
  writings 2, 4–5, 9, 15, 21, 29, 31, 37, 43–44, 52–54, 64, 73, 85–86, 106, 110, 127, 146–47, 155, 164, 174
  wrote 10, 12, 16–17, 22–33, 36–38, 47–49, 53–54, 58, 62–63, 70, 88–89, 92, 105, 137, 156

zeitgeist 12 (see *Weltanschauung*)

Indices

Index of Index of C. S. Lewis's Works
An index of Lewis's works cited or quoted

The Abolition of Man: or, Reflections on Education with Special Reference to the Teaching of English in the Upper Forms of Schools 181, 189

Beyond Personality: The Christian Idea of God 65, 181–82, 189

Broadcast Talks. Reprinted with some alterations from two series of Broadcast Talks "Right and Wrong: A Clue to the Meaning of the Universe" and "What Christians Believe" given in 1941 and 1942 27, 128, 181–82, 189

Christian Behavior 189
Christian Reflections 35, 38, 180–81, 189
The Chronicles of Narnia 4, 25, 28, 31, 52, 62, 64, 66–70, 108, 114–16, 123, 128–29, 146, 148, 170–71, 173, 181, 189
Collected Letters, Vol. I—Family Letters 1905–1931 12, 76, 179–80, 182, 189
Collected Letters, Vol. II—Books, Broadcasts and War 1931–1949 3, 16, 21, 179–80, 182, 189
Collected Letters, Vol. III—Narnia, Cambridge and Joy 1950–1963 15, 105–6, 110, 128, 158, 179–80, 182, 189

The Dark Tower and Other Stories 182, 189
"De Futilitae" 97, 180, 189
The Discarded Image 32, 182, 189

Essays Presented to Charles Williams 37, 180, 189

An Experiment in Criticism 35, 38, 181–82, 189

The Four Loves 182, 189

"God in the Dock" 49–50, 180, 182, 189
"The Grand Miracle" 38, 43, 59, 180, 190
The Great Divorce 27, 83, 146, 167, 170–72, 175–76, 177–78, 182, 189
A Grief Observed 182, 189

The Horse and His Boy, The Chronicles of Narnia 66, 67, 181, 190

"Is Theology Poetry" 37, 53–54, 92, 180, 189
"It All Began with a Picture" 63, 180, 189

The Kappa Element in Romance 37–38, 180, 189

The Last Battle, The Chronicles of Narnia 62, 67–70, 114, 128, 146, 171, 181, 190
Letters of C. S. Lewis (1st and 2nd editions) 32, 182, 189
Lewis to Anne Jenkins, March 5, 1961 179
Lewis to Arthur Greeves, Dec. 6, 1931 21, 179
Lewis to Arthur Greeves from Great Bookham, Oct. 12, 1916 36, 179
Lewis to Arthur Greeves, Oct. 18, 1931 76, 179
Lewis to Clyde S. Kilby, May 7, 1959 105–6, 110, 179

Indices

Lewis to Corbin Scott Carnell, Oct. 13, 1958 15, 128, 179
Lewis to Dom Bede Griffiths OSB, April 24, 1936. 179
Lewis to Dom Bede Griffiths OSB, May 23, 1936 179
Lewis to Emily McLay, Aug 3, 1953 179
Lewis to his father, March 28, 1921 12, 180
Lewis to H. Lyman Stebbins, May 8, 1945 20, 21, 180
Lewis to Lee Turner, July 19, 1958 106, 107, 180
Lewis to Mary Van Deusen, Oct. 20, 1952 158, 180
Lewis to Mrs Hook, Dec. 29, 1958 180
Lewis to Mrs Johnson, Nov. 8, 1952 106, 110, 180
Lewis to Sister Penelope CSMV, May 15, 1941 16, 180
Lewis to The Church Times, Feb. 8, 1952 10, 18–19, 179
The Lion, the Witch and the Wardrobe, The Chronicles of Narnia 70, 128, 181, 190

The Magician's Nephew, The Chronicles of Narnia 62, 129, 148, 170–73, 181, 189
Mere Christianity. A revised and amplified edition, with a new introduction, of the three books Broadcast Talks, Christian Behavior and Beyond Personality 13, 18–20, 22, 28, 70, 97–99, 108, 111–12, 128, 182, 189
Miracles (1st and 2nd editions) 28, 37–39, 43, 49, 59–61, 180, 182, 189
"Modern Theology and Biblical Criticism" 35, 38, 103, 181, 189
"Myth Became Fact" 37–39, 53, 57–58, 181, 190

Of Other Worlds. Essays and Stories 180, 190
"On Myth" 35, 38, 181, 190
"On Stories" 37, 180, 190

"Onward, Christian Spacemen" 138, 181, 190
Out of the Silent Planet 13, 97, 142, 182, 190

Perelandra 64, 142, 160, 182, 190
The Pilgrim's Regress 13, 16, 37, 50, 54–55, 57, 63, 181–82, 190
"The Poison of Subjectivism" 97, 181, 190
Prince Caspian, The Chronicles of Narnia 62, 181, 190
The Problem of Pain 27, 103, 108, 162–64, 171–73, 175, 176–78, 182, 190
"Psycho-Analysis and Literary Criticism" 82, 84, 181, 190

Reflections on the Psalms 28, 77–82, 101–2, 104–5, 124, 182, 190
"Religion and Rocketry" 142, 181, 190
"Religion without Dogma" 38–39, 181, 190

The Screwtape Letters 27, 159, 161, 167, 171, 182, 190
The Screwtape Letters and Screwtape Proposes a Toast 182, 190
The Seeing Eye 138–42, 181, 190
The Silver Chair, The Chronicles of Narnia 62, 115–16, 181, 190
"Sometimes Fairy Stories May Say Best What's to be Said" 63, 181, 190
Studies in Mediaeval and Renaissance Literature 32, 182, 190
Surprised by Joy 1, 13, 38–39, 48–49, 54, 86, 89, 92, 97, 99, 131–32, 143, 156, 182, 190

That Hideous Strength 182, 190
They Asked for a Paper 23, 84, 87, 92, 96, 122, 137, 180–81, 191
They Stand Together: The Letters of C. S. Lewis to Arthur Greeves 1914–1963 32, 76, 182, 191
Till We Have Faces 28, 182, 186, 191

"Transposition" (1st and 2nd editions) 23–24, 87, 95–96, 113–14, 115, 117–19, 121–23, 136, 181–82, 184, 191

Transposition and Other Addresses 23, 87, 96, 181–82, 191

Undeceptions: Essays on Theology and Ethics 37–38, 49, 53, 180–82, 191

The Voyage of the Dawn Treader, The Chronicles of Narnia 62, 123, 181, 191

The Weight of Glory 50, 122, 181, 190

The World's Last Night and Other Essays 181, 191

Index of Writers of Secondary Sources

Adams, Marilyn McCord 165, 183
Alexander, Samuel 99, 183
Appleyard, Bryan 36, 183
Athanasius 15, 24, 118–19, 129, 149, 183
Augustine of Hippo 3, 15–16, 31–33, 46–47, 51–52, 73, 87, 100–101, 145, 147, 151–52, 154–55, 156, 163–64, 173, 183–84
Aulén, Gutav 16, 148–49, 163, 183

Barfield, Owen 13, 48–49, 88–89, 97, 183
Barth, Karl xi, 11, 29, 42, 56–57, 96, 98, 120, 142, 151–52, 154–56, 163, 183–85
Baxter, Richard 4, 9, 17, 19, 22–23, 183
Berkeley, George 3, 6, 14–15, 87, 95, 97, 99–100, 113–14, 131, 183
Berkhof, Louis 11, 183
Black, Max 49, 91, 183
Bonhoeffer, Dietrich 148, 183
Bonting, S. L. 64, 183
Bromiley, G. W. 183
Ronald Brookes 25–26, 185
Bunting, Joel 129, 184

Campbell, Joseph 34, 184
Carpenter, Humphrey 53, 184
Cary, Phillip 152, 184

Christensen, Michael J. 35, 103–4, 107, 110, 184
Coleridge, Samuel Taylor 31, 33, 48–50, 52–53, 73, 85–86, 88, 89–92, 183–84
Collinwood, R. G. 49, 91, 184
Cooper, John M. 186

Dearborn, Kerry 83, 184
Donaldson, James 183
Doody, John 152, 184

Eusebius of Caesarea 17, 185
Evans, C. Stephen 33–34, 44, 185

Ferrier, Jordan 159–61, 185
Fergusson, David 64, 185
Feuerbach, Ludwig 36–37, 185
Fisher, Christopher L. 64, 185
Frazer, Sir James George 5, 31, 36–37, 39–45, 71, 75–76, 185

Geisler, Norman L. 25–26, 185
Gore, Charles 186
Goudge, Henry Leighton 186
Guillame, Henry 186
Gunton, Colin E. 11, 29, 120, 151–52, 154–55, 185

Indices

Harries, Richard 35, 185
Healey, Nicholas M. 11, 185
Hebblethwaite, Brian 64, 185
Heck, Joel 16, 185
Hick, John 34, 185, 187
Hooper, Walter xi, xii, xiii, xiv, 32, 63, 67, 76, 83, 179–82, 185
Huttar, Charles A. 32, 185

Jenson, Robert 11, 185
Johnson, Aaron P. xi, 17, 106, 110, 180, 185

Kant, Immanuel. 2, 48, 85–86, 92, 185
Keller, Timothy 137–38, 186
Kelsey, David H. 49, 91, 186
Kevern, Peter 64, 186
Kierkegaard, Søren 43–45, 51–54, 185, 186
Kilby, Clyde S. 103, 105–6, 110, 179, 186
Kretzmann, Norman 183
Kroner, Richard 49, 91, 186

Lewes, George Henry 49, 91, 186
Lock, Walter 35, 186
Locke, John 3, 12, 186

MacDonald, George 48–49, 54, 73, 82–83, 85, 89–92, 146–67, 176–77, 181, 184, 186
Macquarrie, John 42, 186

Paffenroth, Kim 152, 184
Patrick, James 14, 98–99, 186
Plato 2, 5, 14, 20, 33, 73, 78–82, 87, 98–99, 114, 186

Schaff, Philip 183, 187
Schakel, Peter J. 32, 48, 82, 185–86
Scott, David 15, 42, 128, 179, 186
Seerveld, Calvin 49, 91, 186
Selvanayagam, Israel 42, 186
Sickler, Bradley L. 146, 171–73, 186
Stump, Eleanor 183
Swinburne, Richard 48, 82, 186

Tillich, Paul 11, 96, 186
Tolkien, J. R. R. 13, 15, 32–33, 52–53, 56–57, 69, 73–74, 76, 85, 90, 97, 99, 102–4, 132–33, 145, 167, 184, 186–87
Torrance, T. F. 183
Toynbee, Polly 64, 187

Vincentius of Lérins 18, 187

Wace, Henry 183, 187
Walker, Andrew 14, 100, 103–5, 107, 108–10, 118, 120, 186–87
Ward, Kieth 42, 187
Watson, George 184
Wiles, Maurice 34, 187
Wirt, Sherwood E. 156–57, 187

Sectional Contents

Foreword | xiii

Introduction | 1

1.
***Praeparatio Evangelica*: C. S. Lewis as a Catholic Evangelical, Defined by Method, Technique, and Form** | 9

- I. Introduction | 9
- II. Bible, Tradition, and Creed: How Systematic Was Lewis? | 10
- III. Theological and Philosophical Ground:
  1. The Post-War Zeitgeist | 12
- IV. Theological and Philosophical Ground:
  2. Idealism and Platonism | 14
- V. Theological and Philosophical Ground:
  3. Theological Influences | 15
- VI. Systematic Method, Technique, and Form | 16
- VII. Content-Defined Method:
  1. What has been Held Always, by All | 17
- VIII. Content Defined Method:
  2. A Mere Core | 18
- IX. Content Defined Method:
  3. *Regula Fidei* | 21
- X. Transposition: A Unifying Universal Principle | 23
- XI. Apologetic Technique:
  1. *reductio ad absurdum* | 25
- XII. Apologetic Technique:
  2. Law of Excluded Middle | 26
- XIII. *analogia entis–analogia fidei* | 27
- XIV. Conclusion | 28

2.
Christological Prefigurement:
the Incarnation-Resurrection Narrative—History and Reality,
Imagination and Mythopoeic Intimation | 31

- I. Introduction | 32
- II. Myth | 33
- III. Lewis on Myth | 35
- IV. Myth Became Reality | 36
- V. Myth And Event—A Key to Lewis's Christology | 39
- VI. The Incarnation-Resurrection Narrative | 40
- VII. Ideas of Prefigurement:
  1. Incarnation | 41
- VIII. Ideas of Prefigurement:
  2. Resurrection | 44
- IX. Lewis and Natural Theology, Revelation, and Imagination | 46
- X. Re-Introduction: Interim Conclusion | 50
- XI. Splintered Fragments of the True Light: How do these Prefigured Ideas come to be in Pagan Myths?5 | 2
- XII. How does the Incarnation-Resurrection Narrative Act/Operate on us as a Myth, Whether Spoken or Read? | 57
- XIII. Is there Internal Evidence for a Mythopoeic Interpretation within the Incarnation-Resurrection Narrative? | 59
- XIV. A Temporal Paradox? | 61
- XV. Lewis's "Supposal" | 62
- XVI. Aslan—Lewis's Mythopoeic Sub-Creation | 65
- XVII. Conclusion | 71

3.
Revelation and Second Meanings:
A Philosophical and Pneumatological Justification | 73

- I. Introduction: Christological Prefigurement | 74
- II. Intention and Validity | 75
- III. Plato and The Christ | 78
- IV. Wisdom | 80
- V. Imagination and the Theological Tradition | 82
- VI. Coleridge, Schelling, and Kant's Categorical Imperative | 85
- VII. Primary and Secondary Imagination | 88
- VIII. Macdonald on Coleridge | 89
- IX. Conclusion | 92

Sectional Contents

4.
A Doctrine of Transposition:
Towards a Philosophy of the Incarnation | 95

- I. Introduction | 96
- II. Platonic Idealism | 97
- III. Reason and Imagination | 100
- IV. A Proto Doctrine of Scripture | 101
- V. The Word of God and the Word of God | 105
- VI. Modes of Revelation | 107
- VII. A Hierarchy of Revelation | 109
- VIII. Modes of Revelation as Supra-Theological Categories | 111
- IX. A Doctrine of Transposition | 112
- X. Incarnational Transposition | 117
- XI. The Key | 122
- XII. Conclusion | 125

5.
The Actuality of the Incarnation:
Triune Simultaneity and the Will of God—
Lewis . . . and Shakespeare | 127

- I. Introduction | 127
- II. Incarnation-Atonement-Salvation | 129
- III. How does the Incarnation Work? | 129
- IV. Triune Simultaneity | 130
- V. Lewis, Shakespeare, and Hamlet | 131
- VI. The Incarnation:
  1. An Actuality | 132
- VII. The Incarnation:
  2. Modalism and Individuation | 134
- VIII. The Incarnation:
  3. Trinitarian Ontology | 135
- IX. The Incarnation 4.
  Communicatio Idiomatum and Kenosis | 136
- X. Where is God? | 137
- XI. Conclusion142

209

6.

Election and Predestination:
Decision, Faith, and Responsibility—Whither Humanity | 145

- I. Introduction | 146
- II. Atonement and the Eschaton | 147
- III. Predestination and Election | 150
- IV. Faith, Election, and Scripture | 150
- V. The Tradition | 152
- VI. Potential Universalism: A Gospel Consideration | 153
- VII. Election and Decision: Grace is Resistible, Judgment is Final—There is no Election Outside of Faith | 156
- VIII. Election: An Existential Paradox | 157
- IX. John Calvin and C. S. Lewis: Responsibility and Freedom | 159
- X. An Ontological Riddle | 161
- XI. Arminianism: Grace and Election | 162
- XII. Grace–Election–Faith | 163
- XIII. Arminianism: Central Tenets | 164
- XIV. Faith and Works | 165
- XV. Infernal Voluntarism:
  1. Exile and Banishment | 166
- XVI. Infernal Voluntarism:
  2. How do we Define Heaven? | 167
- XVII. Infernal Voluntarism:
  3. "All Get What They Want; They Do Not Always Like It" | 170
- XVIII. Infernal Voluntarism: 4.
  To Depart, to Conduct One's Own Life | 172
- XIX. Conclusion: A Temporal Paradox? | 176

www.ingramcontent.com/pod-product-compliance
Lightning Source LLC
Chambersburg PA
CBHW062021220426
43662CB00010B/1426